# Busumy FREE

## HOW TO LIBERATE YOURSELF FROM **THE QUEST FOR *BETTER* BREASTS** BEFORE, DURING, AND LONG AFTER EXPLANT

**AMANDA SAVAGE BROWN**
PH.D., LCSW

CW01498381

BUSTING FREE

*How to liberate yourself from the quest for better breasts before, during, and long after explant*

Copyright © 2022 by Amanda Savage Brown

This book contains information to help women whose life journey includes breast implants. It's intended to support them in navigating the psychosocial challenges of living with temporary or problematic breast implants, choosing to replace or remove them, or recovering from their loss. It is educational and not intended to substitute for advice, treatment, or care from a licensed medical or mental health professional. Readers should always consult with their doctor about their personal health-related issues and licensed mental health professionals to receive mental health care. The author is not responsible for any possible consequence of any treatment, action, or application of the information in this book to the reader.

At the time of publication, the URLs throughout this book link to existing websites. The author is not responsible for, and should not be deemed to endorse or recommend, any website other than her own. Although every effort was made to ensure the information in this book was accurate at the time of publication, the author assumes no responsibility for errors, inaccuracies, omissions, or any other inconsistencies in this text and hereby disclaims any liability to any party for any loss, damage, or disruption caused by errors or omissions, whether resulting from negligence, accident, or any other cause.

All rights reserved. Except for brief quotations in critical reviews or articles, no portion of this book may be reproduced, stored in a retrieval system, or transmitted in any form or by any means, electronic or mechanical, including photocopying, recording, or scanning, without written permission from the author.

Paperback: 979-8-9865710-7-2
Ebook: 979-8-9865710-1-0

Library of Congress Control Number: 2022912706 2

Edited by: Chris Nelson
Interior design by: Saqib Arshad
Illustrations by: Kayli Fradin

Open Up Books

amandasavagebrown.com

"This book is a must-read for anyone living with problematic breast implants, considering their removal, getting them removed, or coming to terms with life after explant. Whatever stage of this journey you're in, one thing's for sure: All sorts of difficult thoughts and feelings are guaranteed to arise, especially anxiety and self-judgment.

Amanda Savage Brown takes you step-by-step through how to cope effectively with all this stress, take the impact and power out of those difficult thoughts and feelings, and be there in a compassionate, supportive way for yourself.

Based on the scientifically-validated approach of Acceptance and Commitment Therapy, Busting Free shows you how to handle your pain, free yourself from the tyranny of breast and beauty myths, and find your courage. And above all, it will help you develop a deep sense of self-acceptance and self-worth that's authentic, genuine, and empowering."

**—Russ Harris, ACT Practitioner, Trainer, and author of the bestseller, *The Happiness Trap***

"Busting Free is a must-read for anyone with breast implants wanting to understand why they got them and how they affect their emotional and mental well-being. It helps women heal on the inside before, during, and after breast implant removal and provides much-need guidance on an important topic that's been largely ignored in the breast implant illness community until now."

**—Robyn Towt, Co-Founder, Global Patient Advocacy Coalition**

*For the millions of women who must inevitably choose to replace or remove aging, problematic, ruptured, or recalled breast implants, and the growing population of women adjusting to life after explant. May you trust in your heart that your truest beauty shines from within.*

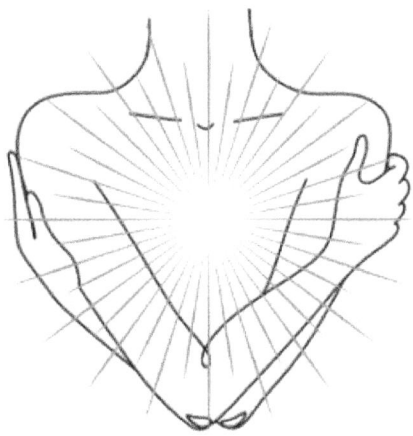

Guided audios, demo videos, and fillable templates enhance your experience throughout this book. While some are optional, others are transformative to your inner healing. To access your *Busting Free* digital library, please scan the following QR code or visit bustingfreeonline.com. For help accessing these, email: amanda@amandasavagebrown.com.

Readers of *Busting Free* have lifetime access to its digital library. To be kept "abreast" of new resources I develop for women's wellbeing, visit amandasavagebrown.com.

# Table of Contents

# Introduction

There's much more to your journey with breast implants than the surgeries to get or remove them. Because of the meaning that breasts hold in our society, these are not mere physical journeys. The pursuit of surgically idealized breast mounds affects your mental, emotional, and financial well-being as well. And because it involves one of the most sexually objectified parts of your body, this journey is far from private. Bottom line: Given the social stakes involving breasts, your journey with breast implants affects your very sense of belonging–and worth.

And here's the kicker: Despite society's reverence of breasts, there's little acknowledgment of (or professional support for) your *inner* experience while living with breast implants that, according to the FDA,[1] become increasingly problematic the longer they're in your body and must eventually be replaced or removed (i.e., **explanted**).[2] Although there are helpful resources focused on the physical side of breast implants and their removal, few focus on the **psychosocial** (i.e., mental, emotional, and social) aspects.

Instead, when you have breast implants for cosmetic reasons, there seems to be an assumption that any anxiety over removing them or grief

---

[1] https://www.fda.gov/medical-devices/breast-implants/things-consider-getting-breast-implants
[2] Words featured in bold text may be new to you or used in an uncommon or specific way throughout this book. For ease of reference, they are included in the Glossary at the end of the book.

over their loss is superficial. And when you reconstructed your breasts with implants after a mastectomy, it's often assumed you haven't carefully thought things through when explanting to flat. Neither of these are true. Irrespective of why you got breast implants or your reasons for removing them, your inner conflict, concerns, and deliberations may, understandably, go much deeper.

Given what the world taught you about breasts, removing breast implants often threatens how you see yourself, literally and figuratively. Because one of the main jobs of your mind is to keep you safe, it wants you to avoid the threatening feeling of being *less than* or *not good enough*. It doesn't want you to do something you might regret. It doesn't want you to feel like you need to be *fixed* again.

Understandably, you might put off doing anything about your aging or problematic breast implants for as long as you can. How long you delay depends on four things:

1. How much your implant-related issues impact your life.
2. Whether you have the resources to pursue change.
3. Your relationship with yourself.
4. What breasts *mean* to you.

Meanwhile, your implant shells are wearing down inside your body, like the tread on tires. And just as worn tires blow, aging implants eventually **rupture**. They may also be recalled or lead your body to develop **breast implant illness (BII)**. And even though it might matter a great deal to you to avoid a rupture, heed a recall, heal from BII, or otherwise reclaim your body, you still might struggle with moving toward explant. Or you may choose to explant, perhaps even be excited or relieved with the decision, and then realize there's some long overdue inner work to be done as well.

Feeling apprehensive over breast implant removal or struggling afterward doesn't mean you're weak, mentally unwell, or broken in any way. You struggle because you were told that breast implants *fix* something about you, and it often feels as if they do. Choosing explant means defying everything you learned to believe about women, breasts, and belonging. Typically, those beliefs sit in the driver's seat while you and your body go along for the ride. And when you must explant to protect your health, it often means pushing yourself forward without knowing how to care for the unpleasant feelings (e.g., regret, anger, guilt, fear, sadness) that understandably show up before, during, and long after.

I know how hard it is to confront the thoughts, feelings, and beliefs that drove you onto the implant table. I'm a fellow traveler on the breast implant journey. I'm also a clinical psychotherapist and women's well-being coach specializing in **Acceptance and Commitment Therapy** (ACT, pronounced as a word, not spoken as three separate letters). It's also known as Acceptance and Commitment Training, depending on its use. I use ACT in my counseling and coaching practice as an evidence-based approach to help women reclaim their bodies and minds from things that cause them suffering, including their own internalized beliefs and self-judgment.

As a fellow traveler, I had breast implants for 12 years. They looked great. They also gave me much more than I bargained for—pretty much the entire time they were inside me. My breasts were cold, barely moved, and did not like to be touched. Snuggling our youngest daughter was painful. Each hug was compromised by self-conscious concern over how it felt to press against my unyielding chest and dread over the pain of tight embraces. I felt fraudulent helping women pursue health and healing while sitting behind two problematic breast implants.

I understand (both professionally and personally) that it can be hard to move toward explant, even when you want to be implant-free. I avoided doing anything about my breast implants until one ruptured after a routine mammogram in 2018. Then, with the help of online resources, I put together and executed an explant plan. Three months later, they were out. Within three more months, and to my complete shock, I recovered from chronic disabling pain and other ailments that I had no idea were related to my body's failing battle against the two bags.

While all that sounds straightforward, it was not easy. My surgery was unexpectedly involved. I loathed the post-surgical drains. And my post-explant chest is permanently distorted. But I would do it all again for two important reasons. First, my journey through breast implant loss helped me forge a long overdue and unshakeable self-acceptance practice. Second, because I witnessed the psychosocial suffering of women on these journeys through the eyes of a psychotherapist and former public health scientist, I emerged with the resolute determination to write *Busting Free*.

*Busting Free* is the first-of-its-kind self-help book for women whose life journey includes breast implants. It's written for the millions of women who must inevitably choose to replace or remove aging, problematic, ruptured, or recalled breast implants, and the growing population of women adjusting to life after explant. As its name suggests, *Busting Free* helps you bust free of your deeply felt and powerfully influential thoughts and feelings about breasts. It helps you find *your* way through the inner journey that starts long before you put breast implants into your body and stays with you long after you remove them.

I call this inner journey **the quest for *better* breasts**. You know this quest well, irrespective of whether you pursued implants to augment, restore, or reconstruct your breasts. You know what it feels like to judge yourself as *not good enough* next to the "ideal" breast or "womanly" body.

You know about trying to surgically "fix" the pain of feeling *less than* or incomplete as a woman. And, you know what it's like to get more than you bargained for from breast implants and to struggle with the idea or aftermath of removing them.

On any challenging journey, it helps to travel with someone who's got your back. This one is no different; you deserve a companion.

*Busting Free* provides you companionship in two ways. First, it's written to be a companion to you, no matter where you are on your journey with breast implants. Whether you're delighted with your implants, coming to terms with getting more than you bargained for from them, urgently need to remove them, or adjusting to life after explant, *Busting Free* helps you move through this journey on *your* terms. Rather than calling the shots or telling you what to do, it helps you find *your* way by using ACT's research-backed theory to shine a light on the harder-to-see inner journey. Like a trusted companion, it helps you prevail over the mental, emotional, and social challenges along the way.

The second way *Busting Free* provides companionship is by showing you how to use ACT's six inner skills to **companion** yourself before, during, and long after explant. By learning how to companion your whole experience—even your unwanted thoughts and feelings—you finally learn how to give yourself acceptance. It becomes an action you take and a choice you make *for the rest of your life*.

Chapter 1 pulls back the curtain to reveal how the human mind creates what I call the **Breast Rulebook**. You learn why you naturally compare yourself to it and why you can never fully unlearn its contents. Knowing these things validates that breasts *matter* and is key to busting the quest for *better* breasts.

Chapter 2 introduces your **inner fixer**. This part of your mind convinces you to fix how you feel on the inside by "fixing" how you measure up on the outside. You'll explore how *your* inner fixer influences you, especially on this journey. You'll see why busting free happens only by learning new ways to respond to this part of yourself.

Chapter 3 introduces you to **BRITE™ Inner Healing.**[3] It's an ACT-based approach I created to help you bust free from the Breast Rulebook and reclaim yourself from your inner fixer. It gives you science-based inner skills to put you in charge of this journey and to live the rest of your life on *your* terms. With its approach, you can work toward inner healing long before you must choose to replace or remove aging breast implants and long after explant.

Chapter 4 presents the **BRITE Roadmap.** I created it based on one of the most respected theories of change. It helps you make sense of what you're thinking, feeling, and doing as you come to terms with getting more than you bargained for from breast implants, move through explant, and fully reclaim yourself for the rest of your life. It orients you to where you are in your journey, like one of those "You Are Here" stars on a directory. It shows you what to expect along the way.

Chapter 5 gives you an inner **BRAKE.** It plays an essential role in helping you steady yourself rather than careening out of control during the more challenging parts of your journey with breast implants or life after explant.

Chapters 6-10 are packed with science-backed strategies to help you bust free, bring your whole self forward, and mindfully move through this journey, no matter if you love your breast implants, want or need to remove them, or are adjusting to life without them. They teach you to be guided by what *you* care about deep in your heart, stay in the here and now, separate what you do from what you think, companion rather than abandon your inner pain, and see beyond your **breast-related self-**

---

[3] **BRITE™** Inner Healing is the ACT-based program I created for women whose life journey includes breast implants. Though it is trademarked, I use the mark only this once to promote ease of readability throughout the remainder of *Busting Free.*

**concept.** These skills might sound abstract to you at this point, but after reading each chapter, you will know how to use each one to navigate and prevail over the mental, emotional, and social challenges that show up on these journeys. And you can use them for the rest of your life, no matter how you "measure up" to any of society's other rulebooks for how you "ought" to be.

Chapter 11 pulls everything together and shows how to use BRITE Inner Healing skills and tools to act on your behalf no matter where you are on the BRITE Roadmap. It includes comprehensive lists of things you can *do* to bust free of the Breast Rulebook long before you must choose to replace or remove your breast implants, as you prepare a **holistic explant plan**, and as you adjust to your post-explant chest.

*Busting Free* is more active and experiential than most self-help books. It's not a "sit with your eyes closed" or journal-intensive self-help book. Though you'll do some of that, the real benefits come from bringing BRITE Inner Healing skills and tools into your life. For that reason, I wrote *Busting Free* intending that you understand how, when, and why to use its content in real life. To show the skills in action, I openly (and rather vulnerably) share how I used them on my explant journey and, now, as a woman living in a breast-obsessed society with distorted post-explant breasts.

I also created several resources to help you experience and interact with the material. They are included in your *Busting Free* digital library at bustingfreeonline.com and the QR code in the front material. Though I provide written prompts throughout this book, some material is better for you to experience (rather than read). There are also several transformational exercises in BRITE Inner Healing that cannot be read at all–they must be felt. I alert you when that's the case. And though your mind may balk at having to access something outside this book, your inner wellbeing is worth the investment of typing a URL into your browser. The following symbols throughout the book alert you when the library has a guided audio, video, or a fillable template for that section's material (each one is uniquely numbered):

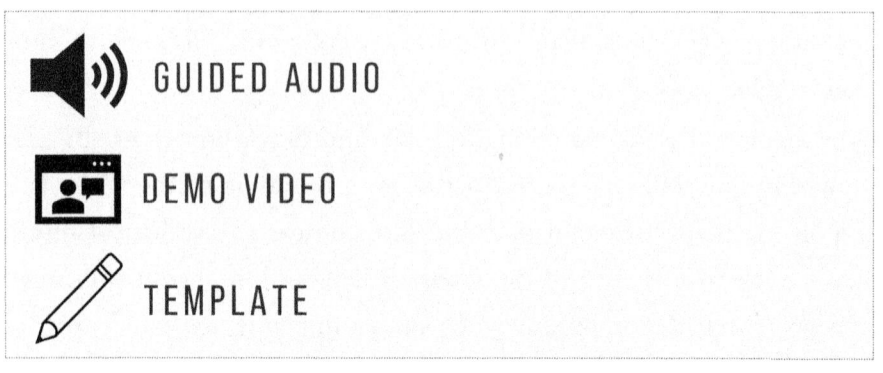

GUIDED AUDIO

DEMO VIDEO

TEMPLATE

Please trust that *Busting Free* is agenda-free. It's not written to persuade you to explant before you're ready. It's not here to convince you that breasts don't *matter*. Instead, it's about forging a more mindful path through your inner journey *because they do*. Although the BRITE Roadmap features an explant experience, *Busting Free* teaches you how to inwardly companion you and bust the quest for better breasts independently of whether you explant.

I hope that *Busting Free* liberates your body, mind, and heart from the Breast Rulebook and *any* of society's other rulebooks about how you *should* look, age, and behave as a woman. Of course, there's nothing wrong with wanting to look your best, so long as you're not doing something that violates your values, puts your body or financial well-being at risk, or feels like you *must* do it to be accepted, worthy, or safe. Rather, by busting free of predatory marketing and domineering social standards, you look your best on *your* terms while knowing how to care for yourself on a deeper level as a woman living (and aging) in an appearance- and youth-oriented society.

Whether you are considering removing your breast implants someday, urgently need to remove them, or want to heal more fully from your explant journey, you can learn to let go of the Breast Rulebook that you never consented to hold. You can learn to care for yourself when feeling *less than* or fear you won't belong, be valued, or be wanted. You can choose a path that reclaims your body, mind, and heart from the quest for better breasts, where you emerge stronger and more resilient than ever before.

*Busting Free* shows you the way.

---

# Chapter 1

# Why You, Me, and Millions of Others Opted for *Better* Breasts

A n essential part of busting free is knowing what *really* drove you to get breast implants. You might be very clear on why you put breast implants into your body yet be unaware of the complicated and ongoing behind-the-scenes process driving that decision. You probably felt this internal process pushing you around, even after you got breast implants. It makes it difficult to consider removing them, even when you want or need to be implant-free. Removing breast implants doesn't shut down this internal process, so it continues influencing you long after explant. Because it's ongoing, understanding this behind-the-scenes process is an integral part of reclaiming yourself from it.

## The quest for *better* breasts

Take a moment to reflect inwardly on how your quest for *better* breasts began. Was it sparked when you were young, against the backdrop of longing to develop like the girls around you, or in response to being ridiculed because you weren't? Did your quest begin later in life after critical words from a partner or something that changed the appearance of your breasts, such as pregnancy, weight loss, or breast cancer? Was it more of an insidious process where you devolved from being okay with your natural breasts to determining they just didn't measure up well to the *ideal* breast? Perhaps your quest was thrust upon you to reconstruct your breasts after breast cancer treatment.

No matter your history, your quest for *better* breasts is fueled in large part by your beliefs about women, breasts, and belonging. These include the idea that there is a normal, better, and ideal way for breasts to appear and the conviction that breasts *matter*. They matter so much, you can surgically place devices inside them to augment their size or change, restore, or reconstruct their shape. Even if breasts don't matter much to you personally, they matter to society. As a result, mastectomy patients, who prefer to go flat, are often pressured to "guard their psychosocial well-being" through reconstruction with implants. Those who do persist in aesthetic flat closure sometimes wake up after surgery with unwanted extra skin left behind "just in case" they change their minds.

If this were a typical self-help book, this chapter would help you take inventory of your beliefs and teach you ways to replace them or stop thinking that way entirely. That might help, but it's akin to putting a Band-Aid on a wound that needs stitches. Busting free from the quest for *better* breasts needs something different because its behind-the-scenes process continues for the rest of your life.

You can test this out for yourself right now by reflecting on how you viewed yourself and your body after getting breast implants. Take a moment to consider if having them stopped your private inner behaviors of comparing yourself to others, judging your body, or fearing you are *not good enough*. (Seriously, take a minute to ponder this before reading further.)

Chances are nearly 100 percent that you continued doing those things after getting breast implants. Even when implants help you feel sexy, confident, or womanly, they don't teach you self-acceptance. No matter why you got them or how happy you are with them, you continue feeling *not good enough*, despite having *better* breasts. After all, there are many other body parts or features you learned are *bad*: cellulite, saddlebags, diminishing thigh gap, "bingo" arms, "Mom bod," thinning lips and eyebrows, "marionette" lines on your face, graying hair, sagging or wrinkled skin, jowls, and so on. This ongoing struggle amplifies your lack of self-acceptance. It makes it painfully difficult when you eventually want or urgently need to be implant-free and have no idea how to care for the part of you that believes they make you *better, good enough*, or complete.

That's why I want to do something different with this chapter. My goal is to pull back the curtain on the behind-the-scenes process driving the quest for *better* breasts. I want you to know how your mind, my mind, and the minds of every person in a breast-obsessed society come to believe that those mounds of flesh somehow magically display a woman's desirability and worth. I want you to finish this chapter knowing that your quest for *better* breasts isn't a *you* thing, a *woman* thing, a *mental* thing, or a *weak* thing. It's a *human* thing. I want you to see how this internal process not only drove you to get breast implants, but also drives your inner struggling before, during, and after explant. Your awareness of this process is the first step to busting free from it.

Please know this chapter is not about looking at the "correctness" of your beliefs. Nor is it about trying to change or cast judgment on any of the beliefs you hold. Instead, it's about understanding how you unknowingly came to believe what you do about women, breasts, and belonging, and why your mind can't simply eject those beliefs when they interfere with moving toward explant or accepting yourself afterward.

## You're only human, after all

While pulling back the curtain on the behind-the-scenes process driving your quest for *better* breasts, there are several things to keep in mind about humans. Although the following information might seem like a detour of sorts, it's fundamentally important to reclaiming yourself from the inside and out.

**We are social creatures who want to belong to our group.**

Humans are social creatures. Your drive to belong is hard-wired. If our ancestors got kicked out of the group, they would die. It was the end of the story: They either froze, starved, or got eaten. Our super-duper great grandparents were probably some of the best hunters, fire makers, and fur seamstresses around! They had to be if they wanted to be of value, belong, and survive. Everyone alive today descended from folks whose minds worried about group belonging. Your mind, my mind, and the minds of (nearly) everyone around you know that *belonging=survival*. Our fear of losing group belonging drives us to find ways to be wanted. Bottom line: The pursuit of belonging and being desired by the group is not some inherent flaw in your psyche. It's a natural state. Please keep this in mind throughout this book anytime I reference your innate desire to belong.

**Our yearning to belong causes us to compare ourselves to others constantly.**

Since group belonging equals safety, you're understandably going to monitor how well you measure up to those around you. Comparing yourself to others helps guard against being *less than* or *not enough* in a way that could lead to displeasure from others and rejection from the group. However, unlike your ancestors, who belonged to small groups, you can compare yourself to the entire world simply by glancing at a device in your hand. This kind of comparison is problematic in many ways. First, when you see countless others conforming and competing to meet group standards, you rarely take time to question the group standards themselves. Second, being focused on everything and everyone around you disconnects you from yourself and diminishes your choice over what you pursue. Finally, predatory marketers prey upon this natural tendency. They surround you with images designed to make you feel *less than* or *not good enough* and promise their products will make you *better*.

**We move away from pain.**

Not only do you seek relief from pain, but you actively avoid it. One of your mind's main jobs is to keep you safe. It takes this part of its job very seriously, keeping vigil for threats to your safety and well-being. It doesn't distinguish between external threats (such as a startled venomous snake trapped in your garage) and internal threats (such as critical self-judgment). It wants to protect you from any pain, including the psychic pain of ridicule, judgment, abandonment, isolation, feeling *less than*, being passed over, loneliness, and so forth. Though this approach works to your advantage with direct external threats, such as a snake, it causes considerable distress when doing something that threatens how you see yourself, such as removing breast implants in a breast-obsessed culture. Chapters 2 and 3 explore this further.

**We learn, think, and suffer through language.**

At a very young age, you were taught to use language to interact with the world around you. That means you learn, think, and suffer through language because your mind *automatically* does the following three things:[4]

1. It sees bidirectional relationships between things. Once it learns how two things are related, it derives their relationship in the other direction. So, for example, once you learn *women have breasts*, your mind derives *breasts are womanly*. This way of relating things might seem super basic and obvious, but it plays a fundamental role in fueling your quest for *better* breasts and is discussed further in the next section.

2. When your mind learns how two (or more) sets of things are related, it combines and derives several other ways they relate to one another. For example, watch what your mind does when told:
   *Sarah is Bob's fraternal twin sister.*
   *Bob is Elle's son.*
   Though given only two relations, your mind can derive four more:
   *Bob is Sarah's fraternal twin brother.*
   *Elle is Bob's mother.*
   *Elle is Sarah's mother.*
   *Sarah is Elle's daughter.*

---

[4] As evidenced by hundreds of studies researching Relational Frame Theory, the underlying theory and foundation for ACT.

The preceding example shows how your mind applies previously learned language conventions, such as familial relationships, to learn and problem-solve more efficiently. As you learn information, it quickly derives new thoughts by applying what you previously learned. Through this union of language and cognition, you imagine, problem-solve, and experience joy and purpose. Your derived thoughts can inspire you to do great things, believe in your dreams, and stand your ground purely on principle.

But this merging of language and cognition also allows your mind to make assumptions and hurtful inferences, jump to conclusions, "read between the lines," catastrophize, and so forth. For example, once you learn about bra cup sizes and the socially derived idea that bigger breasts are better, your mind combines those things. It then concludes that C cups are better than A and B cups. Because your mind automatically sees things bidirectionally, it also derives that A cups have the least value. When you have an A cup in a breast-obsessed society, your mind can easily conclude that your breasts make you less worthy, valuable, desirable, and so forth. Not surprisingly, this plays a significant role in the behind-the-scenes process fueling your quest for *better* breasts.

3. Your mind creates elaborate networks relating everything it encounters and thinks about to what it already knows. It can change the meaning of everything inside these networks depending on how it frames them. For example, if you look at pictures of breast-augmentation patients, you will see bigger, fuller, rounder, perkier breasts with cleavage. In a breast-obsessed society, your mind previously learned that

those are characteristics of *better* breasts. So it now views implanted breasts as *better* breasts. Breast implants now take on all the meaning and possibilities you attribute to *better* breasts, such as desirability, worth, and belonging. Your mind (and you) view breast implants as deliverance from judgment and rejection.

**Humans relate and respond to symbolic meaning.**

The preceding example of seeing breast implants differently after viewing pictures of breast-augmentation patients highlights another aspect of the behind-the-scenes process that drove you to get implants. Humans respond to things based on symbolic meaning through language and cognition processes. For example, humans raised in the USA value dimes over nickels, even though a dime is smaller than a nickel. Responding like this to the two coins is **arbitrary**, meaning it's based on human-made, social whims[5] rather than physical properties. When you were very young, you would choose nickels over dimes based on their physical properties of size. Once you learn their symbolic value, you change your view of their relative worth.

Nonhuman animals relate and respond to things based solely on physical (nonarbitrary) attributes. Even though your pet reacts to the names of different objects, it's only responding to the sound associated with the object. It doesn't do the same complex abstraction of meaning that humans do. For example, a dog learns to relate the sound of a car pulling into a drive with its owner's return. If the owner returns home driving a high-end luxury car one day, the

---

[5] Please note, my use of the word whim here denotes something that changes depending on your social setting. Some cultures do not sexualize or objectify breasts. They are viewed strictly as ways to feed young humans. The idea of fondling breasts during sex is foreign to them, as is the idea of surgically altering breasts for aesthetic reasons.

dog won't be particularly impressed. The dog has no idea about arbitrary stuff such as luxury brands, money, price tags, affluence, financial success, and so on. Responding to something based on its social value is a uniquely human thing. It's why we are the only mammals who suffer over the appearance of our mammary glands.

**You have no inner delete button.**

Though this subsection is short, its information is essential. Research shows that, unlike math, there is no way to subtract (i.e., get rid of) things you learned through language. That means you have no inner equivalent of a "delete" button. You can't consciously eject unpleasant thoughts or unhelpful beliefs. Instead, your mind uses language to build its ever-expanding networks of how things relate to one another. You can learn new thoughts that change what you believe or feel about something, but your old ideas and beliefs don't disappear. Just as you can learn a new language without replacing the one you already know, your deeply ingrained beliefs are with you for the long haul, making it essential to learn more effective ways to deal with them moving forward.

# How this behind-the-scenes process drove your quest for *better* breasts

Now, let's explore how these very human things unknowingly impacted you as a young girl growing up in a breast-obsessed society. At some early point, you learned that *women have breasts*. Then, as we saw earlier, your mind used bidirectionality to derive that *breasts are womanly*. It did this all on its own. I refer to long-ago learned and derived beliefs as **deeply held beliefs**. They're the kind that you rarely think to question; you just see them as the way things are.

As you grew up in a breast-obsessed society, surrounded by images of women and breasts, your mind created a vast network of all the ways it learned to relate breasts and women. This network includes all the arbitrary, human-made, social whims connecting breasts with desirability. For example, once you learned that *bigger breasts are better,* your mind combined it with its prior learning that *women have breasts* and determined that *women with bigger breasts are better.* Because it relates things in both directions, it also derived that *women with smaller breasts are not good enough.* Your mind's ability to do this is staggering. In a breast-obsessed society, where you also learn that breasts are sexy, confidence-giving, body balancing, powerful, eye-catching, and so forth, the human mind creates a massive network of beliefs about women and breasts. I call this network of breast-related beliefs the **Breast Rulebook**.

Something important happens as your young mind continually adds to the Breast Rulebook's content. Just like you learned to see nickels and dimes based on their made-up attributes, once you learned that breasts are desirable, their meaning transformed. Your developing breasts became more than just a part of your body; they became important to your sense of self and belonging. You compared yourself to peers, family members, store mannequins, and images to assess if your developing breasts were *good enough.* You might even have chanted, "I must, I must, I must increase my bust" while furtively practicing exercises promised to promote bust development.

Because everyone around you also grew up in a breast-obsessed society, their minds also hold the Breast Rulebook. Depending on how your developing breasts measured up to it, they garnered you attention, envy, and praise or made you the target of ridicule, judgment, and rejection. The way others treated you reinforced your internalized beliefs that your breasts' appearance impacts your group belonging. Over time, your breasts' size, shape, symmetry, and placement relative to one another influenced not only your sense of belonging, but also impacted your sense of self. I refer to this as your **breast-related self-concept.**

## Your breast-related self-concept

When you grow up in a society where breasts *matter*, so does your breast-related self-concept. Through the language and cognition processes described in the previous sections, your mind makes inferences about you, your breasts, and your worthiness. Then, based on how your breasts measure up, all those derived beliefs are appended to the Breast Rulebook, giving rise to new rules about what you *should, ought,* and *must never do.*

Depending on what your mind concludes, you might feel quite distressed. Unlike the example where luxury-car status does nothing to change a dog's response to an owner's return home, you are *very* capable of feeling differently toward yourself based on social whims about breast size and shape. When you believe your breasts aren't good enough, it's easy to see yourself as *not good enough.* You might feel troubled by how your small, asymmetrical, or non-ideally shaped breasts measure up to the Breast Rulebook. You might want to restore what your breasts lost with pregnancy, breastfeeding, weight loss, or age. You might want to reconstruct what was taken from them by breast cancer. Your mind might tell you that *better* breasts will ease the pain of infidelity, please a critical partner, bring financial success, or boost confidence after divorce. Your mind comes up with thoughts such as:

> *Because bigger breasts are more desirable, my small breasts make me less worthy.*
>
> *There's an ideal way for breasts to be shaped. Because mine are different, I'm wrong.*
>
> *Since breasts are womanly and I am flat-chested, I'm not womanly.*

*My breasts don't fill out tops and dresses; I must be the wrong proportions.*

*With better breasts, I would get more attention, feel better, be more confident, be sexier.*

*He wouldn't have cheated on me if I had breasts like her.*

Rather than questioning societal standards, you seek relief from the **internalized breast shame** of not meeting them. Your mind wants to move you away from the pain of feeling *less than* as a woman. Because you live in a time and place where breast implants are marketed as a solution to a painful breast-related self-concept, you buy into their promises of a *better* you. As you look at pictures, talk with doctors, and connect with other women who have breast implants, the same language and cognition processes that fueled your self-dissatisfaction now derive that breast implants offer you salvation. When breast implants take on this kind of meaning, your quest for *better* breasts leads you to the implant table. You might think nothing of this; after all, you're simply abiding by the Breast Rulebook. Oftentimes, you're quite relieved–even excited–to improve your compliance with it.

Bottom line: Your breast-related self-concept plays a massive role in choosing to get breast implants, tolerating getting more than you bargained for from them, and feeling distressed over their loss. Chapter 10 reconnects you with a powerful inner resource to see far beyond your breast-related self-concept.

## How this behind-the-scenes process interferes with explant

Breast implants are not problem-free or lifetime devices (discussed further in the next chapter). Their temporary and problem-prone nature means you might eventually want or urgently need to remove them. Doing so is no easy thing in a breast-obsessed society. Not only does your quest for *better* breasts remain intact, but your mind now holds powerfully reinforced versions of the beliefs that drove you to implants. You're still wired for belonging, prone to comparative thinking, and avoidant of pain. Your mind still uses the same language and cognition processes. Only now, it comes to all sorts of conclusions about what explanted breasts *mean* to your future as a woman living in a breast-obsessed society.

Even if you're eager to be implant-free, the behind-the-scenes process revealed here continues running in the back of your mind. It can push you around before, during, and after breast implant removal. It leads to the following six inner barriers on explant journeys:

1. Disconnection from what truly matters to *you*, deep down, underneath society's rulebooks.
2. Struggling to stay in the here and now where you can take care of problems needing your attention. Getting caught up in painful memories or scary predictions.
3. Being dominated by your Breast Rulebook-related thoughts, beliefs, judgments, memories, and predictions.
4. Getting trapped by your efforts to avoid or get rid of your unwanted thoughts and unpleasant feelings.
5. Difficulty seeing past your breast-related self-concept. You fear you will no longer be *you* without breast implants or breast mounds (when explanting to flat).

6.   Not acting on your behalf, failing to do things that matter to *you*.

## The curtain's pulled back; now what?

So, what can you do about this ongoing behind-the-scenes process? First, keep reading this book. It teaches you evidence-based inner skills to reclaim your body, mind, and heart from the Breast Rulebook. It helps you change your relationship with yourself and show up as the woman you most want to be, even when this process impacts you in ways that are unhelpful, difficult, or painful.

The end of the preceding sentence makes an important distinction. The behind-the-scenes process is not *all* bad. Wanting to belong, knowing what the group values, striving to be your best, and moving away from pain are helpful things to social beings like humans. Though this leads you to suffer through complex, symbolic, and abstract ways of relating your breasts' appearance to your worth, you can also put this process to work for you. It's what helps you do things that are important and risky. It's how you make sense of your experience with implants, find purpose in your explant journey, and continue pursuing what matters to you *for the rest of your life.*

The second thing you can do about the ongoing behind-the-scenes process is practice awareness of it. The more you become aware of how it works in your mind and leads you to feel in your body, the more choices you have over how it influences you. Practice noticing when your drive to belong is preyed upon by social messaging and marketing. Whenever provocative images and attractive women surround you, anticipate your self-judgment. Watch what your mind does even when you know you're looking at a retouched image featuring an airbrushed model with a filler-injected face, surgically altered body, and artificially extended hair. When you inwardly feel threatened or notice negative self-appraisal, look underneath that feeling or inner behavior. Notice when an arbitrary, human-made, social standard led your mind to conclude that you are *not good enough*. Whenever you find yourself longing to belong, comparing yourself to others, or avoiding feeling *less than*, validate that those things are part of being human.

The third thing you can do is come to terms with the fact that you don't have the inner equivalent of a delete button. That means, even if you form completely new beliefs about women, breasts, and belonging, your mind will still hold the belief that *breasts matter*. Your mind can never fully unlearn what it placed in the Breast Rulebook. Hence, a part of you will likely always care about your breasts' aesthetics.

There's no need to judge your breast-related self-concept or to spend time telling yourself to forget about it. To do either of those things invalidates your lived experience as a woman in a breast-obsessed society. Because you have no inner delete button, trying to get rid of your old unhelpful beliefs is as futile as holding an inflated beach ball underwater. It takes all your effort, keeps you focused entirely on the ball, and nearly always ends with the ball exploding to the surface.

Being unable to get rid of your deeply ingrained beliefs doesn't have to hold you back, though. Accepting that your mind will always hold the Breast Rulebook is like letting a beach ball float around you. You're fully aware of the brightly colored ball when it floats near you or bumps into you, but you're not wasting time trying to hold it underwater. You free yourself to do other things such as swim, lounge, or play water games with friends. Allowing your old beliefs to surface, come, and go on their own doesn't mean you agree with them, like them, or want them. But it does bust you free you from struggling against them. (Obviously, not getting entangled in deeply held beliefs about your belonging is more complex than letting a colorful ball float around you. Chapters 8 and 9 present techniques to help you.)

When breast implants cause you problems, it's easy to feel guilt over getting them. I've seen countless women be rather hard on their younger selves, lamenting that they hadn't loved or accepted themselves more. While that would indeed make a difference, it's just not so easy given this robust behind-the-scenes process working against people who grow up surrounded by breast-oriented messaging. I hope that by knowing what *really* fueled your decision, you give your younger self some nonjudgmental compassion. Furthermore, I hope that by knowing how your mind uses language and cognition processes, you forgive your younger self and catch how those processes impact you moving forward.

In my work with women who have breast implants, I've yet to learn of a set that doesn't rest atop deeply held, powerfully painful, socially derived beliefs. My clients quickly tell me why they got implants:

*My body wasn't normal.*

*I needed bigger breasts to feel sexy.*

*No one would want me without implants.*

*It was impossible to feel like a woman with such small breasts.*

*I was embarrassed over how my body was proportioned all wrong.*

*Cancer was taking my breasts; I would feel incomplete without them.*

But when I ask a client how she learned her breasts were something to be fixed, she sits back and quietly ponders the question. During this tender moment, I imagine her as a little girl and contemplate the many thousands of things her mind derived while growing up in a breast-obsessed society—without her permission or awareness. I'm never surprised when she eventually realizes that she has no idea how she came to believe what she believes about women, breasts, and belonging. If that's true for you, please know it's not unusual to get breast implants without ever questioning the underlying beliefs that drove you to them.

When your beliefs are right on top of you, it's difficult to see them as separate from yourself. When your breast-related beliefs dominate how you see yourself, your problem-solving mind doesn't question them or the social whims upon which they rest. Instead, it stays busy trying to ensure that you measure up to them. I call this part of your mind your **inner fixer**. It significantly influences your quest for *better* breasts. Unlike the behind-the-scenes process discussed in this chapter, you've been aware of and appeasing her most of your life. But, as we'll explore in Chapter 2, she's a huge fan of breast implants, and removing them from your body defies everything she stands for.

*Chapter* 2

# Meet Your Inner Fixer

Y our inner fixer tries fixing how you feel on the inside by "fixing" how you look on the outside. This part of your mind plays a massive role in your decision to get breast implants and is not okay with their removal. Understanding this part of your mind and learning new ways to respond to it are both essential to finding your way through your journey with breast implants and busting free from the Breast Rulebook. This chapter helps you get to know your inner fixer's origin story, her[6] favorite moves, and how you typically respond. It explores the problem with appeasing your inner fixer, particularly when it involves breast implants. You'll learn why she's a huge fan of implants and the six metaphorical moves she uses to keep them in your body. Just as Chapter 1 pulled back the curtain on the behind-the-scenes process fueling your quest for *better* breasts, this chapter exposes a part of your mind committed to its mission so ardently that it's willing to use your thoughts, images, memories, emotions, and body sensations against you.

---

[6] I use she/her/hers to refer to this part of your mind, however, please use whatever pronouns fit best for you.

Unlike the more familiar concept of an inner critic fueling self-criticism, often without justification, your inner fixer is on a mission to protect you from the threatening inner pain of being judged, ridiculed, or rejected. Knowing you live in an appearance-oriented society, she keeps vigil over your outward appearance. She constantly assesses and anticipates how it might threaten your sense of group belonging.

Like a home security system, your inner fixer is fast, nimble, and continually monitoring your body, mind, feelings, and actions. She has full access to your memories, stored images, and awareness of social standards, and she projects them to the front and center of your mind. She convinces you to assess yourself in the mirror carefully and then monitors your comparative thinking. She knows the conclusions your mind derives about you, your body, and your belonging. When you feel *less than*, she sounds the alarm by activating your nervous system's threat response.

She presents you with various self-improvement projects and hammers away at you to complete them. These projects can be noninvasive, such as appraising your reflection or studying photos to determine your *good* side, or they can involve manipulating your body by applying things to it, injecting products into it, and surgically altering it.

Like a confident know-it-all, she predicts the future and warns you of all the terrible things that will happen if you fail to listen to her. She assures you that she knows *the* way to safety. She works strategically and defensively; she takes her job very seriously. She will even use your thoughts, images, memories, emotions, and body sensations against you when she thinks you're risking ridicule, judgment, or abandonment.

## Understanding your inner fixer

Unlike the behind-the-scenes processes described in Chapter 1, your inner fixer is out in front, forward-facing, and remarkably familiar to you. You might even be able to identify when she first came on the scene. Understanding why she's with you and what she's trying to accomplish helps change your relationship with her.

To help you get a read on your inner fixer's origin story, I'll start by sharing my own. My inner fixer made her debut after just *one* comment from a brother about my first cellulite dimple. I had no idea that anyone around me was critically appraising my 12-year-old body. I was simply playing around our backyard pool. Because I was totally off guard, his words hit me hard. My youthful self-*unawareness* evaporated as I registered each of his six thoughtless words, "You better do something about that." I went from laughing, playing, and being totally in the moment to standing frozen in place, unable to think or speak. I felt overwhelmed by the weight of my newfound body shame.

Now that it knew my body's appearance could lead to judgment, my mind quickly determined it was a source of vulnerability. Like all human minds, it wanted to prevent this kind of humiliation from happening again. So it set up a command center to constantly assess my body for flaws and threats to my group acceptance. To enact this mission, it recruited and hired the inner fixer. My brother's words became her mantra: She would *do something about it*. She would fix things.

Like a skilled puppeteer moving a marionette, her commands controlled my actions. To minimize the chance of someone else seeing the offending dimple, she told me to make sure I was always the last one to get into the pool. She said it would be even better if I remained wrapped in a towel until I was at the pool's edge. She also pointed out how it was safer to leave it nearby for quick retrieval. Over time, she developed other strategies when I was wearing a swimsuit. She told me to find reasons to linger behind, just long enough so that no one I knew would end up walking behind me. Because that strategy often failed, she strongly encouraged me to wear sarongs, cover-ups, and swim shorts.

Her efforts to avoid judgment, promote group belonging, and avoid inner pain went beyond monitoring the backs of my thighs. She convinced me that my physical features that met or exceeded social standards were important to my belonging. She encouraged me to protect those assets, and she worried over the parts that were not *good enough*.

"Stay thin," she encouraged.

"Is your nose hump growing?" she worried.

Like a codependent empath, she spent all her time anticipating, avoiding, and fixing my inner pain of feeling *less than*. She offered up solutions, warned me what would happen if I didn't enact them, and comforted me with promises of relief if I did.

I'm sharing these private things about my inner fixer because I believe it will help you get to know yours. I hope it lets you see that your inner fixer is unlike an overactive inner critic, yammering away at you. Instead, your inner fixer is busting her ass, tirelessly hammering away at you so that you can avoid the pain of being cast out from the group. She doesn't tell you that you're not good enough; she jumps into action when someone or something else does. She doesn't intend for her worried warnings and self-improvement projects to tear you down. On the contrary, your inner fixer wants to build you up.

## Your inner fixer's origin story

Guided Audio 2.1 helps you get to know your inner fixer. It includes the information contained in this section and the following two sections as well. If you choose to use the guided audio, it's okay to read through these three sections either before or after listening.

**LISTEN TO GUIDED AUDIO 2.1**

Use the following prompts to reflect on your inner fixer's origin story, how she works inside you, and how you usually respond to her.[7] (Note: If any of these prompts feel triggering, consider working through them with a therapist or coach.)

— Do you recall a time in your younger life when you were self-*unaware* and unconcerned with others' thoughts about your body? If so, connect with any memory from that period of your life. Then sit quietly and give yourself the gift of mentally revisiting the memory and re-experiencing those feelings for one to two minutes.

— Can you identify any event(s) in your younger life that moved you from self-*unawareness* and ushered in your inner fixer?

— Irrespective of whether you can identify what ushered in your inner fixer, recall a memory when you were trying to avoid judgment from others. Then, simply notice the differences between the two memories.

## What worries your inner fixer?

Use the following prompts to look at your inner fixer's agenda.

---

[7] There are many reflective prompts throughout Busting Free. Please respond in whatever way works best for you: using a notebook to record written responses, talking through these prompts with a therapist, coach, or trusted person in your life, joining one of my groups (at amandasavagebrown.com), or sitting quietly in discernment. The most important thing here is that you reflect on the prompts rather than merely read them.

— Does she monitor the relative threat and fixability of your weight, skin color, aging skin, undereye circles, stretch marks, cellulite, teeth, hair, nose, neck, breasts, butt, belly, legs, hips, thigh gap, lip fullness, eyebrow thickness, or something else?

— What does she most try to help you avoid: judgment, ridicule, rejection, abandonment?

— Has she ever disagreed so strongly with you that she used your thoughts and feelings to overwhelm you? For example, even though I longed to wear a typical bikini bottom in hot tubs, my inner fixer convinced me that the risk of judgment from others was too high. She would take over my imagination and create all kinds of unsettling scenes depicting what might happen if others saw my cellulite. Wanting to avoid those possibilities, I repeatedly and dutifully followed her advice. I wore swim shorts in hot tubs, even though they bulged to ridiculous proportions as they filled with air from the jets and interfered with my ability to relax.

Earnestly responding to these prompts improves your understanding of this part of yourself and helps you respond with much more self-compassion and acceptance. It's okay if you can't immediately identify a story or event like mine. I've spent years reflecting on the impact of my brother's words; you've only recently been introduced to the concept of an inner fixer. So, if nothing immediately stands out, let your mind simmer on these prompts for a few days. In your quiet moments, gently reflect on the younger you and her experiences growing up. Then come back to these prompts or repeat Guided Audio 2.1.

## Using Movie Mind

Another way to envision your relationship with your inner fixer is by using a technique I call **Movie Mind**.[8] It's a perspective-giving exercise where you imagine a camera following you and documenting how you appear on the outside. It shows you what you do without any judgmental narration, manipulation of the image, or interpretation of any kind.

You can practice by reviewing footage from how you spent your time yesterday. Rather than watching each minute, simply notice what you were doing at different points throughout your day. See your facial expressions, the way you moved, where you went, and how you used your time. Hear your voice, your words, and your tone. Notice any scenes where you strayed from being the person you most want to be. Notice if you behaved toward somebody in a way you regret, agreed to do something you didn't want to, or wasted time on your phone instead of doing something important to you. Keep in mind: Don't use Movie Mind to shame yourself. Instead, use it to nonjudgmentally observe what you do.

Take one to two minutes now to watch scenes from yesterday as if you're parked at a drive-in movie starring you. (Note: Even when your mind tries convincing you to skip this, *you* can still pause and practice getting a feel for watching yourself from the outside.)

Now that you have a feel for Movie Mind, use it to create a highlight reel starring you and your inner fixer across your life. To select scenes where your inner fixer was orchestrating your actions, take advantage of knowing what you were thinking and feeling, like when you watch a movie after reading a book, and you know the main character's inner world as well.

---

[8] Movie Mind is something I adapted from Dr. Russ Harris, ACT Practitioner and Trainer. It may not be a fit for you when mental imagery doesn't come naturally to your mind. That's okay; you can still use the prompts to comb through your memories in whatever way usually works for you.

For example, my highlight reel includes hiding, lingering, wrapping up, dressing in specific ways, and strategizing around my cellulite. It features all the moments of self-scrutiny in the mirror. I like to include subtitles showing my inner fixer's reactions. For example, my husband once jokingly noted that the way I was sitting, hunched over with poor posture, was the same silhouette as an African lowland gorilla. Though it was a nerdy biologist's innocent observation, my inner fixer suspected it was *really* about my deflated post-nursing breasts. Subtitles to this scene reveal her devastation over failing to notice their threatening devolution.

My highlight reel shows every step I took toward getting breast implants, despite knowing that the human body doesn't play nice with foreign invaders. It shows me as I lived for years with cold, stiff, sensitive, and painful breasts. It includes my quick retreat after initially exploring explant in response to my sister's breast cancer diagnosis. You get the idea.

Now it's your turn. First, pull up to a mental drive-in movie featuring the different ways you appease your inner fixer. Then, gently and *without judgment,* observe what you see yourself doing in moments where you were:

— Overwhelmed by her ominous predictions. Are you avoiding doing things, dressing a certain way, moving, standing, positioning yourself a certain way, buying products, feeling jealous, threatened, or sad?

— Cajoled into doing something by her pretty promises. Notice if buying into those promises required you to compromise on something else important to you. For example, because I never believed the human body would put out a welcome mat to two foreign objects resting atop its heart and lungs, buying into her promises around breast implants meant I had to deny my intuition.

— Doing the same thing repeatedly in response to your inner fixer's relentless hammering away about something you need to fix, protect, or avoid. For example, I have countless scenes of me standing in front of a mirror, twisted at the waist, assessing my desirability and group safety relative to the backs of my thighs.

— Feeling relief by following your inner fixer's advice and suggestions about one part of your body, only to move on to feeling *less than* about another?

Reflecting on your life like this can understandably lead you to feel sadness, regret, anger, or confusion. So please take a moment to support yourself with a deep, slow inhale, followed by an even slower exhale. Then genuinely validate how hard and how long you've worked on your inner fixer's projects. Though it can be uncomfortable to watch this highlight reel, it can also motivate you to learn new ways to show up for yourself when you're feeling *less than* or *not good enough* as a woman in this world.

## The problem with appeasing your inner fixer

To understand the problem with appeasing your inner fixer, consider the following hypothetical question:[9]

If you feed a baby tiger every time it snarls, roars, or approaches, what will you end up with over time?

---

[9] The feeding a baby tiger metaphor is commonly used by ACT practitioners to explore the cost of avoidance of your inner experience.

Answer: A full-grown, eat-you-up, snarling, and roaring-even-louder tiger.

The same is true about your inner fixer. As the Movie Mind exercise revealed, following her advice doesn't lead your inner fixer to go away or stay quiet. Instead, she is emboldened by any relief her advice provides you, even more so if it leads to praise, attention, or desirability. When her advice helps you successfully dodge judgment from others or receive admiration, she makes sure you know she *told you so*. Doing her bidding strengthens her control over you and leads you both to believe that she knows what's best.

There's another fundamental problem with appeasing your inner fixer. She applies problem-solving approaches that work well on the outside to resolve pain on the inside. But unlike a kitchen fire, you can't put out the ongoing behind-the-scenes inner process that fuels human suffering (described in Chapter 1). So even though your inner fixer means well, appeasing her is like an exhausting, repetitive, and futile game of Whac-a-Mole. Your energy and awareness go into striking down whatever leads you to feel *not good enough*. But the game just plays on; other threats inevitably pop up—sometimes, the same one again and again.

For example, you finally achieve your target weight but then find yourself battling loose skin. You get Botox above your brows, and your smoothed forehead now draws your attention to the crow's feet around your eyes. You finally tame your hair into obedience, and then "natural" becomes a trend. If you've ever played Whac-a-Mole, then you know that there are those extra-pesky moles (such as cellulite, wrinkles, graying hair, thinning lips, and so forth) that pop right back up after you smash them down.

Bottom line: Appeasing your inner fixer keeps you busy doing things that never win the game. In a culture of ever-evolving beauty standards, arbitrary measures of worth, and predatory marketing, this part of your mind will never declare you safe.

## The high stakes of appeasing your inner fixer with breast implants

Appeasing your inner fixer with breast implants has high stakes because they are not problem-free or lifetime devices. Though your inner fixer might view them as a safe way to improve your appearance, appropriate studies to demonstrate their long-term safety were not completed by breast implant manufacturers. Until a data dump in 2019 by the FDA, over 450,000 alternative summary reports of problems with breast implants were not available to physicians and patients.[10] In other words, your inner fixer doesn't have all the facts. No one does.

However, there are several ways that breast implants are known to impact you beyond their aesthetics.[11] Though knowing this information is essential when breast implants are in your body, you might find it overwhelming depending on the thoroughness of the informed consent you received before getting breast implants. If you feel overwhelmed reading through this section, please take a moment to slow your breathing and steady yourself as you move through the material. Also, reassure yourself that knowing these things plays an integral part in finding your way through your journey with breast implants.

---

[10] The alternative summary reports not previously known to the public are now available at the FDA's website under MDR Data Files.

[11] Learn more at the breast implant resource list at amandasavagebrown.com

## Local complications

The longer you have breast implants inside your body, the more likely you are to develop problems at or around the implant, such as pain and stiffness with capsular contracture, displacement, shifting, wrinkling, rippling, bottoming out, asymmetry, deflation, or rupture. Not only are these aesthetically distressing, but they negatively impact your health and well-being. These types of complications leave you no option but to remove or replace them. When you are fearful of additional surgeries, you might live with chronic anxiety over the possibility that another one is looming in your future. You might experience regret if they are problematic or disappointing in any way.

## Financial impacts

When implants are placed for cosmetic augmentation, you will nearly always cover the cost of additional surgeries without the aid of health insurance, *even if your implants cause health complications*. Surgeries to safely remove breast implants are often more costly than placing them. You might feel guilt over the total amount of money invested across your lifetime to obtain, replace, remove, or monitor your implants (as discussed in the following section). Alternatively, you might experience insurmountable financial barriers forcing you to live with problematic, ruptured, or painful implants that threaten your health and well-being. These circumstances give rise to anxiety and depression as well.

## Screening concerns

Breast implants require monitoring while inside your body. If you opt for silicone-gel-filled implants, magnetic resonance imaging (MRI) and ultrasound are the only ways to screen for rupture. MRIs are costly and might not be covered by your health insurance when used for implant monitoring. Breast implants also interfere with monitoring your breasts for cancer. Not only do they interfere with the detection of breast cancer via mammography, but they also make mammograms more painful. Mammograms also introduce a risk of implant rupture, which might lead you to forgo the screening. There are alternative diagnostic options for breasts with implants, but you might not live near a facility that uses them, and they are often another out-of-pocket expense. Depending on your family history and personal values around breast cancer screening, particularly as you age, you might experience increasing worry over the increased safety risks and decreased accuracy of mammograms because of your implants.

## Breast-implant-associated cancer

Breast implants place you at risk for a type of cancer of the immune system known as breast-implant-associated anaplastic large cell lymphoma (**BIA-ALCL**). You might develop it many years after implant placement. It leads to persistent swelling and a mass or pain near your implant. BIA-ALCL is typically found in the scar capsule and fluid surrounding your implant. BIA-ALCL is treated by removing the implant and its surrounding scar capsule. If left untreated, this cancer can cause death. BIA-ALCL occurs more often with textured implants. As a result, you might experience the distress of a manufacturer recall if you have textured breast implants.

## Breast implant illness

In response to your body's battle against the bags, you might experience systemic health effects known as breast implant illness (BII).[12] Symptoms can occur immediately after breast implants are placed inside your body or many years later. Though you might appear well on the outside, you

---

[12] Visit the breast implant resource list at amandasavagebrown.com

might inwardly experience inflammation, chronic fatigue, joint and muscle pain, brain fog, memory impairment, heart palpitations, rashes, hair loss, recurring infections, gastrointestinal issues, thyroid and adrenal problems, hormonal disruption, onset of new allergies, food intolerance, headaches, chemical sensitivity, autoimmune disease, anxiety, or depression.

BII symptoms are non-specific and often misattributed to aging and perimenopause. Unrecognized BII might lead you to visit many doctors and specialists, pay for countless procedures, and receive distressing misdiagnoses. For example, I spent thousands of dollars and hundreds of hours pursuing treatment for severe inflammation, chronic body pain, hormone depletion, and disabling peripheral neuropathy in both of my arms. No one, including myself, considered that these things were related to my body's battle with its foreign invaders. Unfortunately, your body can be so overwhelmed by unrecognized BII that it loses the battle.

Although BII was brought to light by activists, investigative journalists, and talk-show hosts in the 1990s, including Connie Chung, Jenny Jones, and Oprah Winfrey, there is still no definitive test for it. It remains a diagnosis of exclusion. Without a diagnostic code or definitive test, it's impossible to know the morbidity and mortality of BII, but it impacts your physical, mental, emotional, and financial well-being.[13] However, many health practitioners refuse to acknowledge a causal link between breast implants and the declining health and well-being of women who have them. Other practitioners are simply unaware of it.

As a result, when you suspect you have BII, uninformed, dismissive, or biased healthcare providers might tell you it's not a recognized medical condition. As so often happens with women's health issues, the

---

[13] For help with BII's mental and emotional repercussions, please visit my blog at amandasavagebrown.com.

implication is that any association between your unresolved health issues and your breast implants is "all in your head." This unhelpful gaslighting leads to a delay in the recommended treatment for BII, which is to remove your breast implants and their surrounding scar capsules without swapping in a new set.

## Explant concerns

Your journey with breast implants is not a round-trip adventure. There's no returning to your natural scar-free breasts. Post-explant breasts and chests might be dimpled, creased, puckered, wrinkled, or have contour distortions. You might experience breast tissue loss or chest wall concavity. When you explant after breast reconstruction, you might face additional surgical challenges to remove any surgical mesh holding the implant in place, achieve aesthetic flat closure, or reconstruct a breast mound using tissue from another part of your body. Surgeons specializing in explant and aesthetic reconstruction often have long waitlists, require you to travel far distances, and come at high prices.

No matter what leads you to choose to remove and not replace your implants, it's no easy thing to do in a breast-obsessed society. Disconcerting and complex feelings often escalate in the days before surgery and sometimes stay with you long afterward. (Chapter 11 offers guidance on using BRITE Inner Healing to care for yourself while planning for and moving toward explant.)

## Other concerns

Your breast implants might interfere with how you sleep, breastfeed, exercise, snuggle, hug, and dress. They might clash with evolving values you hold around natural living or body acceptance. Ironically, the attention you receive because of your breast implants might be unwanted. You might be hyper-objectified in ways you didn't anticipate.

Rather than wearing clothes and swimsuits with the confidence you sought, you might join the ranks of countless women with breast implants who nearly never "show them off." Equally ironic, you might find that your augmented breasts lead to judgmental treatment from others, unwanted comments about your breasts, and a different kind of self-consciousness. You might wonder about your implants' role in intimate relationships when your partner has only known you with implants. Conversely, your partner might make it very clear that your implants matter a great deal to them.

---

There's a saying in ACT: "You hurt where you care." That means breast implants can impact you in many additional ways, depending on what they mean to you. If your breast implants affect(ed) you in ways not included in this section, those experiences also matter and are worthy of your recognition. (Chapter 7 helps you acknowledge your whole experience with breast implants. Chapter 9 enables you to companion yourself through it.)

## How your inner fixer views breast implants and explant

Despite the inevitability of getting more than you bargained for with breast implants, they align with your inner fixer's mission. From her view, they fix the problem of living in a breast-obsessed society with little to no breast tissue or different-than-ideally shaped breasts. Not surprisingly, she's a fan. She views implants as giving you everything that comes with better breasts: worth, desirability, sexiness, power, confidence, wholeness, womanhood, balanced proportions, hourglass shape, and so on. So she floods your mind with images of a better-busted you: happy, desired, confident, and *fixed*. When you face breast loss due to mastectomy, she echoes your surgical team's promise that breast implants offer you an escape route. She repeatedly reminds you that the Breast Rulebook states: *Breasts make you a woman.*

Remember, she isn't doing this to be critical or unhelpful. Whether she convinces you to get breast implants for augmentation or reconstruction, she believes they shield you from judgment and rejection. When she prevails, and your breast implants lead to attention, praise, financial gain, partnership, or soften the emotional loss of your natural breasts to cancer, they become one of her most significant accomplishments.

To your inner fixer, *breast implants=belonging*. And because your mind derives and sees things bi-directionally, she also believes *breast implant removal=threatened belonging*. Smaller, possibly distorted, post-explant breasts and explant-to-flat chests go against everything she stands for. She doesn't want you doing something that defies the Breast Rulebook. She wants you to keep your breast implants, despite any problems, disappointments, or financial or lifestyle impacts from them. She concedes that you could start over with a new set if necessary. *But whatever you do*, she warns from her inner sanctum of influence and authority, *don't even consider life without breast implants.*

## Your inner fixer's metaphorical moves

When you do find yourself considering explant, your inner fixer works to dissuade you. She cues up a disorienting amount of what I refer to as **aesthetic anxiety.** When you persist, she marshals all her inner resources to overwhelm you. In other words, considering or moving toward breast implant removal is one of those times when your inner fixer uses your thoughts, beliefs, judgments, images, and memories against you.

Throughout this book, I use a metaphor that moving through your journey with temporary and problem-prone breast implants is like driving through a series of roundabouts. Chapter 4 gives you a map of these roundabouts and helps you figure out which one you currently circle. But, for now, just keep in mind that your inner fixer takes full advantage of her ability to access your memories, beliefs, feelings, imagination, and threat responses to prevent you from exiting your current roundabout.

She uses the following six metaphorical moves to keep you circling the inside lane (aka **Inner Fixer Lane**):

1.  Prevents you from using *your* values to guide what you do next and how you treat yourself along the way. It's like blocking your vehicle's compass, so you have no way to orient yourself when you veer off course.

2.  Turns on **Bad Boobs Radio**, which plays all your most feared predictions of life without breast implants. She covers the rearview mirror with replays of any memories that led you to get breast implants. She erects roadside billboards of images predicting how you will look and how others will treat you if you exit toward explant. She keeps you so focused on the past and fearing the future that you have no time to care for problems needing your attention in the here and now.

3.  Recruits an army of loud and demanding **backseat drivers** to bully you into following the Breast Rulebook. You're so accustomed to appeasing your inner fixer that you do the same with her backseat minions. When they speak up, you treat what they're saying like commands. Although you're behind the wheel, they control the drive.

4.  Catches you in the trap of struggling against your feelings. Trying to avoid, minimize, or disconnect from unpleasant feelings while defying the Breast Rulebook is like driving a car with your fingers in a finger trap. It doesn't work.

5. Uses your breast-related self-concept to obscure the windshield. You can't see past what your breasts mean to you or imagine yourself without breast implants. You fear that moving forward means losing yourself.

6. Keeps you so busy circling Inner Fixer Lane that you don't take driven actions to reclaim your body, mind, and heart from the inside out.

As many women can attest, it's possible to push yourself through the physical side of explanting, with your inner fixer sounding the alarm and her backseat drivers rioting. But doing so elevates your distress and makes this challenging journey even harder.

## Another way

As I went through my explant journey, I was surprised at my inner fixer's reprisal. The more I moved toward explant, the more she hijacked my mind. I was shocked at the old, familiar thoughts ricocheting around my mind about women, breasts, and belonging. Even though I was eager to be implant-free, my inner fixer erected distressing mental billboards depicting me as being *less than* in various ways without my augmented breasts. She whispered that I would lose social standing, power, and worth. She cautioned me about how it would feel to have post-explant breasts after knowing the joys of a full bust. *Just imagine intimacy*, she scoffed. In the days leading up to my surgery, she was desperate to prevent me from going through with explant. So my entire body trembled with anticipatory fear as she heightened my fear of dying under general anesthesia. After explant, she didn't pack up and head out. Chapter 6 describes how I yielded to her hammering away at me over an incredibly disappointing post-explant crease. Being a specialist in women's self-acceptance, I was humbled.

Given my inner fixer was causing me so much trouble, I wondered how other women were coping with theirs. As fate would have it, three weeks before my explant surgery date, I had to get back on Facebook to receive updates about one of our daughter's extracurricular activities. (I left the platform years earlier because I found it unhelpful to my inner peace.) To my surprise, there were groups filled with countless women considering or moving through explant (primarily due to BII).

In those groups, I witnessed untold amounts of suffering. I saw women overwhelmed with aesthetic anxiety, invalidating their feelings because they "did this to themselves," fearing or experiencing abandonment by breast-obsessed partners, and doubting that explant would improve their health and be worth sacrificing their breast aesthetics. I saw women panicking in the days leading up to their surgeries. My heart broke as I watched women lose their battle with BII because they couldn't afford explant. I witnessed women struggling with gaslighting, medical trauma, and new-onset anxiety disorders, depression, and suicidal thinking. I could fill pages recounting how these temporary, problem-prone, and incompletely studied devices impact women's psychosocial well-being.

For many years, I've used ACT to help women successfully reclaim their lives from anxiety, grief and loss, trauma, body nonacceptance, people-pleasing, and unhealthy relationships with themselves and others. I saw women struggling with all those things before, during, and after breast implant loss. And I *knew* ACT's science-based approach would help women prevail over the psychosocial challenges on these journeys. So, I set out to translate ACT's strategies specifically to help women bust free from living with problematic breast implants and reclaim their body, mind, and heart from the Breast Rulebook. The result is BRITE Inner Healing. The next chapter presents it to you.

Through BRITE Inner Healing, I stopped playing my inner fixer's futile game of Whac-a-Mole. More importantly, I emerged from my journey with breast implants, finally knowing how to give myself acceptance. I did so simply by practicing what I teach to women just like you. That means you don't have to be a trained psychotherapist to do this stuff. You only need the willingness to stop buying into your inner fixer's avoidance agenda and try something new instead.

# Chapter 3

# BRITE Inner Healing Lights the Way

Though getting and removing breast implants involve many conversations, considerations, and concerns over your breasts' appearance, both decisions involve a powerful inner journey taking place on a much deeper level. By finding your way through the complicated internal processes described in Chapters 1 and 2, you take charge of your journey with breast implants. You liberate yourself from automatically following the Breast Rulebook. No longer living a life dominated by your inner fixer's futile agenda, you give yourself the same love, care, and concern you show others, even when you're feeling *less than*. You also reconnect with what matters deep down in your heart, beyond the things society prizes. Instead of falling prey to predatory marketing, you live life on your terms. That's what busting free and inner healing is all about.

This chapter explores why inner healing is often overlooked on your journey with breast implants and explores what you miss when it remains neglected. It also presents BRITE Inner Healing as a solution to the ongoing behind-the-scenes process fueling your quest for *better* breasts. BRITE Inner Healing draws from Acceptance and Commitment Therapy (ACT).[14] So this chapter orients you to ACT's tenets and how they liberate your body, mind, and heart from futile control agendas like the one your inner fixer holds. Then, it explores how that liberation makes a difference on your journey with breast implants. Finally, it ends by helping you be real with yourself about what to anticipate and guard against as you move forward.

## A hidden opportunity

Busting free and reclaiming yourself is a hidden opportunity on your journey with breast implants. I refer to it as hidden because seeing it doesn't come easily. Like the star of the show, the physical aspects of getting or removing implants dominate your awareness. How could they not? After all, these are not minor surgeries, and they involve one of the most sexually objectified parts of your body.

Despite your inner experience directing the show, it's overshadowed by the spotlight-hogging body-based side of breast augmentation, reconstruction, or implant removal. For example, when you experience an implant rupture, recall, or breast implant illness, you often face explant without knowing how to *truly* care for the part of you that opted for implants. Even when you remove your implants without an urgent change catalyst, busting free from the Breast Rulebook might not cross your mind.

Though you're likely very aware of your aesthetic anxiety leading up to surgery, mental and emotional healing might not be at the front of your mind. You might tell yourself you'll get to that part after surgery

---

[14] As mentioned in the Introduction, ACT is spoken as a word rather than three letters. It's also known as Acceptance and Commitment Training, depending on its use.

and recovery. And if you are pleased with your post-explant appearance and feel physically better, it's easy to believe you found an express lane through healing.

However, explant only removes problematic breast implants from your body; it doesn't remove you from the unhelpful messaging around your body. It doesn't quiet your inner fixer, erase the Breast Rulebook, or stop your mind from constantly assessing how you measure up. And, you repeat what you don't repair. So you continue playing your inner fixer's Whac-a-Mole game as you move forward in an appearance- and youth-oriented society with an aging body and a mind that didn't bust free. In other words, there's no detour around inner healing.

## BRITE Inner Healing lights the way

Although BRITE is an acronym for Breast Implant Through Explant, BRITE Inner Healing refers to the ACT-based program I created to help anyone whose life journey includes breast implants. BRITE Inner Healing shines a bright light on your harder-to-see inner journey and helps you find *your* way through it. It enables you to prevail over the mental and emotional barriers that inevitably arise. It repairs your relationship with yourself and changes how you respond to your inner fixer. Once she knows you've got your own back and can care for the inner pain of feeling *less than* or *not good enough*, she reaches for her hammer much less often.

You can use BRITE Inner Healing's skills and tools to bust free from the Breast Rulebook, whether you are:

— enjoying your current set of breast implants;

— considering removing your breast implants;

— living with problematic implants that you can't afford or aren't ready to remove;

— actively preparing for explant;

— adjusting to your post-explant chest;

— yearning for complete healing after explant.

No matter where you are in your journey with breast implants, you deserve to be in charge of the drive. BRITE Inner Healing puts you there.

## What is ACT?

ACT is a mindfulness-based approach for changing what you *do*, inside and out, so you live a life that's meaningful to you. It's known to ease many types of suffering and help overcome numerous life problems, from test-taking anxiety to trauma recovery. Though you may not have heard of ACT, it was developed several decades ago based on scientific principles. Its effectiveness is continually examined.[15] It's my honor to use its strategies to help others transform their lives.

After practicing ACT for many years, I know that *acceptance* and *commitment* are often misunderstood. I've even seen suggestions that ACT is a sadistic therapy, teaching you to like pain! That is simply untrue. Furthermore, ACT is not about compliance, giving up, or tolerating pain. Instead, ACT uses acceptance strategies to help you turn toward, allow, and make room for your inner experiences. Just like you can accept a gift that you don't want, acceptance helps you make room for all your thoughts, feelings, and sensations, even the unwanted ones. It doesn't do this to be sadistic; it helps you do this because struggling against your inner experience often interferes with living life. Chapter 9 focuses on the role acceptance plays in BRITE Inner Healing. For now, though, rest assured that ACT doesn't leave you simmering in your

---

[15] As of March 2022, there were over 900 worldwide randomized controlled clinical trials on ACT, listed on the Association for Contextual Behavior Sciences website, https://contextualscience.org/ACT_Randomized_Controlled_Trials.

suffering because *commitment* means doing things, no matter how small, to move toward the life outcomes you desire. It's not "something weird involving couples or marriage therapy," as my hairdresser once said to me.

Working with an ACT practitioner like me is different from the stereotypical psychotherapy sessions frequently depicted on TV and in films. Though sense-making and purpose-finding are important in ACT, you learn how to use its tenets by experiencing them. For example, if you and I were working together, I would help you experience present moment awareness in your body and mind, rather than just talking about it. I would teach you to catch when you're stuck in the past or frozen with fear over the future. I would ensure that you knew how to bring yourself back to the here and now. (As you'll see, the material throughout this book is written with the same spirit. This book isn't just to read. It's a book to *do*.)

Just like learning another language doesn't replace the one you already know, ACT acknowledges that your mind maintains what it has already learned and derived, despite any new thoughts, feelings, and beliefs you acquire over time. That's why this book doesn't include material aimed at convincing you to *stop* caring about your breast aesthetics. Instead, it helps you deal with the reality that a part of you might always care about how they (and the rest of you) appear to others.

ACT distinguishes between the "clean pain" you inevitably experience throughout life (most often because you deeply care about something, like group belonging) and the suffering your mind adds by drawing its own conclusions, like determining you're worth *less* because of your breasts or post-explant chest's appearance. Rather than wagging a finger at you for comparing yourself to others or for hoping that breast implants would help you feel better, ACT sees the pain of feeling *less than* or *not good enough* as a universal human experience. It normalizes the pain of not measuring up to society's standards and recognizes that no one's life is struggle-free. Unlike traditional views on mental and emotional health, ACT doesn't view struggling with thoughts and feelings as indicators that something's wrong with you. In ACT, psychological well-being is about how you respond to your disturbing thoughts and feelings, not their absence.

Like yoga, Pilates, and stretching improve your body's flexibility, ACT uses six strategies to improve your **psychological flexibility.** Though that sounds rather clinical, psychological flexibility simply means staying present and doing what's important to you in any given situation, even with challenging thoughts, unpleasant feelings, and uncomfortable body sensations. But, rather than gritting your teeth through challenging moments, ACT's processes help you be less impacted by them.

ACT's tenets include:

1. Using your **values** to guide your choices and actions.
2. **Present moment awareness** to stay focused on the here and now and notice your whole experience.
3. Using your **Observing Self** to see yourself and your experiences with flexible perspectives.
4. **Cognitive defusion** to separate what you do from what you think.
5. **Acceptance** of your inner experience so you can free yourself from struggling against it.
6. **Committed action** to do what it takes to move in your chosen direction.

Figure 3.1 shows the **ACT hexaflex.** It's a schematic showing ACT's six processes as points around a hexagon, with lines showing their interconnectedness. To me, it looks like a diamond with many facets.

But those lines aren't just drawn for effect; they show that when you're working on one process, you're relying on and reinforcing the others. They also show that all the processes work individually and collectively to improve your psychological flexibility; there's no starting point or rigid sequence to follow. None of the processes is more important than another.

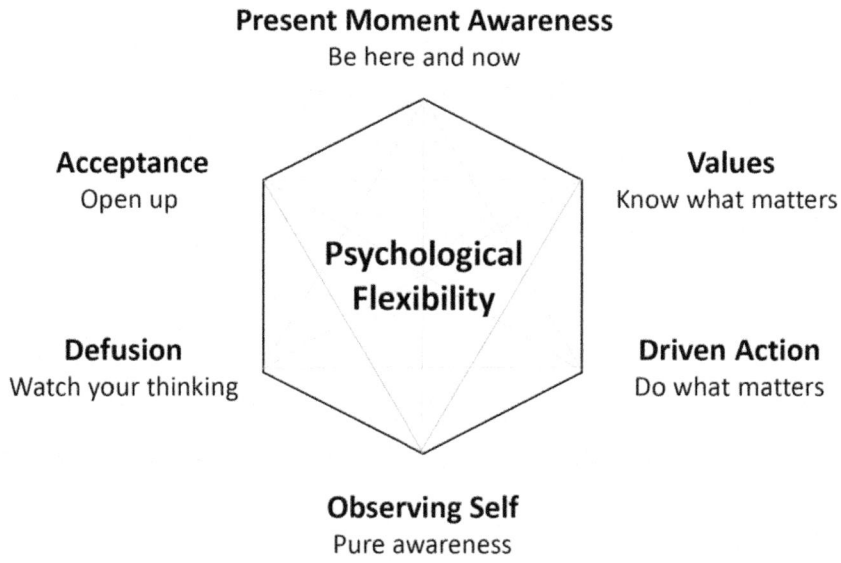

Figure 3.1 The ACT Hexaflex

Rather than discussing these processes further at this point, Chapters 6-11 explore each one in a way that makes it relevant to your journey with breast implants. I translate each of them using language that's less clinical and more relatable. At this point, keep in mind the following two things: 1) You will use each of these processes to reclaim your body, mind, and heart from the Breast Rulebook; and 2) because the processes are interconnected, as soon as you start working with one, you are building and strengthening the others.

## Acting on the control agenda

ACT's processes focus on something you can choose to *do* privately in your mind and body or publicly in your life. It does that because your actions are the only thing you control in life. Reading that might surprise you because chances are high you've been told throughout life to "stop thinking like that" or to "get over something." As a result, you probably buy into the myth those feats are possible. But here's the truth: *Your thoughts and feelings are not entirely under your control.*

Usually, when I say the preceding ten words to a client, her eyebrows furrow in disagreement or shoot up her forehead in surprise. Yours might be as well, so let's explore the concept further through two easy, brief exercises:

1. To test your power of thought control, let's see how you do with not thinking about something. To put this in your favor, I won't ask you to work with a distressing thought. Instead, just pay careful attention *right now* to what happens in your mind when I invite you to sit quietly for the next several seconds and, no matter what, *do not* think about a puppy.
   (Seriously, take about 30 seconds just to sit here and not think about a puppy!)
   If your mind is like nearly every other mind, it immediately thought of a puppy. You might have seen an image of a puppy in your mind. If you tried distracting yourself by thinking of something else, your mind's clever enough to know it was doing that to avoid thinking about a puppy, which means you were *still* thinking about a puppy.

2. To test your ability to control your feelings, we'll make it a bit easier and work with an emotion commonly regarded as "positive." All you need to do is love the next stranger you meet.

But it can't be that general "love one another" type of love. Instead, it should be deep and abiding love; the kind of love where you're willing to die for that person. Now, go ahead and command yourself to turn that type of love on *right now* and have it ready to go for whomever that next person might be.

Are you ready to go with deep, abiding love?

Typically, when I do this exercise with a client, she looks curiously at me and tentatively smiles. If your mind is like hers, mine, and most others, it scoffs at this proposition. It offers up several reasons why the idea is ridiculous. It points out how impossible it is to love on command. It states that you can't just turn on an emotion. It also points out that your feelings just don't work like that. When considering this scenario involving a "positive" emotion, your mind knows that feeling love involves more than telling yourself to do so. Yet that's exactly what it tries to do with unpleasant feelings.

Bottom line: The mythical control agenda doesn't work. After a lifetime of being told it's possible, you might hold the unrealistic self-expectation that you *should* be able to control your thoughts and feelings. As you will see, letting go of that notion is an integral part of BRITE Inner Healing. But unfortunately, your mind and society continually promote those ideas, so please remember your experience with these two exercises.

## BRITE flexibility

Given the futility of trying to control your thoughts and feelings, BRITE Inner Healing targets other things you can do to promote your **BRITE flexibility**. Like the ACT concept of psychological flexibility, BRITE flexibility helps you bust free from your old ways of responding to the Breast Rulebook and move on a new path toward reclaiming yourself.

As you move through your journey with breast implants, BRITE flexibility helps you catch when your inner fixer is using your thoughts, memories, feelings, beliefs, and nervous system against you. For example, when you're delighted with your breast implants, BRITE flexibility helps you monitor their evolving impacts on your body, lifestyle, and well-being. When you're unsure if you want to remove or replace them, BRITE flexibility helps you bring your whole self to bear on that decision. When you remove your breast implants, BRITE flexibility helps you show up to each tender moment leading up to the surgery and throughout recovery. And when you continue struggling with your inner fixer after explant, BRITE flexibility offers you another way.

No matter where you are in your journey with breast implants, moving through it with BRITE flexibility helps you emerge with a long-overdue practice of self-acceptance that serves you far beyond this journey. BRITE flexibility gives you the inner skills to companion your inner fixer rather than appease her. You know more helpful ways to respond when feeling *less than* or *not enough* in a profit-driven society that will forever prey upon your innate human drive to belong.

Figure 3.2 shows the ACT hexaflex converted into the **BRITE diamond**. It provides a snapshot of what you do to foster your BRITE flexibility. By practicing the inner skills presented throughout *Busting Free*, you will forge your own BRITE diamond.

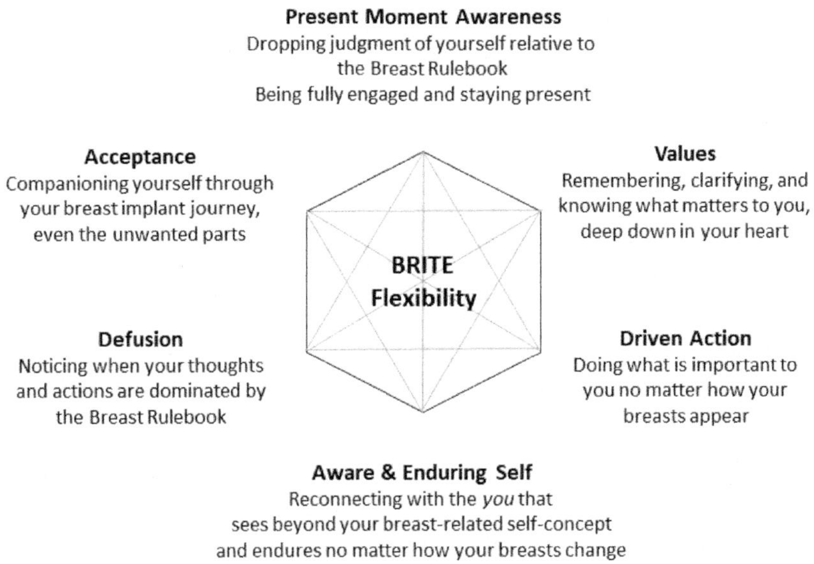

**Present Moment Awareness**
Dropping judgment of yourself relative to
the Breast Rulebook
Being fully engaged and staying present

**Acceptance**
Companioning yourself through
your breast implant journey,
even the unwanted parts

**Values**
Remembering, clarifying, and
knowing what matters to you,
deep down in your heart

**BRITE**
**Flexibility**

**Defusion**
Noticing when your thoughts
and actions are dominated by
the Breast Rulebook

**Driven Action**
Doing what is important to
you no matter how your
breasts appear

**Aware & Enduring Self**
Reconnecting with the *you* that
sees beyond your breast-related self-concept
and endures no matter how your breasts change

*Figure 3.2 The BRITE diamond*

# Hidden and unhelpful hopes

After only a minute or two of searching online, you can quickly see how
breast implant marketing promotes the Breast Rulebook. When you opt
for them, it's with great hope. However, when you eventually consider
or follow through on removing them, it usually means there's a rather
large gulf between what you wanted for yourself by getting breast
implants versus what you got from them. That gulf fills with unwanted
thoughts and painful feelings, such as sadness or anger over how it
worked out for you, anxiety over surgery and recovery, or
apprehensiveness over post-explant aesthetics. When you suspect you
have BII, the gulf might also fill with worry over not feeling better after
explant. After breast reconstruction, you face additional layers of grief
and loss with explant.

It makes perfect sense to feel confused, distressed, or angry over getting more than you bargained for from breast implants. However, since you can't command your thoughts and feelings, it's unreasonable to move toward explant and pressure yourself to feel *only* gratitude, care *only* about your health, or *stop caring* about your breasts. You also invalidate yourself afterward by commanding yourself to *be happy with your post-explant body*. You might feel those things *and* experience other thoughts and feelings worthy of support and care. (Chapters 8 and 9 provide more-practical alternatives to these well-intentioned but often unhelpful approaches.)

Hidden hopes and self-expectations like those are risky because when you (naturally and understandably) continue to worry or feel concerned, your inner fixer convinces you it's because you're making (or made) a mistake. She declares that the skills throughout this book *just don't work for you.*

"See?" she asks.

"It *really* is better for you to just listen to me," she declares.

You've had enough of that kind of self-sabotage. It's also the last thing you need when doing something that defies social programming about your breasts and belonging.

Don't get me wrong: I want you to suffer less as you find your way through this messy inner stuff. It's the entire reason I'm writing this book! I even anticipate that you will notice many moments where you feel happy, grateful, and peaceful as you work through BRITE Inner Healing. But goals to *stop worrying, caring,* or *thinking* about things are known in ACT as **dead-person goals**, meaning they are something a dead person does much better than you.

More helpful and realistic goals with BRITE Inner Healing include having your own back, no matter what your breasts look like, or not allowing fear of judgment, rejection, or feeling *less than* to dominate how you live your life. You might still feel those things, but with BRITE Inner Healing, you'll know what to do for yourself when they're with you. As you work through this book's material, it's helpful to guard against any hidden and unhelpful goals you might hold around controlling or changing your thoughts and feelings, and instead focus on learning beneficial ways to respond to them.

## Taking back the wheel

I want to acknowledge that the road to reclaiming your body, mind, and heart from breast implants is often paved with difficult and painful moments. I was so afraid of the surgery and drains that I put off removing my breast implants until one ruptured. In the weeks leading up to my explant surgery, my inner fixer warned that breast implant loss might devalue me. Since removing my breast implants, I frequently grieve my unnatural aesthetic outcome. Though I don't miss having implants, I also don't like having a distorted post-explant chest.

As ACT's tenets show, having difficult thoughts or feelings before, during, and after my explant journey doesn't mean there's something wrong with me. Nor does it mean that my inner skills aren't working or that I haven't inwardly healed. Instead, they alert me that I'm facing something that feels difficult to me, as inevitably happens in life. Those thoughts and feelings help me recognize that it's time to *do* something helpful for myself. So, I care for my inner pain rather than abandoning it or telling myself to *get over it*. I describe how to do that for yourself throughout this book.

I'm disclosing these things about my journey to reinforce that BRITE Inner Healing isn't designed for dead people. In other words, it doesn't eradicate your breast-related concerns. Instead, it honors the reality that a part of you will likely always care about your breasts' aesthetics simply because you're a human with a mind and heart capable of caring about things that hold symbolic meaning. Struggling on your inner journey with breast implants doesn't indicate you're vain, weak, or misguided. It happens because breasts are the icon of femininity.

Not surprisingly, getting and removing breast implants involve a great deal of concern about how your breasts look. And both decisions involve a powerful inner journey that impacts you far beyond your breasts' appearance. Fueled by the ongoing behind-the-scenes process described in Chapter 1, it pushes you around before, during, and long after explant. But it doesn't have to take you for a ride.

Through BRITE Inner Healing, you take back the wheel. You stop buying into your inner fixer's futile control agenda. In doing so, you free yourself to set out on a completely different journey. Like kintsugi pottery repaired with bright golden lacquer, you put your best effort into healing yourself.

By translating ACT's tenets to the breast implant-through-explant journey, BRITE Inner Healing offers you inner skills that transform self-acceptance from a "wouldn't that be nice to have" concept into a choice you make and actions you take. It empowers you to step back from your unhelpful beliefs, see beyond your breast-related self-concept, take care of yourself as a woman in a breast-obsessed society, and do the things that matter most to you. Though your body may be scarred, BRITE Inner Healing helps you emerge from your journey more resilient than ever before.

As you'll see in Chapter 4, choosing to work on your inner healing puts you on a path to reclaiming yourself. You can take this path no matter where you are in your journey with breast implants, even if you want to keep them or long ago removed them.

All that matters is that you choose to take it.

# Chapter 4

# Know Where You Are on The BRITE Roadmap

This chapter presents you with the **BRITE Roadmap**. It's part map and part travel guide. It extends the metaphor (introduced in Chapter 2) that moving through this journey is like driving through a series of roundabouts, with your inner fixer working to keep you circling rather than exiting. The BRITE Roadmap helps you visualize an alternate, more mindful path through your journey with breast implants. You'll learn each roundabout's defining characteristics, including what you're doing, thinking, and feeling while circling them, and what helps you finally exit each one. You'll finish this chapter oriented to your deeply felt and harder-to-see inner journey with breast implants. Irrespective of where you are in your journey or why you are reading this book, the BRITE Roadmap helps you make sense of past struggles and know what lies ahead.

# The BRITE Roadmap

I developed the BRITE Roadmap based on one of the most respected theories of change: the **Transtheoretical Model** (TTM).[16] The TTM shows how you move through a predictable process when considering a "good for you" change (such as giving up cigarettes, drinking less alcohol, exercising regularly, learning mindfulness, or leaving a neglectful partner). This process unfolds over time, sometimes many years, while you consider the benefits and costs. I like the TTM because it validates that most of us struggle with change, particularly in the earlier stages. I also appreciate how it normalizes that setbacks are part of the change process and points to ways to minimize and learn from them.

The TTM shows how you typically think, feel, and act as you move through the following five stages of change:

1. **Precontemplation:** You're building awareness of the need to change.
2. **Contemplation:** Your mindset goes back and forth as you accumulate more pros toward making the change than cons.
3. **Preparation:** You decide that the change is worth it and develop a plan for moving forward.
4. **Action:** You implement your plan.
5. **Maintenance:** You integrate the change into your life.

The TTM works well for modeling what you do when you get more than you bargained for from your breast implants, and what you might

---

[16] The Transtheoretical Model was developed in the late 1970s, by Prochaska and DiClemente, to conceptualize what we think and feel as we ready ourselves to act on a new, healthier behavior. By understanding how a person is typically thinking and feeling at each stage, interventions were optimized to help people progress through change. Its framework is now widely applied across many health-promoting behaviors (e.g., mammography screening, developing an exercise habit, using sunscreen or condoms, anti-bullying, etc.) and addictive behaviors (e.g., smoking cessation, drinking less alcohol).

typically think, feel, and do as you move through the health behavior change of breast implant removal. But these journeys are not straightforward, especially given the ongoing behind-the-scenes process giving rise to the Breast Rulebook and your inner fixer's devotion to it.

So, I created the BRITE Roadmap using a series of roundabouts (Figure 4.1). Each has unique challenges, opportunities, and inside lanes. You circle your current roundabout until something in your life, health, or mindset changes. The BRITE roundabouts also model that your progress isn't one-way: You can be so overwhelmed, unsupported, or disappointed that you take a "**reversal route**" to an earlier stage. Reversal routes are explored more in the next section.

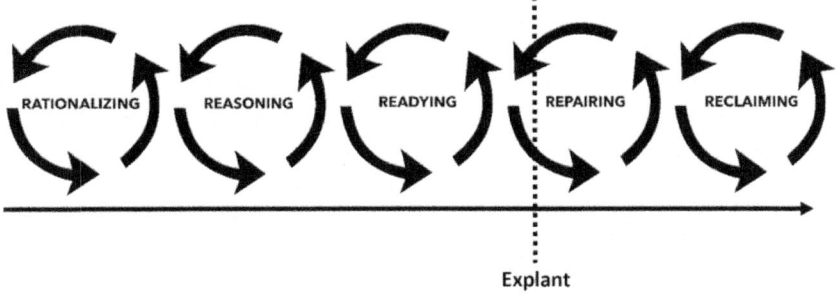

*Figure 4.1 The BRITE Roadmap*

Important things about the BRITE Roadmap:

— Although it shows an explant experience, there are things you can do to reclaim yourself from the Breast Rulebook long before and long after breast implant removal.

— The names of each roundabout reflect what you're doing on your inner journey with breast implants and their removal. Conveniently, the names of the Readying and Repairing Roundabouts also describe what you're physically doing relative to explant surgery.

— On the far left, you're dominated by your inner fixer and focused mainly on aesthetics. As a result, you aren't interested in change, even if you have problems with your breast implants.

— You move right as two things increase: problems with your breast implants and your awareness of those problems.

— The inside lane of each roundabout is called Inner Fixer Lane. As discussed in Chapter 2, your inner fixer floods you with unpleasant thoughts, painful memories, distressing images, uncomfortable feelings, and so forth to keep you circling the inside lane of your current roundabout.

— Depending on what your breast implants mean to you, it's possible to circle the first three roundabouts until you've accumulated more problems than you can tolerate, or you're forced to move by an external event such as BII or a ruptured or recalled implant.

— Even when you explant, you can only move through the Repairing Roundabout by fully reclaiming yourself from the Breast Rulebook.

BRITE Inner Healing offers you a different path through the BRITE Roadmap. Though you still pass through each roundabout, you catch when you're circling Inner Fixer Lane. Because you know different ways to respond to your inner fixer's agenda and the Breast Rulebook, you spend less time circling and suffering. You make choices based on what matters to *all of you* (noted throughout this book as *you*). You become your own inner companion and repair your relationship with yourself, irrespective of when and if you explant. You bust free and continually act on your own behalf to live on *your* terms as a woman in a youth, breast, and beauty-obsessed society. (Chapter 11 helps you visualize what that means to you.)

# The Five BRITE Roundabouts

By exploring what you're doing outwardly and inwardly in each roundabout, you can find your "You Are Here" pointer on the BRITE Roadmap. Knowing which one you currently circle helps you move through the material in this book. So as you read through each roundabout's characteristics, see which one feels like the best fit for you. If you think you might be in more than one, that indicates you're in a time of transition. If you already explanted, it's okay to focus on the last two roundabouts. But to optimize your understanding of this journey and the change process in general, I encourage you to read through the first three as well.

## Rationalizing Roundabout

Rationalizing is something we all do. It helps you tolerate how you feel when you're doing something that doesn't feel quite right or goes against your values. For example, if you value reducing your impact on the environment, you'll feel guilty throwing away an empty plastic bottle when there's nowhere to recycle it. The emotion of guilt shows up when you're doing something against your values. Your discomfort with guilt is designed to get your attention, so you choose differently next time. Because guilt is uncomfortable, you might use rationalization to feel better.

In the recycling example, you might tell yourself: *I needed to be hands-free* or *I had too many other things to carry* or *There wasn't any room for it in my bag.* Rationalizing like this helps you feel better about prioritizing your convenience over your value of recycling. However, although rationalizing lets you "off the hook" and gives you relief, it disconnects you from what you care about when you do it too often. And while it might not be a big deal with a random plastic bottle here and there, it can be a huge deal when compromising on things related to your health and well-being.

Rationalization shows up on your inner journey with breast implants in two different ways. One way is to help you feel okay about getting breast implants put into your body when doing so goes against something important to you, such as living naturally, organically, authentically, or with body acceptance. This was *absolutely* the case with me. I took months to rationalize my way onto the implant table. I knew that the human body would be irritated by two foreign objects. After the safety issues in the 1990s, I still didn't trust that they were safe. I was also terrified of being put under general anesthesia and not waking up. I dreaded the recovery because, years earlier, I helped care for my older sister after she got breast implants to achieve symmetry in her breast size. It seemed rough on her at the time, and I didn't want anything to do with it for myself. I also disliked that breast implants promote the sexual objectification of women. Bottom line: Even considering getting them violated my values of self-care, safety, and respect.

So I rationalized that breast implants *must be safe*; otherwise, they wouldn't be FDA-approved, and doctors wouldn't put them into our bodies. I comforted myself that the high viscosity gel-filled implants were safe after being told they wouldn't leak. To make my choice more credible, I pointed out that I was simply restoring the shape and volume I lost in my breasts after dutifully making the lauded maternal sacrifice of breastfeeding for a year. To appease the concerned scientist in me, I also enrolled in a clinical study.[17] My story is an excellent example of how rationalizing leads to self-abandonment. Everything in me was

---

[17] Not only did the study in which I enrolled abruptly end and fail to provide meaningful longitudinal outcome data on its enrollees, but it also asked many subjective and leading questions about my experience with breast implants. I remember feeling concerned that the data being gathered was incomplete at best and misleading at worst.

alerting me not to move forward, but I didn't honor my intuition or values.

Not every woman has to rationalize her way onto the implant table. My sister skipped into the surgical center for her breast augmentation. She didn't feel conflicted in any way. Instead, she had painful feelings and memories from living with mismatched breasts. She trusted the medical industry and viewed her surgery as deliverance from suffering. Because my sister didn't feel bad, there was no need for her mind to rationalize what she was doing.

Whether you're like my sister or me, you still spend time circling the Rationalizing Roundabout because breast implants are not problem-free devices. Moreover, the longer you keep them in your body, the more you risk developing problems.[18] You inevitably get more than you bargained for from breast implants. Even the inherently biased studies conducted by breast implant manufacturers show that nearly half of first-time augmentation patients and nearly three out of four reconstruction patients experience issues within the first three years.[19]

As you circle the Rationalizing Roundabout, your mind guards against acknowledging implant-related problems as anything serious. You label them as *minor* or tell yourself, *I'll get corrective surgery if needed*. You might feel defensive, dismissive, rebellious, or resigned when confronted with emerging information regarding breast implant safety, or you might avoid it altogether. You might judge women who experience BII or other implant-related problems as gullible, "crazy", or overly sensitive. You might comfort yourself, like I did, with beliefs that regulatory agencies wouldn't approve breast implants if they were harmful. You remind yourself that breast augmentation is among the

---

[18] https://www.fda.gov/medical-devices/breast-implants/things-consider-getting-breast-implants
[19] What you need to know about breast implants, National Center for Health Research, https://www.center4research.org/breast-implants/

most common plastic surgery. You reassure yourself that women have lived with implants in place for decades.

Engaging in rationalization like this is a classic avoidance move. In Chapter 9, you'll learn more about it and other thinking strategies commonly used to avoid your feelings. Just know that you're not willfully trying to dupe yourself. You might not even realize you're doing this. You're simply trying to disconnect from feeling guilt, disappointment, or other uncomfortable feelings involving your breast implants.

With the development of any issues related directly to your breast implants, there is likely an underlying fear that maybe your breast implants are, in fact, *not* problem-free. Though you might be disappointed with whatever issues you notice, rationalization lets you avoid the discomfort of contemplating that your breast implants might not be the panacea you imagined. In addition, it helps you avoid the fearful possibility of someday reexperiencing the painful feeling that you are *less than*, *not good enough,* or *incomplete* as a woman.

You also circle the Rationalization Roundabout because your inner fixer likely stopped hammering away at you about your breasts. (And that's the deliverance and relief we're all seeking!) Still, she monitors how you perceive appraisal from others. She gauges how you feel while shopping for bras, swimwear, lingerie, or clothing. When you feel more confident, womanlier, sexier, and enjoy more attention, your inner fixer praises you for "fixing" this part of your body.

When your implants give you pleasure and relief, *and* you start developing problems with them, you might understandably rationalize those concerns away. Of course, that's the entire point of this thinking strategy. By rationalizing away the early-onset problems in your journey with breast implants, you get to enjoy having *better* breasts and avoid the possibility of returning your body to something you deemed needed fixing.

Given all this, you're likely wondering how anyone ever exits the Rationalization Roundabout. It works the same as with anything that gives you pleasure and causes you problems (e.g., binge eating or drinking, using tanning beds, smoking, lying, having an affair, people-pleasing, skipping the workout, scrolling social media, and so forth). You stop doing things that give you pleasure because your life circumstances change, your values shift, or your problems intensify. So when it comes to breast implants, you might start thinking about the possibility of someday removing them for many reasons, including:

— focusing on fitness and a desire to be free of the exercise limitations sometimes experienced by women with breast implants;

— increasing concern over implant interference with mammography results and cost of breast MRIs;

— changing values, perspectives, and priorities that shift with motherhood, age, breast cancer in close female relatives or friends, pursuing natural and organic living or body acceptance;

— cost of repetitive replacement surgery or difficulties in managing complications such as rupture, deflation, capsular contracture;

— worsening systemic impacts on your overall health and well-being unattributed to other causes (i.e., BII);

— reaching a point of intolerance with other effects such as neck, back, and shoulder pain, capsular contracture, or localized breast pain;

— tiring of unwanted attention, compromised hugs, appearing "matronly" in clothing;

— feeling done with them.

Though less common, I have worked with some women who skip the Rationalization Roundabout altogether. This detour happens when you feel no need to rationalize getting breast implants and realize that they are not a fit for you shortly after putting them into your body. You don't rationalize keeping your breast implants because you immediately feel unrelenting discomfort from having them in your body. When your journey with breast implants is like this, though you spend less time with them in your body, you are still impacted by longing for, living with (albeit briefly), and removing your breast implants. Your inner healing matters too.

## Reasoning Roundabout

Once you determine that your breast implants might be impacting you in problematic ways, you move into the Reasoning Roundabout. At this point, you acknowledge that your breast implants are creating some problems for you, and you sometimes even consider what life would be like if you didn't have them. This acknowledgment doesn't mean you are ready to make a change. Usually, you are nowhere near prepared. You are just moving into a different mindset. You are less defensive and protective of your implants, and fully aware that they're causing you issues. Unlike your earlier avoidance and rationalization, you want to understand more. So you begin reasoning your way through the potential cause and effect between your implants and your well-being.

You circle the Reasoning Roundabout with much ambivalence. You swing back and forth on a mental pendulum between the pros and cons of doing anything about your breast implants. For example, even if you've heard about BII, you might wonder if something else is causing your declining health. As a result, you might spend a lot of time in the Reasoning Roundabout with health professionals who chase the source of your declining health while never considering, or actively dismissing, that breast implants might be to blame.

Whether you suspect BII or are impacted in some other way by having breast implants, you might genuinely feel conflicted when you enjoy your breasts' appearance and worry about how you'll look without them. That inner conflict feeds ambivalence. You can spend years circling the Reasoning Roundabout in a state of indecisiveness and inaction. I spent about a decade in it.

Another major factor in how long you spend in the Reasoning Roundabout, weighing the pros and cons, going back and forth, is that although you are open to learning information about problems with breast implants, your inner fixer is most certainly *not*. As discussed in Chapter 2, she considers the notion of explant a threat to your well-being. The possibility of returning to smaller post-explant breasts or explanting to flat after breast reconstruction violates her mission. She wants to prevent the inner pain of not "measuring up." She doesn't want you doing something that defies social programming around women, breasts, and belonging. She reminds you of your disappointing pre-implant breasts. She points out that your breasts might appear worse after having implants stuffed inside them. She erects mental billboards depicting images of your "imbalanced" body with a tummy that protrudes farther than your distorted, deflated, saggy post-explant breasts or flat post-explant chest. Other billboards show sad scenes from your future where others judge, devalue, or abandon you.

When you haven't learned helpful ways to respond to her moves, you might be shocked to see yourself reacting in the old, familiar, and unhelpful way you thought you moved past. You might be disappointed to realize that breast implants only temporarily quieted your struggle with the Breast Rulebook. You might learn that breast implants didn't "fix" anything inside you. They didn't teach you how to show up for yourself as you do for everyone else. So you might try abandoning this confused part of you. But, with only the inner fixer for company, this old, familiar part of you does not fare so well.

I struggled like this after my sister was diagnosed with breast cancer. Her diagnosis propelled me into the Reasoning Roundabout. It amplified my concern about my implants' interference with mammograms. They sat atop my pectoralis muscle and obscured the breast tissue next to them. Plus, I have extremely dense breast tissue which also reduces the efficacy of mammograms. So with the additional concern of breast cancer in a close relative, I investigated the surgery for breast implants removal.

I *immediately* retreated.

It was 2014, and there were only a few published case studies with pictures of women with explanted breasts; they were absolute deal-breakers for my inner fixer. Plus, I was fearful of the surgery due to my lifelong unfounded fear of general anesthesia. The idea of having surgical drains also overwhelmed me. I helped my sister with hers after her double mastectomy, and my hands shook the entire time with fear that I would accidentally do something to cause her more pain.

My mind began deal-making around how it would keep me safe with my breast implants in place: It pointed out that I could get a referral for breast MRIs and avoid activities that might cause accidental trauma to my breast implants. I also held tightly to what my implant doctor said about gummy bear implants being safe and lifelong. Once again, I didn't use my personal values to guide my actions. Instead, I was pushed around by fear. So I went back into the Rationalization Roundabout, where I created more distance between myself and the terrifying prospect of enduring the surgery and life with post-explant breasts.

According to change theory, retreats like these are part of the change process. They commonly happen when moving forward brings too much discomfort. I refer to them as "taking a reversal route."

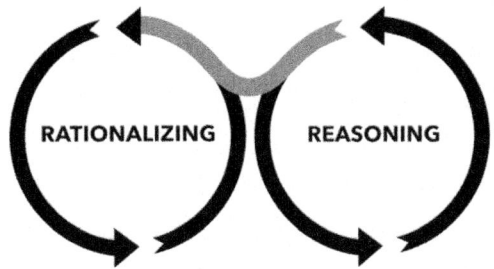

*Figure 4.2 A reversal route on the BRITE Roadmap*

No matter how many reversal routes you take, you exit the Reasoning Roundabout once you decide you don't want to (or cannot) continue living with your breast implants and commit to change. For many women with breast implants, change requires an urgent catalyst such as severe health impacts from BII, implant rupture, or a recall. That was true for me. After noticing a sudden shape change in my right breast, I firmly (and correctly) suspected that it was a mammogram-related rupture.

As odd as it sounds, I feel indebted to my promise-breaking gummy bear implant.[20] Without it, my implants would have remained in my body longer. Though I didn't realize how much they impacted my health, it became apparent several weeks after explant when my chronic body pain relented, and my misdiagnosed disability resolved *completely*.

---

[20] I was told it would last my lifetime so long as I didn't experience major chest trauma (i.e., a car crash). I was also told that even if it were to rupture, it would maintain its shape like a sliced gummy bear candy.

I had no idea those things were related to my body's ongoing battle with my breast implants.[21]

## Readying Roundabout

You enter this roundabout once you determine that your breast implants impact you in ways best resolved by removing and not replacing them. You intend to explant, and soon. But deciding to remove your breast implants doesn't mean you resolved *all* your doubt or worry. Those feelings simply become less unpleasant than whatever implant-related issues you experience. Most likely, you are moving forward despite your complex and unwanted thoughts and feelings. Your challenging inner experience can stay with you right up until surgery and long after explant. I've companioned women who were solid in their decision to remove their breast implants who felt tremendous fear the morning of their surgeries (myself included).

The Readying Roundabout can be intense. The human mind prefers predictability and preparedness, but breast implant removal is an evolving area of women's health with controversial and confusing topics (e.g., BII, best practices for explant surgery, and after-care). Depending on your health and age, you may fear your body's ability to handle surgery and recovery. You might encounter informational resources that warn you'll be unhappy with explanted breasts. You see post-explant pictures that inspire you and others that alarm you. Because your inner fixer keeps vigil for threats associated with your decision, you might "doom-scroll" and look for every awful possibility that could happen. As you seek reassurance online, you might experience "Google overload" which can lead you to take a reversal route and spend more years circling in limbo.

---

[21] To read more about my breast-implant-related health decline and explant-related recovery, visit my blog at amandasavagebrown.com

Although BII is a common reason to explant, you may enter this roundabout without awareness of it. As you explant plan and inevitably learn about BII, you may feel it doesn't apply to you and quickly move on. Or you may identify with its symptoms and wonder if your body's battle against the bags is to blame. Fortunately, there are many resources that help you learn more about BII and navigate the special considerations for BII-related explant surgery.[22] Depending on the intensity of your health-related struggles, you may feel hope *and* betrayal, doubt, confusion, regret, anger, fear, and sadness. When that's true for you, please use the strategies throughout this book to give your BII-related feelings room to move and to offer yourself forgiveness and compassion.

No matter your reasons for entering this roundabout, anytime you do something important and risky, you do better by steadying and readying yourself beforehand. Consider how a public speaker, athlete, or even a person proposing marriage might pause, take some centering breaths, review their plans, or do something physical to get their blood flowing. They do these things to soothe their nerves and help them feel ready for the task.

The Readying Roundabout serves the same purpose. By developing a plan, you soothe the part of your mind that dislikes ambiguity, cares about your breasts' appearance, or feels threatened by breast implant removal. This readying of yourself is essential. Based on change theory, if this part of your journey isn't done thoroughly, you risk stumbling as you move forward and encounter challenges. After all, it's much easier to be pushed over when you're unsteady.

For example, at one of my consultations, a surgeon suggested removing my implants in his office under light sedation. He said he would cut open my scar capsule and pull my implants out. He assured

---

[22] The resource list at amandasavagebrown.com is good place to get started

me that explant was a minor surgery and that my body would reabsorb the implant's scar capsule over time. Because of the investigation and learning that I did beforehand, I knew that scar capsules are not reabsorbed, and they cause problems for some women when left behind.[23] I also knew that this approach was unsafe with silicone implants, especially given my concern that one was ruptured. If his low-cost, low-pain promise had swayed me, silicone from my broken and dripping implant would have been released into my body. Instead, I recognized that his recommendation was likely based on his surgical skills rather than what was best for my body.

In addition to ensuring you understand the surgical considerations, you can promote your inner healing in the Readying Roundabout by preparing yourself mentally, emotionally, and socially for breast implant removal.[24] But to truly explant plan on *your* terms, you must know how to guard against automatically following the Breast Rulebook and care for the part of you that learned breasts *matter*. Otherwise, your focus and inner well-being can be hijacked by your inner fixer's aesthetic anxiety; you may overlook the affordability of additional surgeries, fail to fully consider their risks and benefits for your circumstances, or be pushed around by the same beliefs that led you onto the implant table. And in the end, as discussed in Chapter 3, it often leads to continued domination by your inner fixer's obsession with the Breast Rulebook, the Age Rulebook, the Weight Rulebook, or any other rulebook society creates for women.

---

[23] Visit amandasavagebrown.com for resources that help you learn more.

[24] Although your digital resources at bustingfreeonline.com include a holistic explant plan checklist, I encourage you (when possible) to work through the material in this book before you explant plan. As you will see, Chapter 11 helps you pull all this together and take a values-guided approach to holistic explant planning. If you are currently in the Readying Roundabout, it's okay to review the checklist now and use *Busting Free* to move through its items on *your* terms.

I've seen countless women on these journeys struggle with the challenge of planning for explant while mentally gripping the Breast Rulebook. It happened to me as well. The more I explored how to safely explant, the more I noticed the resurgence of powerful thoughts about my worth and desirability. I feared I'd be more vulnerable without reasonably sized breasts. I felt I'd have to work harder at being lovable, likable, and valuable. As incredibly disappointing as that was to me, I loosened the trap by using the same strategies I share throughout *Busting Free*.

But if you are reading this book after white-knuckling your way through explant's harder-to-navigate inner journey, you're most likely circling the following roundabout. That doesn't mean you're stuck. You can still use BRITE Inner Healing to bust free.

## Repairing Roundabout

The Repairing Roundabout is where change happens. No longer planning, you are doing. You select a surgeon, set a date, and explant. You do things to help your breasts and body recover from living full-time with foreign objects inside them. While these physical changes are highly anticipated and prepared for, they are only part of the total change. When you use BRITE Inner Healing to companion yourself through the events in the Repairing Roundabout, you repair the inner damage caused by all the unhelpful things you learned about women, breasts, and belonging.

At this point in your journey, you are more open to receiving help from others. You seek support from family and friends, trusted health providers, or online support communities. You are more willing to tell others about your surgery plans and look to share your fear and anxiety with people who understand. Connecting with others is so helpful to your well-being that this roundabout could be called the Reach and Repair Roundabout.

Reaching out to others makes perfect sense, considering how women react to stress and threats. You've undoubtedly heard of the fight-or-flight response to stress and danger. Interestingly, that stress response is more commonly the go-to response for males. Original studies into the human stress response from the early 1900s mainly included male participants and dismissed the "outlier" female responses, regarding them as negatively affected by hormonal fluctuations (insert eye roll). Decades later, additional studies revealed that those responses were, in fact, meaningful. In 1959, a social scientist named Stanley Schacter, Ph.D., designed experiments to understand affiliation among women when they perceive a threat.[25] He observed two notable behaviors. First, women approach and connect with each other when threatened. Second, we prefer to be with other women going through the same thing.

Additional studies on the stress response by Shelley Taylor, Ph.D., also extended our understanding of how women respond to stress and threats. Although we sometimes react to threats with a fight-or-flight response, we often use a **tend-and-befriend** approach. Like Schacter, Taylor observed that women reach out and connect with one another when distressed. However, she also observed that men tend to isolate themselves. (These behaviors were observed in rodents as well.) Taylor argued that these responses make sense from an evolutionary and biochemical perspective.

---

[25] Women were divided into two groups: One group was told that they would receive an electric shock that was harmless but quite painful; the other group was told that they would receive a shock that was entirely painless. Members of the group anticipating the painful threat were significantly more likely to approach and interact with one another as they waited for the test to begin. When non-study participants were included in the waiting room, the women experiencing distress from the perceived threat congregated preferentially with each other.

Imagine a human female living eons ago; let's call her Mama Cavewoman. If she was pregnant, nursing, caring for young, and facing an overwhelming threat to her safety, she was likely unable or unwilling to fight or flee on her own. Depending on the predator, Mama Cavewoman would end up eaten, stolen, raped, murdered, or forced to endure whatever other fresh hell was thrust upon her. These early women, and their offspring, improved their chances of survival by tending to their young (e.g., quieting a baby through nursing) and relying on protective bonds previously formed with those around them.[26] A group can overcome a threat better than an individual, so it's likely that early women using this tend-and-befriend response survived and ultimately became our ancestral Great-Grandmamas.

We continue this approach today. When under stress, modern women call friends, family, and co-workers, seek professional advice, and join online support groups. All these behaviors play out among women anticipating explant; we seek out others who know what we feel and fear. If you know a woman who explanted, you will likely reach out to her. If your surgeon or someone on their staff represents this shared emotional experience, you might be comforted by conversations and interactions with them. You might also join social media or other online groups (including mine) committed to helping women on explant journeys connect. You can find resources with links to dozens of groups at the resource list at amandasavagebrown.com.

Another important repair in this roundabout involves changing your relationship with your inner fixer. Comparative thinking naturally and frequently shows up after explant, even when you're thrilled to be implant-free. You compare your aesthetic outcome to others on this

---

[26] The hormone **oxytocin**, responsible for human bonding, is higher in females. During stress, it likely inhibits the female fight-or-flight response, promotes the tend-and-befriend response, and ensures the survival of the species.

journey. Or you compare your recovery to women who transform their bodies and health after explant. And, of course, you continue comparing yourself to images on TV, social media, store posters, etc. By learning how to be there for yourself during these moments, you repair the unhelpful history shared between you and your inner fixer.

Of course, you might back-burner this kind of inner repair, especially when you're pleased with your aesthetic outcome. But, as discussed in Chapter 3, it's only through intentional investment in yourself that you learn new ways to respond to the ongoing internal processes that naturally lead you to compare yourself to society's rulebooks. At this point, all this might sound abstract. But rest assured, the remaining chapters help you acquire the inner skills that repair your relationship with yourself and your inner fixer.

## Reclaiming Roundabout

Reclaiming means "to retrieve or recover something previously lost, given, or paid; to obtain the return of." So this roundabout is named the Reclaiming Roundabout to:

1. Evoke an image of you working hard to bust free from the Breast Rulebook and win back a sense of safety and belonging that comes from within yourself;
2. Remind you that you can lose this hard-fought sense of inner safety;
3. Urge you to live with a consciousness that prevents its loss.

Remember, learning another language doesn't replace the one(s) you already know. So, even though you might feel differently about breast implants and your self-worth, it doesn't mean your mind forgets that breasts *matter*. So, the BRITE Roadmap's final roundabout is where you continually reclaim yourself and practice ongoing self-acceptance. You want to continue circling this roundabout because reclaiming yourself isn't a goal; it's a constant way of being. That's why these journeys never truly end.

The Reclaiming Roundabout also has an Inner Fixer Lane. You circle it anytime your inner fixer urges you to follow a rulebook, even when it might harm your health or well-being. It even offers you a reversal route back to rationalizing your way to another set of breast implants (as shown in Figure 4.3). I've seen countless women take this reversal route in the absence of BRITE Inner Healing. It's understandable, however, because removing breast implants doesn't stop you from caring about your breasts' appearance, and as previously discussed, we repeat what we don't repair.

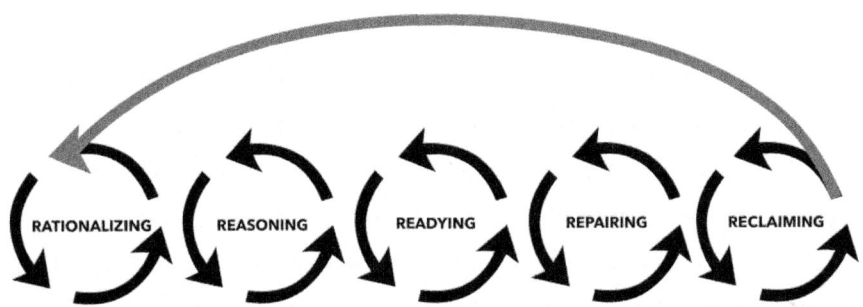

*Figure 4.3. Post-explant reversal route to another set of breast implants*

There's nothing wrong with wanting to look your best, so long as *you* drive your decisions instead of being driven to them by unhelpful beliefs. This autonomy is essential when you live in a society that offers you costly, temporary, and problem-prone ways to "improve" yourself. Autonomy over your decisions is imperative when you don't want to violate your values, put your body or financial well-being at risk, or feel like you *must* comply with a rulebook to be accepted, worthy, or safe. It's also pivotal when you want a future life without breast implants and surgeries, but your post-explant aesthetic outcome disappoints you.

Speaking from personal experience, I know that finding your way after explant can be challenging. There are plenty of moments in my post-explant life where the *not good enough* story gets cued or my inner fixer picks up her hammer. Although it happens much less frequently than in the past, it still happens. It's nearly impossible for me to look at anything online, watch a movie or TV show, go clothes shopping, or wear a bathing suit without comparative thinking lighting up my brain circuitry. Despite the trend for displaying more realistic mannequins and posters throughout retail stores, none of them feature women with breasts like mine. I can spot breast implants within half a second. I also quickly notice natural, unblemished breasts. When I see my undressed body each day, I am reminded of my earlier choices and their lasting effects. When I see a picture of myself before implants, I regret having done anything to alter my natural breasts. When I see a photo of me with implants, I feel tremendous relief that they are out *and* long for things to have turned out differently. Sometimes my reflection stops me in my tracks. It's as if I forgot that I now lack the coveted upper half of the breast mound. No matter how amazing my husband is to me, and no matter how much I believe he fully and completely accepts and cherishes me, I must be very intentional during intimacy to be the partner I want to be despite my unwanted thoughts and feelings. (I describe exactly how I cope with the vulnerability of post-explant intimacy in Chapter 9.)

I share all this in hopes of helping you see that reclaiming yourself and living with true-self acceptance is an *ongoing process.* I would never want you to think you were failing because old familiar thoughts and feelings show up. Remember, it makes sense for them to be there. But, thankfully, how you respond is entirely up to you.

# Your Journey Through the BRITE Roadmap

You likely have a long list of things you've successfully changed and an equally long list of changes you failed to make or keep. Even when you consider making a change that's known to be "good" for your health and well-being, you only move forward once you believe the advantages outweigh the disadvantages. Things get even more complex when you're considering a change that requires you to give up something addictive or something that means a great deal to you, like having *good enough* or *better* breasts.

When you are delighted with your breast implants, you're not in a change process. But once it occurs to you that you got more than you bargained for from them, your problem-solving mind inevitably considers their removal. The BRITE Roadmap shows how your mind progresses through a series of mental roundabouts as you weigh the pros and cons of keeping, replacing, or removing your breast implants. It also shows that change is a process. It's possible to spend years tolerating lifestyle impacts or minor problems related to your breast implants.

The BRITE Roadmap also honors that you might take a reversal route whenever you feel overwhelmed. When you do, don't judge yourself too harshly. A reversal route often indicates that you were pushed too far or too quickly, either by your own doing or something beyond your control such as a rupture, recall, or BII. Understandably, when you feel coerced or forced to move toward breast implant removal before you're ready, your inner fixer will convince you to retreat to familiar terrain. By reflecting on how she succeeds, you can support yourself differently moving forward.

Although most everyone moves through predictable stages when considering a health-related behavior change like no longer living with breast implants, your journey is as unique as you. What leads you to continue circling your current roundabout, or move to the next one, might be very different from someone else. For example, I did many laps around the Reasoning Roundabout because I feared dying under general anesthesia. But you might circle it because of something powerfully painful from your past or worry that explant might impact your relationship or job. In other words, the bigger picture of your life matters.

How long you circle and what propels you through the BRITE Roundabouts are influenced by what your breast implants mean to you, how much discomfort or unwellness you attribute to them, and how supported you are in moving toward their removal. When you determine that your breast implants negatively impact things that matter greatly to you (e.g., health, well-being, unrestricted physical activity, authenticity, or comfort), then you're willing to consider life without them. Your ability to follow through, however, is heavily influenced by how you respond to your inner fixer.[27]

According to change theory, your journey through the BRITE Roadmap will go quite differently when you know and use strategies that undermine your inner fixer's moves. Chapters 6-11 give you those strategies and show how to use them in each roundabout, after a reversal route, or in advance of doing something that you find particularly difficult. These strategies help you navigate the BRITE Roadmap on *your* terms.

It's important to finish this chapter knowing where you are on the BRITE Roadmap. It helps you make sense of your journey so far.

---

[27] At the time of this writing, your ability to follow through with breast implant removal is also heavily influenced by your financial circumstances. When you find yourself physically stuck in the Readying Roundabout due to an inability to finance the costs of explant surgery, you can still use BRITE Inner Healing to move through your inner journey. Though you may be unable to reclaim your body from the problematic implants inside it, you can still reclaim your mind from the toxic social messaging that drove you onto the implant table and the ongoing behind-the-scenes process that fuels unhelpful comparative thinking and painful feelings of *less than* and *not enough*.

Moreover, it serves as a reference point for much of the material throughout the remainder of this book. Please note that when you come to this book after explant, you are most likely circling the Repairing Roundabout with an inner fixer who continues to hammer away at you about your post-explant breast aesthetics and the rest of your body. I applaud you for circling back to repair your relationship with yourself and bust free from the Breast Rulebook.

No matter where you are in the BRITE Roadmap, there are two fundamental things to know as you set out on your BRITE Inner Healing journey: how to use your inner BRAKE and when to shift into Park. Chapter 5 walks you through both.

# Chapter 5

# Steady Yourself Using Your Inner BRAKE

W hen Rollerblades emerged in the late 1990s, I was eager to try the new in-line skates. I went to a sporting goods store with an indoor track. After a few spins around it, I decided that they seemed easy enough to use. With my newly purchased skates in hand, I headed to a park to try them out. I imagined gracefully gliding along the paved walking trail.

I had *not* anticipated the difference between wheeling around an obstacle-free track at the sporting goods store and a real-life trail crowded with other people and occasional intersections with busy entrances to parking areas. All three challenges converged upon me as I picked up speed on a barely noticeable decline while navigating slower-moving people and approaching an intersection with a continuous line of cars moving through it.

But I hadn't practiced for this terrain or these conditions. My few spins around the store's track weren't enough to build the skill of effectively raising the front of my skate to lower its rear brake. I tried but felt unsteady. I continued to gain momentum as I rolled toward the intersection. I had only one option. I aimed for nearby grass and hurled myself to the ground. I ended up with a road burn so severe that I had to abandon my plans for the day.

That was not the scene I'd envisioned at all.

That day, I learned the importance of knowing how to steady yourself anytime you're doing something where things can potentially overwhelm you (even when you're eager to do it). The same applies to your journey with breast implants. Like my highly anticipated adventure with rollerblading, you can't just roll through your journey with problematic breast implants hoping for the best. Instead, you need to be able to steady and ready yourself when facing difficult or overwhelming decisions, conversations, and experiences. Being able to steady yourself is particularly helpful when you have prior medical or relationship trauma, are prone to harsh self-criticism, or have been dominated by your inner fixer for decades.

This chapter teaches you how to use your inner BRAKE. I created this ACT-based inner skill to help you learn five science-based ways (one for each letter of BRAKE) to steady yourself as you move through your journey with breast implants or anytime life feels overwhelming. Knowing how to use your inner BRAKE is a fundamental part of BRITE Inner Healing. It steadies your nervous system so you can steer with purpose and intention rather than careening out of control during the more challenging aspects of your journey.

This chapter also highlights three important things to keep in mind about using your inner BRAKE so you have realistic expectations of what it can do for you. It also provides practical suggestions for practicing with your inner BRAKE, so you know how to use it when you need it. Finally, it shows you the differences in a hypothetical scenario for a woman attending an explant consultation with and without knowing how to use this inner skill.

The chapter ends with a few words about the importance of putting in "behind-the-wheel" time with this and the other BRITE Inner Healing skills and tools so you know how to use them while busting free.

## Your autonomic nervous system

Your **autonomic nervous system** has two branches that automatically act on your behalf. However, as you'll see, the social complexities of this journey can activate your nervous system in ways that aren't helpful.

Your **sympathetic nervous system** (SNS) is the branch that lights up when you feel threatened. It's your threat-response system. It activates without you even thinking about it, whether you feel threatened by something around you, such as finding a snake in your home, or because of something internal and deeply felt. So, for example, when your inner fixer feels that your breast implants make you desirable, worthy, sexy, normal, complete, appealing, feminine, or womanly, removing them feels threatening (even when they cause you problems). Unfortunately, she sits at command central and can activate this part of your nervous system to send you circling Inner Fixer Lane.

No matter the threat, when your SNS activates, it releases chemicals that keep you on high alert and ready for quick action. Think of the SNS as a gas pedal that quickly moves you out of danger. As briefly discussed in Chapter 1, it's helpful to have an automatic and quick response when facing an external threat that you can separate yourself from, such as a snake. But it becomes problematic when you feel threatened by the stuff inside you: the thoughts and feelings that show up when doing something (removing breast implants) that goes against a deeply ingrained belief (*breasts matter*). No matter how hard you smash down your metaphorical gas pedal, you can't escape your inner experience. Instead, you remain in distress, making it hard to think clearly or act intentionally.

Moving through the BRITE Roadmap involves considering many things and making important decisions. The very last thing you need is your inner fixer revving up your SNS and hijacking your ability to think clearly, plan, and move through this journey on *your* terms. Instead, you need a way to steady yourself.

Steadying, grounding, and centering refer to ways to activate the other branch of your autonomic nervous system, known as the **parasympathetic nervous system** (PNS). You can think of the PNS as a brake pedal. When a threat has passed, it slows you down by releasing chemicals that calm the mind and relax the body. You can stimulate it through the largest nerve in your body, called the vagus nerve. This nerve wanders through your body, connecting your brain to vital organs such as your heart, lungs, stomach, and intestines. Working with your body in specific ways stimulates the vagus nerve and presses your inner brake (i.e., PNS).

## Your inner BRAKE

To help you remember to press your metaphorical brake pedal, each letter of BRAKE represents an easy way to steady yourself by doing something that's under your control:

**B**: Breathe slowly in and out
**R**: Rub your lips lightly
**A**: Attune inwardly
**K**: Keep connecting to your body
**E**: Expand your awareness

BRAKE harnesses the two-way connection between the body and mind. Just as your mind can rev up your body's threat response, you can use your body and awareness to calm your mind. The following sections walk you through how to perform each of these actions. A demo video is available in your *Busting Free* digital library.

 **WATCH THE BRAKE DEMO VIDEO**

## B: Breathe slowly in and out

A well-known way to pulse your vagus nerve is to modify how you breathe. It's my go-to move when I want to steady myself. I teach this to nearly every client early in our work. There are many variations on this simple skill, but I present it in ways that work for busy women, whether you're always on the go or rarely have a moment to yourself. You can do this in pretty much any setting and even while talking. Over the years, I have worked with women who feel distressed with breathwork, so I use an eyes-open approach that involves more external awareness than most breathwork. I've also learned that traditional breathing exercises intensify feelings of discomfort and distress for some. When that's true for you, please read through this approach and determine your willingness to try it. If you decide not to try it, or you try it and it feels unhelpful, use the modified version of BRAKE described in the Rub Your Lips Lightly section.

To get started, direct your awareness to your breath cycle. You don't need to change it. Instead, simply notice that you are breathing in and out; observe whether your chest rises and falls or your belly expands and contracts.

You can stimulate your vagus nerve by directing your breath toward your belly. Imagine your stomach is like a balloon. As you breathe in, you expand the balloon. As you breathe out, you deflate the balloon by bringing the front of your belly back toward your spine. By shifting your breath from your chest to your belly, you stimulate the vagus nerve in a way that gently presses your inner brake.

Please experiment a bit with this now. (*I seriously cannot stress this enough.*)

Belly breathing can feel uncomfortable at first, given the social programming and messaging that this part of your body *should be flat.* Most of us hold it in tightly, especially when we are more body-conscious. When that's true for you, please compassionately acknowledge this part of your experience and still allow yourself to relax this part of your body.

Another practice is to place your hand atop your belly and watch your breath cycle raise and lower your hand. Then, slow down and allow your inhale to expand your belly completely. Pause for a moment. Then, exhale *super slowly.* Your mouth can be closed or slightly opened. The most important things here are to see your belly rising and falling and slowing your exhale way down. Honestly, that's all there is to it.

Please take a moment to experiment a bit with this now.

You might be wondering if you should breathe in or out for a certain amount of time. Because we all have different lung capacities, I do not endorse a one-size-fits-all count that you must follow. Plus, I find it distracting to count. However, many of my clients prefer to count when initially working with this skill. So if counting helps you learn this valuable skill, go right ahead. However, to prevent overdependence on counting, be sure to also practice belly breathing without counting.

Learning to belly breathe without counting allows you to do it more naturally during challenging experiences. (Imagine how awkward it might be to try steadying yourself while counting during a conversation with a dismissive physician or an unsupportive partner.) For the same reason, I don't encourage making odd sounds or loudly exhaling, as you might do in a yoga class. However, it can be helpful to slightly open and adjust your mouth while exhaling, as if you are *quietly* trying to fog a mirror. This modification can also help to slow your heart rate.

To build the muscle memory needed for this skill, please practice belly breathing frequently throughout your day, during conversations and when alone, during periods of stress, *and when you're perfectly calm.* To integrate this practice into your life, consider writing a small "B" on your hand. Then, do a few cycles of slow belly breathing whenever you notice the letter. Remember, practicing this doesn't require a time investment; you're always breathing. You're just breathing slowly in and very slowly out.

## R: Rub your lips lightly

This step is super straightforward. Your lips have parasympathetic fibers throughout them, and anecdotal reports suggest that lightly brushing your lips with one or two fingers can activate the PNS. You can experiment with this by varying the pressure you apply as you run one or two fingers gently over and around your lips. Notice how you feel when you lightly trace the border between your lips and face.

---

This alternate version of **BRAKE** accommodates those with sensitivities to breathwork:

**BR:** Brush your lips lightly
**A:** Attune inwardly
**K:** Keep connecting to your body
**E:** Expand your awareness

---

## A: Attune inwardly

Attuning inwardly is an essential part of steadying yourself. According to attachment theory (one of the most researched and science-based theories explaining human relationships and bonding), attunement makes humans feel safe. In relationships with high levels of attunement, partners can anticipate and genuinely feel each other's needs. Just as attunement is helpful between two people, it's also important to reclaim your relationship with yourself.

Self-attunement is particularly important when considering, doing, or recovering from something that impacts your body, mind, and heart, such as breast implant removal. Though it's natural to press the gas pedal (activate your SNS) in response to fearful thoughts and feelings around explant, you abandon your underlying need for reassurance when trying to escape your inner experience.

Just like children calm down with a safe other's presence, and partners feel soothed by having their partner nearby during distress, this part of BRAKE helps you attune inwardly and be there for yourself. For example, you can reassure yourself by letting yourself know, "I'm here for this struggle." That statement might seem odd because you're always in your struggle, but it helps you be there for yourself without pressing your gas pedal. Instead, you stay with yourself by acknowledging that unpleasant thoughts or feelings are with you. For example, you might say any of the following (or whatever feels like an authentic way for you to connect with yourself):

*I see this pain right here, right now.*

*What I'm doing is hard for me.*

*I know.*

*Fear is here.*

*Self-judgment is with me.*

Note: Attuning to your inner experience is different than identifying with it. It's different than saying, "I *am* afraid" or "I *am* critical."

## K: Keep connecting with your body

When your inner fixer interprets a threat, your body responds by pressing the gas pedal. For example, when you see a picture of a woman's post-explant breasts and your inner fixer interprets something about it as threatening (e.g., their size, shape, loss of volume, scars), your heart might race, palms can sweat, or you might feel an urge to flee. In other words, you can feel uncomfortable just *thinking* about removing your breast implants.

Have you ever noticed how threatened prey do not draw attention to themselves? Instead, they hold still, breathe shallowly and rapidly into their chests, look around with rapidly darting eyes, and tense up in anticipation of springing into action. When you feel like threatened prey, you can soothe your nervous system by taking advantage of the two-way relationship between your mind and body. When you move your body as you would *outside a threatening situation,* your mind follows your body and sends "threat over" signals that press your inner brake.

You can choose to behave unlike prey by doing the following:

— Look around with your head, not just your eyes.
— Intentionally move your body.
— Check on the parts of your body where you usually tense up, and purposefully soften them.
— Sit up straight so you can take those full belly breaths.
— If circumstances permit, you can even walk around, stretch your arms, or make some noise.

Choosing to behave unlike prey redirects your focus on actions under your control. This part of BRAKE is called *keep connecting with your body* because you might need to continue doing these things repeatedly during distress.

---

Note: You're not trying to trick yourself with these moves. They are not intended to serve as distractions. And they absolutely aren't intended to minimize your inner experience. You do these moves because you recognize that you are in a challenging situation, and you want to soothe your body and steady your mind.

---

## E: Expand your awareness

You can also steady yourself by expanding your awareness. When you're hyper-focused on overwhelming stuff around and within you, you can ground yourself by also noticing other things. Using your five senses is one way to expand your awareness. For example, you can use a classic grounding technique known as 5-4-3, where you ask yourself, "At this moment, what are five things I can see, four things I can hear, and three things I can touch, taste, or smell?" This simple tool helps you reconnect with the world around you.

It's also helpful to expand your inner awareness by asking, "What else is happening inside me?" This curiosity is critical when you might simultaneously feel two opposite feelings but only focus on one. For example, you might feel fearful *and* eager, disappointed *and* relieved, or angry *and* calm. Unfortunately, your mind is naturally inclined to focus on the more difficult or threatening one, which leads you to miss other parts of your experience that might be helpful or important to acknowledge. For example, I was very aware of feeling trepidation during my surgical consults. Unfortunately, that spotlight hog overshadowed my more subtle feelings of relief and pride over moving forward with removing my problematic implants. Honoring all three feelings helped me open up to my whole experience. If I hyper-focused on trepidation, my inner fixer might have used it to convince me I was making a mistake.

## Three important things about BRAKE

There are three things to keep in mind about using this BRITE Inner Healing tool. First, BRAKE doesn't change your challenging circumstances. Instead, it changes how you move through them. For example, imagine driving down a road, and your speed suddenly increases while entering a series of roundabouts with exits you want to take. To have more control, you would press the brakes. But slowing down wouldn't make the challenging terrain disappear. So, please don't use BRAKE with the hope of changing your circumstances. Instead, use it to steady yourself when you're revved up and want to regain control of your awareness and actions.

Second, using your inner BRAKE is more like pumping a brake rather than smashing it down and keeping it there. Not only is that impossible to do with your nervous system, but it would also be super unhelpful because *you* would stop completely. So instead, what you are going for is more like pulsing the part of your nervous system that helps you steady yourself.

Third, if you feel disappointed by how often you find yourself needing to hit the BRAKE while traveling through the BRITE Roadmap, it might be helpful to think about how often you use your brake and gas pedal on any journey. You get where you're going only by using both. Without knowing how to do both, you leave a lot up to chance and limit your options for safely maneuvering obstacles.

## BRAKE on the go

After years of teaching distress tolerance and grounding skills (and learning to do them myself), I know it can feel awkward to practice grounding skills when you aren't distressed. But unless you practice, you won't know what to do when you need it. That didn't go well for me on my maiden rollerblade journey; the stakes are much higher on your journey with breast implants.

To learn how to use BRAKE, I suggest the following:

— Use your phone to take a picture of the BRAKE acronym so you have it for reference. Label a reminder on your phone and set it to alert you every few hours. Also, if your circumstances allow, write BRAKE on sticky notes and place them all around your home (e.g., bathroom mirror, car dashboard, near the kitchen sink, on the door to the fridge, and anywhere else you frequently see throughout the day). Each time your alarm goes off or you see a note, practice any of the letters. These informal practices should take maybe one minute or less.

— After a day or two of practicing each letter on its own, start combining them. Practice belly breathing while attuning to yourself on the inside. After working with that combo, practice keeping connected to your body and expanding your awareness. Experiment with different physical actions to learn which ones help you feel more connected and steadied. Explore your senses to see if one enables you to steady yourself more than others.

— Fully expect your mind to balk at and judge these moves. It might say, *This isn't working* or *You're not doing this right* or *These are stupid.* Those thoughts just reflect your mind trying to keep you safe. It doesn't want you to waste time or be duped. When ideas like that show up, thank your mind for looking out for you.

(You'll learn much more about thanking your mind in Chapter 8.) And keep choosing to practice BRAKE randomly throughout your day so you are familiar with how to steady yourself in times of distress.

I know you're busy, so here are some ways to practice an element of BRAKE on the go for no more than one to two minutes:

— Do about five slow breath cycles: Inhale deeply into your belly, exhale super slowly, eyes open, while nearly silently fogging up an imaginary mirror super close to your mouth.

— Direct your awareness inwardly for about 10 seconds, and see if you observe contentment, neutrality, discomfort, or something else. Then, simply acknowledge whether your current inner experience feels easy, neutral, or challenging. As you repeat this, attune more specifically to noticing the characteristics of your thoughts and feelings in the moment (e.g., busy, scary, neutral, scattered, foggy, distressed, worried, bored).

— Practice being unlike prey by moving your head side to side, rotating your chin toward each shoulder, raising your chin up to the ceiling, and dropping your chin down toward your chest. Also, sit up straight, stretch out your arms, and take a deep breath. Press your fingertips together from each hand. Interlace your fingers, and twirl your thumbs around each other, alternating directions. Check on areas where you typically hold tension, and intentionally relax those body parts.

— Look around and direct your attention to five things you don't usually notice. Then listen for four sounds, like something you hear in the same room, outside the room, inside your body, and when you move your body. Finally, notice three things you can touch, smell, or taste; these can be three things you touch or a mixture of any of those things.

---

Be creative.

Experiment.

Find what works best for you.

The only wrong way to practice is not doing it at all.

---

## BRAKE through the BRITE Roundabouts

Your inner BRAKE works the same, no matter which challenges you encounter along the BRITE Roadmap or when life overwhelms you. This section shows how differently you might move through an event in the Readying Roundabout by using your inner BRAKE. It features a woman named Anya, who is experiencing BII as she maneuvers the (often anxiety-producing) experience of attending a surgical consult for explant surgery. She's not entirely sure if removing her implants will ease her symptoms, but she's tried everything else to address her declining health, with no real improvement. As a result, she has a mix of powerful emotions. She feels inspired by other women's recovery stories and worries that she won't feel better after explant. Anya struggles with self-doubt and wants to use her consultation to gain clarity. At her first consultation, the surgeon seemed annoyed with her questions. Now she feels even more apprehensive about meeting this one.

Without knowing how to use her inner BRAKE, Anya passed the time in the waiting room by using her phone to distract herself. Now, as she waits alone in the exam room, she is aware of a display case showcasing the latest trend in breast implants. Her mind floods with memories from years ago, when she sat in a similar room, eyeing the implant case, eager to get them into her body. Now she ponders the quality and condition of her implants and her anxiousness over removing them. It bothers her to imagine the surgery. Disturbing mental images of discolored and leaking implants, drainage tubes, and newly explanted breasts come to her mind. Next to the display case sits a small, glossy poster sponsored by the implant manufacturer. It features a smiling woman with full breasts, glowing skin, thick hair, and a toned body. It looks to Anya that the model has breast implants.

She fills with sadness and anger as she anticipates going back to being flat-chested, while comparing herself to the woman in the ad. She's covered in rashes, her hair is thin and falling out, and she's gained weight despite dieting and exercising. She remembers how she looked before implants and BII. Anya both longs to be healthy and dreads feeling incomplete as a woman once again. Her heart races as her fear, sadness, anger, regret, and self-doubt intensify. She breathes shallowly. Her hands shake as she reaches for her list of questions. She's sure her voice will tremble when she speaks. Anya tries to clear her mind and calm down, but she knows how dismissive some surgeons can be of BII. A surge of anxiety shows up and unsteadies her even further. At that inopportune moment, the door opens, and the surgeon walks into the exam room.

In the preceding scenario, Anya didn't know how to steady herself or respond to her inner fixer's distress. Instead, her mind and body moved into fight, flight, or freeze mode. She could not think clearly or steady and ready herself before meeting the surgeon. This experience likely adds to Anya's self-doubt, which is unfortunate because change theory shows that she needs a sense of self-efficacy and a belief that she can handle what lies ahead. She might continue pushing herself toward explant or stall out for a bit. That latter option is particularly unhelpful and dangerous, given that she is symptomatic with BII. Either way, without knowing how to be there for herself, her already taxed body will take on the unhelpful burden of processing additional stress-induced chemicals (such as cortisol) during difficult situations.

Now let's explore what this scenario looks like with Anya knowing how to steady herself using BRAKE. These new ways of responding to her inner experience are in **bold**.

**Anya recognized her discomfort in the waiting room. So she attuned inwardly rather than distracting herself by using her phone. Anya noticed how painful it feels to consider removing her breast implants, given her history of disliking her natural breasts and feeling incomplete as a woman with a nearly flat chest. She chose to steady herself by doing belly breathing until called back.** After settling into the exam room, she is aware of a display case showcasing the latest trend in breast implants. Her mind floods with memories from years ago, when she sat in a similar room, eyeing the implant case, eager to get them into her body. Now she ponders the quality and condition of her implants and her anxiousness over removing them. It bothers her to imagine the surgery. Disturbing mental images of discolored and leaking implants, drainage tubes, and newly explanted breasts come to her mind. Next to the display case sits a small, glossy poster sponsored by the implant manufacturer. It features a smiling woman with full breasts, glowing skin, thick hair, and a toned body. It looks to Anya that the model has breast implants.

She fills with sadness and anger as she anticipates going back to being flat-chested, while comparing herself to the woman in the ad. Her skin is covered in rashes, her hair is thin and falling out, and she's gained weight despite dieting and exercising. She remembers how she looked before implants and BII. Anya both longs to be healthy and dreads feeling incomplete as a woman once again. Her heart races as her fear, sadness, anger, regret, and self-doubt intensify. She breathes shallowly. Her hands shake as she reaches for her list of questions. She's sure her voice will tremble when she speaks.

**Anya remembers to use her inner BRAKE when she feels overwhelmed like this. She resumes belly breathing for a few breath cycles. While slowly breathing in and out, Anya attunes to her inner experience. She recognizes how much distress she's feeling in that moment. She sees how fear and regret showed up in response to her mind recalling explant images and her personal and painful memories of feeling *not good enough*. She silently acknowledges that this is hard stuff. She keeps connecting to her body by moving her head side to side, up and down. She purposefully softens her jaw because she knows that is where she tenses up the most. She expands her awareness to notice other features of the exam room in addition to the display and poster. She observes that she is wearing her favorite shoes and purposefully notices five details about them that she usually overlooks; she also listens to the sounds in and out of the exam room. She hears the surgeon talking outside the door.** She recalls how dismissive some surgeons can be of BII, and a fresh wave of anxiety shows up. **She takes another belly breath, acknowledges that this is hard, and expands her awareness to recognize that getting her questions answered and advocating for herself is important to her as well. Just then,** the surgeon walks into the exam room.

In this scenario, Anya took time in the waiting room to attune inwardly and recognize that she was doing something that felt uncomfortable and hard. Once she got to the exam room, her inner experience intensified with complex thoughts, feelings, images, and memories, so she used BRAKE to steady herself. However, it didn't change her circumstances or magically make her feel better about being in that situation. Instead, it steadied her and helped her show up more helpfully. The consultation mattered to her, and she wanted to be fully present to gain clarity around her questions and discern if this surgeon was a good fit for her. BRAKE helped her steady herself and move toward her goals.

## Final words about using your inner BRAKE

Learning to use your inner BRAKE gives you the ability to steady yourself when you feel overwhelmed or distressed. It returns your focus to actions under your control, including where you place your awareness. It provides tangible alternatives to white-knuckling your way through an unpleasant experience or hoping for the best.

You don't have to master all five of BRAKE's letters. You may find that one of them simply doesn't resonate with you. Likewise, you may find one or two that become your go-to approach for steadying yourself when you feel overwhelmed. Mine is a combination of belly breathing and sliding my shoulders down my back (as I tend to hold them up when feeling stressed).

Ideally, you will also use your inner BRAKE to prepare yourself *before* doing something difficult, such as talking with a partner about possibly removing your implants or seeing yourself (or others) after surgery. For example, I anticipated that returning to a plastic-surgery office would be difficult with its waiting-room ads, posters, products, and videos playing on loop. I knew that being exposed to those things while contemplating explant would make for a rough ride with my inner fixer. I knew that she would view the marketing messages as proof that these were problems needing fixing, and then bombard me with rulebooks around my breasts, body, cellulite, and aging face.

Rather than letting her rev me up, I went into those appointments ready to use my inner BRAKE, much like I would hover my foot over a car's brake going into a dangerous stretch of road. I proactively chose to attune inwardly by silently acknowledging: *What I'm doing right now is hard for me. Sadness is here. Comparative thinking and self-judgment are with me.* By attuning inwardly, the distressed part of me felt seen, heard, and held. I also chose to expand my awareness to include the bigger picture of why I was in that setting in the first place. I reminded myself of why it mattered to me to remove my breast implants.

It doesn't matter how you end up using your inner BRAKE. All that matters is that you know how to use it. If you wait until you're distressed to learn how your inner BRAKE helps you steady yourself, you're setting yourself up for frustration because it's hard learning something new when you're under duress. To guard against that, use this chapter's suggestions to randomly take one to two minutes throughout your day to experiment with this inner skill. In addition to those, look for opportunities to use your inner BRAKE in real-life settings, such as a difficult conversation or an uncomfortable work meeting. Practicing BRAKE in small, simple, and brief ways when you're not overly distressed builds mental muscle memory that stays true even when your inner fixer works against you.

## Putting in time behind the wheel

Just as reading about driving doesn't enable you to drive, reading about BRITE Inner Healing skills doesn't enable you to use them. If you want to learn how to *do* something new or different, you must practice doing it. For example, all effective driver's education programs include in-class learning and behind-the-wheel time. Imagine how difficult, even impossible, it would be to become a skilled driver if you only read about driving.

It's the same when learning to use ACT-based skills to learn new ways of responding to your inner fixer and bust free from the Breast Rulebook. To develop a self-acceptance practice, you must know how to use BRITE Inner Healing skills and tools. If you only read about them, you'll likely end up like me at the park, unprepared for the challenges of real-life conditions.

While I am committed to providing you with why, what, how, and when to use the inner skills, only you can invest the behind-the-wheel time that will genuinely foster your BRITE flexibility. However, please know that this behind-the-wheel time doesn't have to be time-consuming. It's different from a formal mindfulness practice where you sit on a cushion with your eyes closed. It would NOT end well if you tried that approach while learning to drive!

It can be helpful to remind yourself of *how* you learned to drive. (If you're not a driver, it's okay to imagine what it would be like to learn.) You kept your eyes wide open. You directed your full awareness to what was happening around and inside you. If you felt unsure of yourself, you would slow down or ask for help. You kept vigil for difficulties ahead, such as confusing intersections or turning onto a busy road. You understood that you couldn't just drive straight and maintain a steady speed. You did things that you had little to no experience doing, even very challenging things such as parallel parking. Of course, you weren't flawless in your execution: You likely drove too slowly at times, went into turns with too much speed, and drifted out of your lane. Nevertheless, this experience boosted your skills, confidence, and self-reliance as a driver. Although you initially stayed in familiar areas, you eventually traveled new routes without questioning your ability to handle the drive.

The remaining material in this book is like a driver's ed program for moving through the BRITE Roadmap without being dominated by your inner fixer. After you read about these inner skills, put time into *using* them. As you do, you'll (mostly) keep your eyes open. You'll stay fully aware, be willing to do things differently, and recognize that you will not have flawless execution as you experiment with these new ways of responding to your inner fixer and the threatening feeling of being *not enough*.

Most of the skills presented throughout Chapters 6-11 are learned best through behind-the-wheel time. To help, I provide many suggestions for taking the skills off the page and using them on the go. When you are doing something requiring more focused inner reflection— that's best experienced with your eyes closed—I point out when it's necessary to shift mentally into Park (denoted by **P**). There are also many reminders to visit the guided audios, demo videos, or worksheets to help you experience these inner skills.

I'm pointing all this out because I want this work to translate into real change for you. I know you can learn to companion your inner fixer's distress rather than continue being dominated by her well-meaning but unworkable agenda. I know you can emerge from your journey with breast implants fully healed from the inside out, stronger, and more radiant than ever before. And I know both of those things are more likely to happen if you integrate these techniques *into* your life rather than see them as something separate *from* your life.

I also know that's not as straightforward as it reads. Doing something helpful for yourself (e.g., exercising regularly, practicing mindfulness, or improving your diet) nearly always lands at the bottom of your proverbial to-do list, *even when you want to do it*. I also know that you might feel unwilling to take on one more thing when you feel drained. I could try to convince you that it's time to invest in yourself or use the logic that you can't care for others if you don't care for yourself, but I know those approaches aren't always effective or helpful.

Instead, I'd like to ask you to recall *why* you learned to drive. (If you're not a driver, choose another thing you've learned to do.) Most likely, it was because of something important to you, such as living with more autonomy, independence, or convenience. It's the same with BRITE Inner Healing skills. Learning them is part of something important to you, such as busting free from the Breast Rulebook, reclaiming your body, mind, or wallet from the quest for *better* breasts, or learning to live with true self-acceptance, no matter how your body or breasts change over time. You're holding this book for a reason. There is something here that matters deep down to *you*. Whatever it may be, use it to inspire your behind-the-wheel time through Chapters 6-11, no matter what your inner fixer says about it.

To help you consider what matters to you on this journey, the next chapter helps you build another essential tool in BRITE Inner Healing: your BRITE compass. Rather than using the Breast Rulebook to dictate what you do, you use your BRITE compass to move through your journey with breast implants on *your* terms.

*Chapter* 6

# Find *Your* Way Using Your BRITE Compass

Busting free from the Breast Rulebook means rediscovering the kind of person *you* most want to be, deep down in your heart, far beyond your inner fixer's rigid and fear-based agenda. Growing up in an appearance-oriented society and being hyper-focused on everyone and everything around you can lead to self-disconnection. That disconnection intensifies when painful experiences lead you to prioritize your inner fixer's futile agenda, as I did in response to the shame I felt after my brother's unsolicited warning about my cellulite dimple. You become adept at fixing the problem of feeling *less than* and gain little experience doing things differently. When you're accustomed to automatically following your inner fixer, you often lose connection with other things that matter to *you*.

Your inner fixer warns that doing other things, such as accepting yourself, might lead to "letting yourself go" or being judged, rejected, or abandoned by others. She highlights the relief of feeling *good enough* (and savors the pleasure of feeling *better than*). She convinces you that pursuing those things is what matters most. But, by doing so, she also prevents you from knowing and living by *your* values. As your life becomes all about being *good enough*, you might no longer realize you have a choice over how you show up to it. Even when surrounded by people who love and accept you completely, your inner fixer's agenda reigns supreme.

Being disconnected from your values and not knowing how to act on them undermines your self-reliance when doing something that defies group standards, such as breast implant removal. It's easy to lose your way when your inner fixer stirs up a confusing mental and emotional storm. Chapters 7-11 give you the skills and tools to see beyond, and drive safely through, this inner storm. This chapter helps you know the kind of person you strive to be while moving through it.

## The BRITE compass

As its name suggests, a **BRITE compass** guides you. It's labeled with your values and is an important tool for changing how you react to your inner fixer. Within our driving metaphor, a BRITE compass is like a dashboard feature that's easy to consult while driving. It helps you bring your whole self forward when choosing to keep, replace, or remove your problematic or aging breast implants. In the Readying and Repairing Roundabouts, it plays an essential role in companioning yourself before, during, and after breast implant removal. And it's a must-have tool for staying in the Reclaiming Roundabout while living in our beauty- and youth-obsessed society. As you'll see in later chapters, though your BRITE compass is a stand-alone tool, it works in tandem with the other BRITE Inner Healing skills.

This chapter helps you build your own BRITE compass. It's based on the tenet of ACT that focuses on your values, so this chapter clarifies how ACT defines and uses values. Then it helps you discern your values and label your own BRITE compass. Next, it shows how to use your BRITE compass when being pushed around by your inner fixer or dealing with other difficulties, such as unsupportive people. Next, you'll see how to use your compass before doing something difficult and after taking a reversal route. Finally, I close the chapter by sharing how my internalized BRITE compass helped me find my way when struggling with my distorted post-explant breasts and circling Inner Fixer Lane instead of caring for my disappointment and grief.

## What are values?

In ACT, values describe ongoing ways that you want to *be*. They're how you want to show up to the things that matter to you, deep down in your heart. They inspire you, get you fired up, and motivate you to act. Your values aren't something that you complete like goals. (Imagine someone proudly declaring they finished their efforts to treat you lovingly and then crossing it off their to-do list!) Values differentiate between *wanting a life partner* and *wanting to treat your partner lovingly*.

Unlike ethics, morals, or laws, you freely choose your values. One way to get a sense of your values is to think about people you admire, either in your life, from history, or even fictional characters. Often your hero's qualities of action reflect your chosen values. For example, when you feel admiration toward someone who thoughtfully speaks their mind, you value acting confidently, authentically, or bravely. Just as you don't need to justify your preferred ice cream flavors, your values need no justification. You might care deeply about acting kindly toward others and treating animals and nature respectfully, while someone else might care about living playfully or productively.

Unlike rigid rules you must follow, you prioritize your values depending on your circumstances. For example, when you find yourself alone in a dark alley, with a shadowy figure approaching, you prioritize acting safely over being friendly. Being flexible with your values is like rolling dice. Each roll, your move is guided by the side that faces upward. Even though you're not using the other sides, they remain intact (including the one you can't see). That's important to keep in mind because your values remain true, even when you don't act on them.

Our work in this chapter is to help you discern *your* values and learn how to use them to guide yourself while busting free.

## Discerning your values

To help you personalize and build your BRITE compass, let's explore how you most want to show up to life. This exploration goes beyond wanting to look your best, have your clothes fit better, or feel like a whole, complete, or "normal" woman. Remember, this book isn't about convincing you to let go of those things, and it's not about judging you for caring about them. But those are goals—not values—and they're often driven by inner processes over which you have no control, as previously discussed.

By discerning your values, you begin taking back the wheel. You reconnect with yourself, deep down underneath the social standards that understandably matter to you and drive so much of your suffering. So, while doing the work in this chapter, allow your concern over your appearance and belonging to be there, *and* give yourself permission to explore other things that matter to you as well.

Guided Audio 6.1 helps you build this important tool. It includes this section's prompts and can be listened to before or after reading through the remainder of this section. If you feel very disconnected from your values, I recommend reading through this section first to orient yourself to its material. Either way, keep in mind that when you're reflecting on your heartfelt values, you aren't asking what you think is possible for you to do. You're focused on how you care about being.

**LISTEN TO GUIDED AUDIO 6.1**

Now please mentally shift yourself into **P** as you envision how you want to treat yourself as you live and age in a breast-, beauty-, and youth-obsessed society. Thoughtfully reflect on the following questions:

— How do you most want to treat yourself as you move forward in life?

— How do you want to respond when you're flooded by toxic messaging and engaging in comparative thinking or feeling *not good enough*?

— What do you want to stand for on this journey to reclaim your body and mind?

— How do you most want to see yourself behaving in your relationships, during difficult interactions, and as you pursue and protect your inner healing in a breast-obsessed society?

In early sessions with a client, her mind often goes somewhat blank when considering these questions. If that's happening to you, give yourself some compassion. Validate that not knowing how to answer these questions often indicates that you had painful past experiences that brought forward a very committed (and domineering) inner fixer.

It can be helpful to see how others have answered these questions:

— How do you most want to treat yourself as you move forward in life?
*I want to talk respectfully to myself instead of tearing myself down.*

*I want to give myself the same care and concern that I so freely give to everyone else in my life.*

*I want to protect myself, even from myself.*

*I want to liberate myself from being driven by fear; I want to live bravely.*

— How do you want to respond when you're flooded by toxic messaging and engaging in comparative thinking or feeling *not good enough*?

*I want to notice that I'm doing that to myself; I end up drowning in those feelings. I want to know how to give myself a life preserver when that happens.*

*I want to be gentle and kind to myself and do things that are supportive to me when I'm hurting.*

— What do you want to stand for on this journey to reclaim your body and mind?

*I want to be real.*

*I want to show up to the world as I am.*

*I want to take care of myself, especially when I'm afraid it will end with me getting hurt.*

— How do you most want to see yourself behaving in your relationships, during difficult interactions, and as you pursue and protect your inner healing in a breast-obsessed society?

*I want to be authentic, speak my truth, and do a lot less people-pleasing and praise-seeking.*

*I want to be dedicated to taking care of myself, even when that means disappointing others or my inner fixer.*

*I want to respond compassionately when I see someone else who looks amazing, and I feel bad about myself in comparison.*

Once you have a sense of your responses to the preceding prompts, look through the following list of values and determine which ones resonate with you.[28] I suggest reading through the list entirely while reflecting on what your life would be like with these things as your guides. Imagine what would be different if you used each of these values to respond to your thoughts and feelings, others, and the world. Then ask yourself which ones would help you pursue inner healing.

When labeling my own BRITE compass, I mentally experimented with different values. For example, I was so adept at caring for others, I pondered what it would be like to treat myself with the same kindness that I so freely give to those around me. I also wondered what it would be like to prioritize self-care or act bravely. I considered how differently I would regard myself if I were more self-accepting. I contemplated how different my life would be if I chose to respond gently, playfully, or compassionately to the distress my inner fixer represents. I considered what would be different if I approached my inner fixer with curiosity and treated her as my ally rather than a dictator. I wondered what she might tell me if we were companions on this journey, where I listened to her worries, and she stopped trying to fix me. Reflecting like this helped me see that my inner fixer was simply trying to honor that I wanted to safely belong, be genuinely loved, and be truly accepted. By investing time to consider these things, I set self-acceptance as the North on my BRITE compass.

As you do this for yourself, keep it light and imaginative. Notice and drop any judgment that comes up as you do this.

---

[28] There are countless online resources with comprehensive lists of values. If you choose to explore your values further, it's most helpful to use lists from Acceptance and Commitment Therapy-based resources and practitioners because those will be consistent with how values are used in BRITE Inner Healing. The values list provided here is adapted from a longer list included in *ACT Made Simple* by Russ Harris.

**Self-acceptance:** to allow my thoughts, feelings, beliefs, and judgments around myself and my body; to struggle less against my inner experience and offer myself true companionship instead.

**Assertiveness:** to respectfully stand up for my rights and request what I want.

**Authenticity:** to be authentic, genuine, and real in my interactions and with myself.

**Bravery:** to be courageous and persist in the presence of fear, threat, or difficulty.

**Self-care:** to be caring toward myself.

**Self-compassion:** to recognize my inner pain and be willing to help.

**Connection:** to engage fully in whatever I am doing and be fully present to others.

**Curiosity:** to be curious, open-minded, and interested; to explore and discover.

**Encouragement:** to encourage and reward behavior when doing things important to me.

**Fairness and justice:** to be fair and just to myself.

**Fitness:** to maintain or improve or care about my physical and mental well-being.

**Flexibility:** to adjust and adapt readily to changing circumstances.

**Self-forgiveness:** to be forgiving toward myself; to give me what was lost by my own choices.

**Freedom and independence:** to choose how I live and help others to live freely as well.

**Fun and humor:** to be fun-loving; to seek, create, and engage in fun-filled activities.

**Gratitude:** to be grateful for and appreciative of my body, my mind, and my life.

**Honesty:** to be honest, truthful, and sincere with myself and others.

**Intimacy:** to open up, reveal, and share myself emotionally or physically.

**Self-kindness:** to be kind, considerate, nurturing, and caring toward myself.

**Self-love:** to act lovingly or affectionately toward myself.

**Mindfully:** to be open to, engaged in, and curious about the present moment.

**Persistence and commitment:** to continue resolutely, despite problems or difficulties; to act on my own behalf and follow through on what matters to me.

**Self-respect:** to treat myself with care and consideration.

**Responsibility:** to be responsible and accountable for my actions.

**Safety and protection:** to secure, protect, or ensure my safety.

**Sensuality and pleasure:** to create or enjoy pleasurable and sensual experiences.

**Sexuality:** to explore or express my sexuality.

**Skillfulness:** to continually practice and improve my skills and apply myself fully.

**Supportiveness:** to be supportive, helpful, and available to myself.

**Self-trust:** to be trustworthy, loyal, faithful, sincere, and reliable in my relationship with myself.

The following image shows a labeled BRITE compass. I suggest writing the labels as adverbs (e.g., bravely, kindly, authentically) to remind yourself that they describe how you want to behave. However, it's awkward to write values such as self-acceptance, self-care, and self-trust like adverbs. So, it's helpful to think of them as completing the sentence: *I want to be guided by* (insert your chosen value).

## Labeling your BRITE compass

Now it's your turn to label your own BRITE compass. Rather than pressuring yourself to identify the *right* labels, use the previous values list to identify the top eight values you want to guide you on this journey. It's okay to choose values you hold in your heart but struggle to bring into your daily life, even when your mind tells you that *You could never act that way* or *That's just not how you are*. You're just experimenting with what's helpful to you right now. You can modify your BRITE compass over time (and you will be redirected here again once you reach Chapter 11). However, when you do know what matters most to you on this journey, place that as North on your BRITE compass. A fillable template is available in your *Busting Free* digital library.

## DOWNLOAD THE BRITE COMPASS TEMPLATE

Once completed, it's helpful to take a picture of your labeled BRITE compass using your phone so that you have it with you on the go. It also helps to set it as your phone's lock screen so you see it throughout the day. You can also print it off or re-create it informally on sticky notes and place them all around your life, even your vehicle's dashboard. The goal is to become so familiar with your BRITE compass that you no longer need a visual representation. By internalizing your BRITE compass, you can shift your awareness toward it, even when your inner fixer manages to block its view.

## Using your BRITE compass

A tool serves you only if you know how to use it. The following material highlights several different ways to use the labeled BRITE compass shown earlier in this chapter.

### To guide how you respond on the inside

Chapter 4 introduced the metaphor that your journey with breast implants is like driving through a series of roundabouts with your thoughts, memories, beliefs, feelings, imagination, and threat response frequently hijacked by your inner fixer. Without consulting your BRITE compass, getting caught up in the ensuing mental and emotional storm keeps you circling Inner Fixer Lane. For example, when you feel overwhelmed imagining life without breast implants or consumed with self-doubt over whether you have BII, a natural response is to avoid moving toward explant. That avoidance amplifies when your inner fixer erects distressing billboards, plays Bad Boobs Radio, and fills your car with backseat drivers insisting you must follow the Breast Rulebook.

Consulting your BRITE compass inspires you to respond differently to explant-related anxiety. You might use a combination of compass points or focus on only one. Either way, the moment you turn your awareness toward this inner tool, you reclaim how you show up for yourself. Instead of being dominated by your inner fixer, your BRITE compass helps you respond more helpfully to that part of your mind and the internal distress it holds.

Using the BRITE compass with the labels shown earlier in this chapter, you might choose *bravely* to guide how you respond to your explant-related fear. Let's look at how you would use bravely to guide your actions in each of the BRITE roundabouts.

— When circling the Rationalization Roundabout, acting bravely might lead you to schedule MRIs to ensure your implants' integrity, even though it might reveal a problem needing your attention.

— In the Reasoning Roundabout, acting bravely might look like researching breast implant safety, even when it feels scary to contemplate what's going on inside your body.

— In the Readying Roundabout, bravery helps you meet with explant surgeons, even when a part of you is scared, unsure, or dealing with past medical trauma.

— In the Repairing Roundabout, acting bravely helps you during tender and vulnerable moments, such as seeing yourself for the first time after surgery, being intimate, or returning to work or other settings where you expect people to notice.

— And in the Reclaiming Roundabout, acting bravely helps you live life on *your* terms and do what you want, even when your inner fixer warns that your post-explant chest isn't *enough*.

Pursuing your values is often not the easiest path to take through the mental and emotional storm stirred up by a distressed inner fixer. As you read the preceding examples, you might be envisioning yourself white-knuckling your way through it all. But rest assured, your BRITE compass is only one of many tools you'll have after reading this book. As you work through the chapters ahead, you will learn how to prevail over uncomfortable thoughts, feelings, and sensations that naturally show up when busting free.

## To guide how you respond on the outside

Many things are beyond your control on these journeys. For example, you might experience partner abandonment, unsupportive friends and family, medical trauma, or gaslighting (i.e., being treated like you're mentally unsound). Mistreatment from others kicks up an intense emotional storm, swirling with self-shame, self-doubt, humiliation, disempowerment, self-abandonment, confusion, resentment, sadness, and anger. It's hard to think straight. As a result, you might shut down, lash out, retreat, people-please, go along to get along, or respond in other unhelpful ways that further erode your relationship with yourself. Women with BII who are gaslit often rank the experience among the hardest to manage.

By internalizing your BRITE compass, you can mentally access it when an interaction is unfolding in a surprisingly unpleasant way (e.g., you're having a conversation with someone who questions your plans to explant to flat or dismisses BII as being *all in your head*). Your compass remains steady when you can't think straight and when your emotions are storming. It reminds you to advocate for yourself. It inspires you to bring into these moments the qualities you admire in others. No matter how you historically respond to being mistreated, your BRITE compass reminds you of the person you want to be *now*. When directing your awareness to a compass labeled like the one earlier in this chapter, it reminds you to pursue your value of acting assertively. That might inspire you to tell the other person they don't have your permission to challenge your actual lived experience. Or you might choose to be guided by self-respect and end the conversation rather than tolerate it for fear of offending the other person.

## Before doing something difficult

You can also proactively use your BRITE compass to help you visualize how you want to move through something you expect will be hard. For example, I knew that seeing my breasts for the first time after explant surgery would be a difficult adjustment. Even though I was eager to be implant-free, I still cared about the appearance of this highly sexualized part of my body. I felt concerned about the aftermath of my skin stretching so far to accommodate the implants, particularly in the cleavage area. Plus, my explant surgeon warned that there would be aesthetic impacts because my left breast's inframammary fold (where the breast tissue meets the chest) was surgically lowered during augmentation to "correct" the horizontal asymmetry of my natural breasts. Having been warned of this possibility mere moments before going into surgery, I didn't fully understand what those implications might entail. But I did know that I wanted to be very intentional with how I stepped through the tender and vulnerable moment of seeing my newly explanted breasts. I knew my inner fixer would be very alarmed.

By proactively consulting my BRITE compass (which looks exactly like the one shared earlier in the chapter), I acted kindly to that distressed part of my mind and treated myself respectfully. I chose to do that by minimizing my use of judgmental language. For example, I knew that words such as "deformed" and "disfigured" would further distress my inner fixer (and me). But I also knew that I wanted to be authentic. Well-meaning affirmations just don't help me much.

I wanted to use a word that nonjudgmentally reflected my breasts' surgical trauma and manipulation by the drains. So I chose "distorted." It means *pulled or twisted out of shape; contorted.* This small act of treating myself authentically and respectfully acknowledged my reality and prevented my inner fixer from escalating my breasts' appearance to an all-consuming threat level.

I also chose to respond to my unwanted thoughts and feelings with acceptance. Rather than struggling against them, I allowed them to come and go on their own. I didn't like or want them, but I accepted that they were showing up in ways that made sense given my circumstances. I supported myself while they were with me. (You'll learn much more about doing this type of work for yourself in Chapters 8 and 9.)

Did doing these things make my inner fixer (or me) feel better about my breasts' appearance? No, but feeling better wasn't the point. I simply didn't want to amplify, escalate, or worsen how I felt; I wasn't trying to control or change it. Instead, by showing up for myself in values-guided ways, I had my own back, rebuilt self-trust, and stayed out of Inner Fixer Lane.

## After taking a reversal route

When under significant distress, you likely default to old coping mechanisms. For example, when you're very overwhelmed, your inner fixer tries convincing you to stay put or head back to an earlier roundabout. You often feel relieved when you take a reversal route. After all, you got away from the unpleasant thoughts, feelings, and predictions that overwhelmed you. But as time passes, you realize you're compromising on your values once again. It's easy to beat yourself up or even delude yourself after taking a reversal route. But as discussed in

Chapter 4, reversal routes are opportunities to reflect on what overwhelmed you and to do things differently next time.

By referring to your BRITE compass, you can reorient yourself to being the person you aspire to be. Doing so is akin to a hiker pulling out her compass after realizing she's lost her way. She pays extra attention to its guidance until she is sure she's once again heading in her chosen direction.

Using the BRITE compass shared earlier in this chapter to reorient yourself would ensure that you treat yourself kindly. You wouldn't engage in negative self-talk about what you *can't handle,* or how you *look like a boy,* or that *no one will ever want you.* Instead, you'd recognize those are things your inner fixer says to keep you circling; they don't represent how *you* want to treat yourself moving forward. Your BRITE compass would remind you to embrace your value of acting with self-trust, which is especially important after a reversal route. It would also reorient you to acting authentically. As a result, you'd be real with yourself and address what overwhelmed you, rather than pushing yourself forward and hoping it will somehow turn out differently.

## Inner healing and pursuing what matters

Knowing your values might seem like a straightforward concept. But, to find your way through this journey, you must hold your values in your awareness and use them to bring your whole self forward. Otherwise, you default to familiar and unhelpful ways of treating yourself privately on the inside and while navigating the world around you.

As previously discussed, your deeply ingrained beliefs are reinforced by the ongoing behind-the-scenes process described in Chapter 1, an inner fixer that's here to stay, and a Breast Rulebook you can never fully unlearn. After living for decades with those things pushing you around, the thoughts, feelings, and sensations that come with them travel pathways in your mind like superhighways. They are much faster and easier for your mind to use.

Although your mind can build new pathways of thinking and behaving, *you* must choose to use them instead of your mind's superhighways. To help understand why you must be so intentional, imagine the difference between crossing a dense field with waist-high grass using a pathway used once or twice compared with taking a heavily used path. The well-worn path is easy to see, offers less resistance, and requires less awareness.

In contrast, using a new path requires motivation to put in the additional effort. That motivation often comes from knowing and embracing your values. They remind you to forge ahead despite resistance from your inner fixer. They inspire you to bust free of the superhighways built in your mind by society's obsession with breasts. Perhaps most importantly, they guide you to be the woman you most want to be and live life on your terms, even when your mind derives that you are *not good enough.*

Your values are pivotally important when you inevitably must choose to replace or remove aging or problematic breast implants. Likewise, being guided by them is essential when your mind naturally compares your post-explant chest to the Breast Rulebook. Pursuing your values makes the difference between caring for your body and mind on *your* terms versus doing whatever it takes to meet society's standards or missing out on life because you don't.

To close the chapter, I will share how my internalized BRITE compass helped me find my way after explant. The "**Fluff Fairy**" visited me sometime after the one-month mark. (The Fluff Fairy refers to the phenomenon of post-explant breasts filling out.) I returned to my former and familiar pre-augmentation silhouette. It was a homecoming of sorts. Overall, I felt great when dressed because I simply felt like me.

My undressed appearance was something altogether different. Despite the promises and pictures proving that explanted breasts changed tremendously in the months after the surgery and often returned to a natural appearance, I had a sinking feeling that would not happen with mine. By about week six post-op, my breasts settled into a close approximation of their final appearance. Their overall contour maintained a depression in the area previously under the implant. The skin between my breasts was unable to recover from its earlier demand to accommodate the high profile of my implants; it resembled a partially deflated air mattress.

Most distressing to me was the aftermath my explant surgeon predicted mere moments before the surgery when he noticed that my implant surgeon surgically lowered the inframammary fold on my left breast. This lowering is routinely done during breast augmentation to maximize horizontal alignment of the implant (i.e., to honor the Breast Rulebook). As a result of that surgical decision, my left breast now has two inframammary folds: the natural one and the surgically created one.

To me, it looks like it has a double chin. Because I'm a South Park fan, it reminds me of Cartman. (If you're not familiar with him and want help visualizing this, Google his image.) I often joke that I should draw some eyes over the nipple and put a little hat on my left breast. Sometimes I even personify it with Cartman's attitude. While this imagery helps me step back from my painful thoughts about my breast's appearance (an inner skill described further in Chapter 8), it takes a lot of intentional effort to make room for my disappointment. (Don't worry, Chapter 9 shows you how to do this for yourself.)

I could fill pages listing how I struggled with thoughts, images, and feelings involving my explant aesthetics. Instead, I will simply say that feeling regret is among my least-preferred experiences. I was swimming in it as I reflected on the loss of my natural and unblemished left breast. My inner fixer was eager to address this regret. She knew there was no convincing me to have further surgeries, but she was hell-bent and determined to fix "The Crease."[29]

For several weeks, I struggled mightily against The Crease. Because post-explant creases are not uncommon, I reached out to an online support group asking what to do and when to start. Many well-intentioned women told me it was much too soon to be concerned and that my breasts would change on their own over the next year. Others encouraged me to work hard now to remove the crease before it permanently settled in.

My inner fixer knew a permanently creased breast would lead to many moments of feeling *less than*, so she elevated The Crease to the highest threat level. She took inspiration from the story of a woman with a crease nearly identical to mine. That woman's crease resolved after a painful manipulation by a health provider. Her before and after pictures filled me with painful longing. Because I couldn't find any nearby providers experienced with manipulating post-explant breasts, I tried acupuncture in hopes it would minimize the double chin appearance. I also put significant effort into self-massage and cupping. Unfortunately, these attempts caused my embattled breasts more pain and did not improve the stubborn crease.

Fortunately, a part of me silently watched all my unsuccessful efforts to get rid of The Crease. (You also have this *incredibly* helpful inner resource and will learn how to use it in Chapter 10.) To tap into this resource, I used the Movie Mind tool (from Chapter 3) to watch a movie showing how I reacted to The Crease. Watching my actions from that perspective helped me see similarities between how I was behaving now

---

[29] Naming something helps lessen its hold over you. It's discussed further in Chapter 8.

and other futile quests, such as hiding cellulite. I saw that I was once again following my inner fixer's agenda.

I was unsuccessfully attempting to fix my grief and loss with cups, massages, and needles. My efforts were ineffective, and they caused me physical pain. Moreover, they amplified my inner suffering by introducing a cycle of hoping *this* cupping session or *this* acupuncture visit would make a difference. Fueled by denial, that unhelpful hope dominated my actions during this tender healing and recovery period.

As I watched this newer footage play out, compassion swelled inside me. Instead of hurting myself, I needed to do the more difficult inner work of accepting that my crease was unlike the kind that eventually gave way–mine was anatomical and permanent. That self-compassion set the stage for the moment I dropped the struggle against The Crease.

I was lying in bed one night about six weeks post-explant. My hand began exploring my left breast's trauma in hopes the crease was improving. I noticed the old familiar judging of my body and longing for it to be different. Without even thinking about it, I shifted from exploring my breast's contours out of fear, regret, and longing, to giving this part of my body compassion, caring, gentleness, acceptance, and love. I softened my hand and allowed it to rest gently, just like I would if I were touching something painful on one of my daughters. I even lightly patted this poor, battered, and traumatized part. I allowed myself to notice the warm support of my hand connecting to this innocent part of me that never asked to be cut once, let alone twice, and was changed without its permission. I noticed it was doing its best to heal like a champ. And, to my surprise, tears filled my eyes.

My internalized BRITE compass helped me shift from anxiously hoping for improvement to companioning myself like I would someone I care about. I finally pursued the previously mythical concepts of self-love and self-acceptance after four decades of trying to *fix* the painful feeling of being *less than*. That was a turning point for me.

Moving forward, I continued pursuing self-care. I stopped applying those painful suction cups and started touching The Crease with loads of self-compassion.[30] (Chapter 9 shows you how to do this for yourself, no matter what you're struggling against.) I acted with self-respect as I apologized to that poor part of my body, recognizing that it never asked to be surgically lowered to accommodate a silicone-filled bag. I treated myself kindly by simply being with my sadness. To this day, my BRITE compass helps me take those infinitely more helpful paths and behave like the self-accepting and self-loving woman I aspire to be.

By sharing that experience with you, I hope to illustrate that using your BRITE compass doesn't require some formal stance or massive time investment. Once you've done the work in this chapter to label your compass, you simply need to bring its guidance into your heart and recognize that it's often in the most tender, unsuspecting moments that you need it most.

You also need concrete ideas of the kinds of things you will and won't do when guided by your values, because *knowing* what matters goes hand in hand with *doing* what matters. Chapter 11 focuses on doing what matters. For now, you can draw from the examples throughout this chapter to develop your own ideas of what busting free looks like to *you*.

In the next chapter, you'll see how your inner fixer pulls you from the here and now by flooding your mind with painful memories and fear-filled predictions about explant. Then you will learn how to use present-moment awareness and another tool, your BRITE lasso, to stay present and take care of things needing your attention.

---

[30] Cupping can promote physical healing after explant. It can be an important way to act with self-care. In this context though, I was using the cups inappropriately in hopes of fixing an issue that they are not designed to improve.

# Chapter 7

# Stay Present Using Your BRITE Lasso

ave you ever driven somewhere while mentally doing something else, such as planning what to wear to an event or preparing your words for a difficult conversation? It's easy to get lost in your thoughts rather than pay attention to the road. You're more likely to miss your exit, lose your way, or veer into danger. The same holds true for your journey with breast implants. To safely find *your* way through your journey with them, you need to stay fully present, inside and out.

Unfortunately, your inner fixer is skilled at using your memories and imagination against you. She keeps you busy ruminating over the past and fearing the future, which compromises the attention you give to problems in the here and now. Your inner fixer has several metaphorical moves within our driving metaphor to disconnect you from the present moment and keep you circling Inner Fixer Lane. For example, when you're in the first three BRITE Roundabouts, she turns up the volume on Bad Boobs Radio anytime you consider what to do about getting more than you bargained for from breast implants. She uses it to reinforce your implants' importance by broadcasting excerpts from the Breast Rulebook. She covers the rearview mirror with scenes from your past where you felt incomplete or *not good enough* because of your breasts. She erects roadside billboards of distressing images predicting how you will look and be treated if you take the exit toward explant. She places warning signs near the exits stating things like, *You won't feel sexy and confident* or *No one will find you attractive* or *Exit here for misery.*

Each time you near the exit while circling the first three roundabouts, your view from the driver's seat looks somewhat like this:

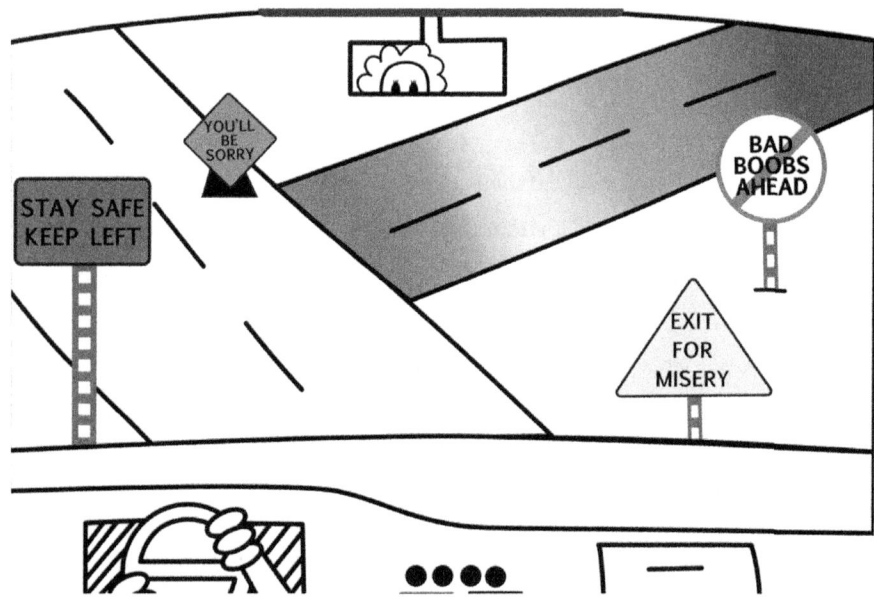

*Figure 7.1 Your view when approaching a roundabout's exit*

She changes these billboards and signs using whatever content is most distracting to you. For example, when your journey involves BII, your inner fixer bombards you with *What ifs* over its lack of a definitive diagnosis, nonspecific symptoms, and conflicting opinions on surgical approaches to explant. These mostly sound like, *What if I don't feel better after explant?* or *What if I don't have BII?* When you got breast implants because you "felt like a boy" or experienced ridicule, she reminds you what it was like to live with that threatening lack of breast tissue. When you're a mastectomy patient who reconstructed your breasts using implants, she reminds you of the many health professionals, family, or friends who said that you *needed* breast mounds to feel normal, happy, or whole, and predicted you'd be miserable without them.

She continues these moves once you explant, particularly in the early days after surgery, or when you have difficulty adjusting to your new silhouette or breast aesthetics. She'll predict what others will think the first time they see you or how a partner might judge your post-explant chest. She cautions against doing activities where the way you dress might reveal your post-explant chest (e.g., going to the beach, swimming, or wearing a formal gown). She draws your attention to other parts of your body that are more noticeable without your breast implants (e.g., a less-than-flat tummy).

Even when you're not struggling with your post-explant aesthetic, she remains concerned about weight gain, changes to your body's shape, wrinkling skin, thinning hair, lips or eyebrows, etc. To avoid feeling *less than* or *not good enough,* she can even lead you to miss out on doing things, going places, or spending time with people you enjoy. She continues convincing you to invest money and time into "fixing" yourself with unproven or costly products and procedures.

Busting free from your inner fixer's agenda happens in the here and now. Only in the present moment can you make informed decisions, work on problems needing your attention, and skillfully take care of yourself when surrounded by predatory marketing of products and surgeries to fix your "flaws." For example, being fully plugged in during a surgical consult helps you discern if the surgeon is a good fit for you. Likewise, paying attention to and absorbing words of reassurance from a partner or friend enables you to feel supported and safe. Recognizing when you're feeling insecure or avoidant after explant, whether related to your breasts or not, alerts you to pull out your BRITE compass and be the person you most want to be.

You can learn to stay in the here and now, no matter what memory or feared prediction your inner fixer conjures. To that end, this chapter features the ACT process of **present moment awareness**. It helps you stay present to yourself and your surroundings. It lays the foundation for a more mindful path through your inner journey with breast implants and is a key feature of BRITE flexibility.

Keep in mind that moving mindfully toward reclaiming yourself is unlike the popularized idea of using mindfulness to relax, feel better, calm down, clear your mind, get rid of negative thoughts, and so forth. In BRITE Inner Healing, mindfulness is about nonjudgmentally and purposefully being aware of what's going on inside and around you to know how to show up.

You take a more mindful path through this journey by:

1. Being able to focus on what you choose, despite your inner fixer's efforts to distract you (this chapter).
2. Stepping back from your breast-related thoughts and feelings rather than treating them like commands (Chapter 8).
3. Companioning your inner experience (Chapter 9).
4. Seeing beyond your breast-related self-concept (Chapter 10).

This kind of mindfulness is the antidote to mindlessly following your inner fixer.

The first half of this chapter explores ACT's tenet of present moment awareness (PMA) and introduces you to your **BRITE lasso**, an inner tool to rein in your wandering attention. To help you practice PMA and learn to wield your BRITE lasso, you're provided with many different options to bring them into your life. (Rest assured, you won't be sitting cross-legged on a cushion with your eyes closed!)

The second half of this chapter shows how to put the practice of PMA into action to move more mindfully through the BRITE Roadmap. It provides examples of using your BRITE lasso to counteract your inner fixer's efforts to hijack your attention, prepare for something that feels hard, and reorient yourself after a reversal route. I close the chapter by sharing several examples of how I used PMA and my BRITE lasso before, during, and after my breast implants were removed.

## Present moment awareness

PMA is an inner skill that helps you have your own back. By paying attention to what's going on inside and around you, you're better able to meet your needs at any given moment. Instead of hoping for the best or fearing the worst, you take things as they come (and use your BRITE compass to guide your way through). When you flexibly show up to problems needing your attention, self-trust grows.

Although paying attention to the here and now is a straightforward concept, its practice doesn't come easily. Your mind naturally wanders, ruminates, and plans. While a wandering mind helps daydream your way through a repetitive task, it gets in the way when you're doing something important that feels risky (e.g., asking for a raise, preparing for a big speech, leaving an abusive partner, removing breast implants), especially when it leads to unhelpful procrastination or overwhelmed shutdown.

On your breast implant journey, PMA is a mental muscle that helps you:

— Direct your focus and do what matters to you, even when your inner fixer brews up a ton of difficult thoughts and feelings.

— Notice and describe (rather than judge and predict) the discomfort that naturally shows up when doing something that defies your deeply held beliefs around your breasts, belonging, and worth.

— Pay purposeful attention to what you (and your inner fixer) are thinking, feeling, and doing moment by moment.

Just as you do reps at a gym to strengthen your body's muscles, you can do things that build your PMA muscle. But keep in mind, you don't go to a gym to be good at going to a gym, and you don't do PMA exercises simply to be good at doing them. The exercises in this chapter build a mental muscle that catches when you're hooked by toxic social messaging. It helps you see when you're being lured to "fix" yourself without awareness of the risks, costs, and impacts on your inner well-being. You use this muscle continually to ensure that your self-improvement projects are carried out on *your* own terms and guided by *your* values, rather than motivated by your inner fixer's judging, predicting, and rulebook following.

Guided Audio 7.1 reviews this section's material and provides your first experience with using your BRITE lasso (introduced in the following section).

 LISTEN TO GUIDED AUDIO 7.1

# Your BRITE lasso

Building a mental muscle might seem abstract but working with PMA involves something quite tangible and under your control: *your focus.* Because your mind naturally wanders, especially when you're caught in a mental and emotional storm, practicing PMA isn't about overcoming a wandering mind; it's about noticing when your mind wanders *and bringing it back.*

When you do PMA exercises, you're building an inner lasso to redirect your wandering mind back to whatever you've told it to do. (I like imagining that you're traveling this journey with your BRITE compass in hand and a lasso hanging from your hip, like Wonder Woman.) Just like Wonder Woman's golden lasso forces whoever is bound within it to obey her commands, your BRITE lasso tells your mind to follow *your* focus. On your journey with breast implants, that means you tell your mind where to focus rather than your inner fixer. Sure, her billboards will still be there, but you notice when you're staring at them and redirect your attention to other things that also matter to you.

Let's walk through an example of how your BRITE lasso works. I know this might sound odd, but for the next two minutes, just mindfully pay attention to the sounds around you. During the two-minute exercise, your only job is to catch when your mind wanders from paying attention to sounds and bring it back to paying attention to them.

Go ahead and shift into **P** for the next two minutes. (Set a timer on your phone if you prefer.)

If you practiced the exercise, you now know that doing it wasn't so easy despite its simple directions. Most likely, after only a few moments, your mind moved on to planning what you're going to eat next, judging the exercise, anticipating the two minutes being over, or noticing countless other distractions both within and around you. You may have spent the entire two minutes just catching your wandering focus and bringing it back. Like a skilled ranch hand roping a stray, you lassoed your focus and redirected it back to the exercise. You were just listening and lassoing, again and again. The exercise wasn't about clearing your mind, reaching some transcendental state, or gaining insight by listening to the sounds you hear. It's not about listening. It's not about the sounds. It's about lassoing.

By doing exercises like this, be they focused on sounds or anything else, you become skilled at catching your wandering mind and using your BRITE lasso to redirect your attention. You can then wield it anytime you're ruminating on the past, judging the present, or making unhelpful predictions. You can lasso your awareness back to whatever needs your attention in the here and now, including sadness over the past or apprehension over your future.

## Practicing PMA and using your BRITE lasso

There are countless ways to practice directing your attention to the present moment. My goal is to help you find ways to integrate this into your daily life, so you build the mental muscles needed for PMA and lassoing. And, here's a welcome change: To get a feel for using your inner lasso, these exercises don't have to focus on anything related to your breasts. This flexible focus brings us to two important points about PMA:

1. **Though it doesn't matter where you choose to direct your attention during an exercise, you absolutely must set your focus each time you practice.** Otherwise, you can't catch when your mind has wandered, and you don't know where to return your focus.

2. **Practicing PMA is not about relaxing, feeling peaceful, or being happy.** Sure, you might feel calm, centered, or relaxed sometimes, with some exercises, but if you put pressure on yourself to feel those things, you might think *I'm doing this wrong* or *This doesn't work for me.* (Sometimes, my mind is busier than Chicago's O'Hare Airport, and it is *not* relaxing to watch my thoughts fly by and occasionally collide!)

   As you work on building your BRITE lasso, don't burden yourself with those unrealistic expectations. You likely do that more than enough as a 21st-century woman; let's not add more to your already overflowing plate. Instead, I encourage you to gently keep in mind that this is just one way you're **building a skill set to companion yourself mindfully through BRITE inner healing.** Though the following exercises aren't about feeling "better," they are part of a skill set that often *does* turn down the volume on inner suffering, including the kind that comes when you feel like you don't measure up to beauty standards or don't like something about your appearance.

In each of the following PMA exercises, you will do the following four things:

1. Set your focus.
2. Specify an amount of time to practice, and (ideally) set a quiet timer.
3. Direct your attention to whatever you set as your focus.
4. Notice when your attention wanders and lasso your focus back to the exercise.

As you read through the exercises below, please shift into **P** and actually do each one. Your BRITE lasso is an essential tool for your

BRITE journey and life. You build it only by doing exercises. It is *not* enough to simply read this chapter. However, you don't have to master all of these. You're simply looking for a few that resonate with you and that you're willing to practice. It's best to do only one or two exercises at a time. Try working them into your life for a couple of days. Then come back to this section and choose a couple more. There are many from which to choose, so don't force yourself to do any that are uncomfortable to you. Guided audio for each of these exercises is included in your *Busting Free* digital library.

## Describe Without Judging

As discussed in Chapter 1, your mind comes to its conclusions, reads between the lines, and makes unhelpful inferences. That kind of judgmental thinking often drives your suffering and choices without your awareness or permission. It pushes you around on the inside and dominates how you treat yourself, interact with others, and move through the world. This exercise helps you build the inner skill of noticing your judgmental thinking and being able to let it come and go while doing something else. Over time, this skill helps you catch unhelpful judgment *before* it sends you circling Inner Fixer Lane.

Practicing this exercise isn't to eradicate judgment from your life. Lots of judgments can be quite helpful in making decisions, like judging if a surgeon is *too far* or *too expensive* or *too impersonal* for your comfort level. However, judgmental thinking is problematic when you don't notice you're doing it, and your reaction to it disconnects you from your full experience or interferes with what you care about or need to get done. For example, if you judge that you are *too unattractive* without implants, you might continue tolerating problematic implants or struggle with their loss each time that judgment shows up. Your BRITE lasso helps you redirect your focus to the here and now, where you can care for problems needing your attention, including the feelings fueled by self-judgment.

I recommend mentally shifting into **P** and practicing the first version below. Then take it on the go by randomly practicing it (and its many variations) throughout your day.

For this exercise, you will:

— Spend two minutes with your attention focused on describing a handheld object as it is, without adding or subtracting anything.

— Either aloud or silently to yourself, describe what you can see, feel, hear, and smell about the object.

— When your mind engages in any other mental activity, use your lasso to gently return your awareness to describing the image.

— Notice when judgmental thinking shows up around yourself, *I'm probably not doing this correctly*; the exercise, *This is really weird*; or the object, *This is cute/old/nice.*

— When that happens, inwardly note *judging,* and return your focus to nonjudgmentally describing the object.

You can work with this exercise using Guided Audio 7.2, by reading through the following prompts, or both.

🔊 ))) LISTEN TO GUIDED AUDIO 7.2

Go ahead and choose any nearby object to hold in your hand. It doesn't matter what you select. It can even be a box of tissues, a pen, or a pet. Set a timer and spend two minutes using nonjudgmental language to respond to the prompts below (either out loud or silently in your mind).

— Describe the size of the object: length, width, thickness.

— Describe the shape.

— Guess its weight. If you're unsure, compare it to something tangible such as a slice of bread or an athletic shoe.

— Describe any colors.

— Describe the texture, noting any distinct areas.

— Describe any movable or detachable parts.

— Are any words written on it? If so, count the words and their letters, vowels, and consonants, or notice the font color and size.

— Describe the sounds you hear when you tap or scratch it.

— Describe any scent when you hold it near your nose.

— How do you use this object? What purpose does it serve?

— How did this object come to be in your possession?

Using prompts can artificially corral your focus. So to experience how your mind wanders typically, please take two more minutes to describe another object *without* using the previous prompts. By observing how your mind naturally wanders with a neutral object, you can validate when it's hard to focus on something your mind interprets as threatening. Seriously, put it in **P**, and see how this exercise goes without the prompts.

There are many ways to vary how you do this exercise moving forward:

— Nonjudgmentally describe a handheld object with your eyes closed.

— Another eyes-closed variation is to have someone place an unknown object in your hand. Tell yourself that you can open your eyes after two minutes of mindfully exploring the object with your eyes closed. Notice the urge to open your eyes. Notice and name the feelings and judgments that show up once you open your eyes and visualize the object. (Note: This version is my clients' favorite.)

— Pick an object, picture, photograph, or article of clothing and describe your inner experience in the present moment as you interact with it. But, instead of describing its attributes, notice and name the thoughts, feelings, and body sensations that show up for you moment by moment. Gently acknowledge when judgment shows up. (I suggest starting with more neutral objects before asking your mind to nonjudgmentally describe something such as a bra or an old photo of you. Remember to use your inner BRAKE as a grounding tool if needed.)

— Spend time people-watching and silently describing their age, height, weight, clothing, shoes, accessories, the sound of their voice or laughter, and the color of their skin, hair, and eyes. Notice any biases or comparative thinking showing up in the moment while continuing to describe them using nonjudgmental language. This variation is a super-useful way to gain experience using your inner lasso because it's easy to wander into the Land of Judging and Comparative Thinking when people-watching.

## Breathing

Watching your breath cycle is an excellent on-the-go way to practice PMA because, no matter where you are or what you are doing, you are always breathing. When practicing PMA of breathing, you don't need to modify your breath. You don't have to slow down, speed up, count, or put your hand on your belly. Just set a timer and turn your awareness to noticing the sensations of breathing. When you notice your mind wandering, lasso your attention back to focusing on the sensations of breathing. That's it!

You can also work with this exercise using Guided Audio 7.3.

Tips for extending your practicing of mindful breathing:

— Start with only a minute or two. If you wish, you can add time as you get more practiced at watching your breath. Alternatively, spend several minutes of each day informally doing this practice. For reference, I practice PMA of my breathing for a couple of breath cycles, a couple of times, every couple of hours.

— Do this practice with your eyes opened and closed. We move through life mostly with our eyes open, so it's important to get used to using your inner lasso that way as well.

— As you breathe in and out, notice differences in temperature between the air you breathe in and the air you exhale, the sounds you make, the pauses between inhaling and exhaling, your body rising and falling, and the rate of your breathing. When practicing this, you can notice all of these or focus on only one or two.

— Remember: Your mind will wander. Success with this practice means noticing when it does and returning to observing your breath. Notice if your ability to maintain your focus changes when you silently say to yourself, *breathing in* while you inhale, and *breathing out* while you exhale.

## Moving

Another on-the-go technique for practicing PMA is to direct your awareness to an activity such as walking, dancing, washing dishes, brushing your teeth, driving, typing on a keyboard, getting dressed, washing your face, petting a pet, gardening, doing yoga, etc. The possibilities are endless, and it doesn't matter what you choose. When practicing this kind of PMA, go all in and purposefully direct your attention toward what you are doing. Most women, out of necessity, are rather skilled at multitasking. Take a break from it and give yourself the gift of doing just one thing for a few moments. You don't need to set a timer for many of these. Instead, practice PMA for the duration of the activity or a specified distance (when walking, jogging, etc.) or mindfully dance for the duration of a song. You get the idea. No matter what activity you're doing, build your BRITE lasso by directing your awareness to doing only that one thing and gently returning your focus to the activity any time it wanders. That's it!

You can also work with this exercise using Guided Audio 7.4.

 LISTEN TO GUIDED AUDIO 7.4

Tips for practicing PMA of movement:

— This practice is done mainly with your eyes open. You can mindfully notice differences by closing your eyes and feeling them from the inside. (Do this only when it's perfectly safe, such as while you're brushing your teeth or washing your face. I did this one time on a treadmill and ended up with my feet flying out from under me, tons of skid marks, and more than a bit of embarrassment!)

— As you do the activity, notice the sensations of moving inside your body, the sounds, what your body touches as it moves. Describe the intention behind your movement (self-care, fun, creativity, productivity, responsibility). When washing dishes, notice the water temperature, iridescence on the soap bubbles, and fragrance of the soap. When brushing your teeth, notice the taste of the toothpaste, sensations in your mouth, and sounds. Notice how you feel as you do the activity. Notice judgments (praise-based and critical) that show up around it (*This is great/boring/too hard*) or the way you do it (*I'm good/bad at this*), and gently lasso back to the experience of moving.

— Success with PMA of movement involves noticing when you're no longer focused on what you are doing and mentally plugging back into the activity.

## Eating

Eating is something you do every day that provides another way to practice eyes-open PMA. When doing this practice, you're not eating and watching TV, scrolling through social media, listening to music, or chitchatting. Instead, you're directing your complete awareness to the sensation of eating.

You can work with this exercise using Guided Audio 7.5, by reading through the following prompts, or both.

LISTEN TO GUIDED AUDIO 7.5

Tips for practicing PMA of eating:

— Before taking a bite, notice the food's colors, aromas, and texture.

— As you look at the food, consider all the effort that went into making it available to you at this moment. Consider how it was grown or processed, packaged, shipped, displayed, and prepared.

— When judgment shows up around your food choice, notice it and redirect your awareness back to the experience of eating.

— Before bringing a bite into your mouth, allow it to linger a bit longer at the edge of your lips. Allow it to sit on your tongue and notice the way it feels in your mouth. Push the food around your mouth with your tongue. Savor the flavors. Notice the temperature.

— Notice the sounds of chewing and how long you chew before swallowing.

— Notice the sensation and sounds as you swallow.

— Once the food is in your belly, consider how it serves your body by providing fuel for your cells.

— When your mind wanders, gently return your focus to the experience of eating.

There are many ways to extend this practice:

— One bite: This can be a forkful, spoonful, a single bite of a piece of fruit, a single slice of a vegetable, or one nut, berry, mint, raisin, chip, etc.

— One sip from whatever you're drinking.

— Mindfully eat an entire meal or drink an entire beverage.

— My personal favorite is to mindfully eat a piece of fruit that requires peeling—a clementine, for example. Doing this offers you the chance to mindfully notice the details of the rind and listen as you remove it. You can then notice the differences between the outside and inside of the fruit. Also, notice the delicate, lace-like vein patterns on the individual wedges. Finally, consider how sunlight provides energy to grow the fruit-bearing tree and how the fruit of that tree is now providing you with energy to move through life.

## Listening

There are many sounds around and within us for hearing-abled persons. So practicing PMA of sounds varies depending on the type of sound you choose.

**Music:** When practicing PMA with music, you don't need to set a timer. Just choose a piece of music, and mindfully listen to its instruments, tempo, melody, rhythm, and other sound patterns. If there are lyrics, notice the words. Notice changes in the volume and pitch of the voice(s). Music is emotionally evocative, so when your mind wanders, use your inner lasso to return your focus to hearing the music.

**Sounds in and out, near and far, or random and rhythmic:** Set a two-minute timer. First, direct your awareness to sounds you hear inside your body, such as breathing and swallowing. Then, notice sounds outside your body. Shift to listening to sounds in the same room as you. Then notice sounds outside your room. Notice the farthest sound you can discern. Notice sounds as they appear and fade away, coming and going on their own. Notice sounds that are constant and unchanging or repetitive and rhythmic. Anytime you notice your mind wandering, use your inner lasso to bring back your focus to listening.

You can work with this exercise by listening to Guided Audio 7.6.

LISTEN TO GUIDED AUDIO 7.6

## Connect with the Natural World

When was the last time you looked up at the sky, listened in on the world of birds, or watched sunlight sparkling on the water, the acrobatic antics of a squirrel, the sun slipping down the horizon, or noticed trees swaying in a breeze? The natural world is full of sights, sounds, smells, and other living things, all constantly interacting and changing, perfect for practicing PMA. It comes with the bonus of *not* having to do, prepare, or gather anything. You don't even have to be outside to practice PMA of nature; you can look through any window. You can also view nature-based videos (e.g., a waterfall, the sun rising over the ocean, birds flying in perfect synchrony, or a time-lapse video of a flower blooming).

You can work with this exercise using Guided Audio 7.7, by reading through the following prompts, or both.

LISTEN TO GUIDED AUDIO 7.7

Tips for practicing PMA while connecting with nature:

— Choose where you will direct your attention and for how long. It's helpful to set a timer.

— Be more observational than descriptive; just let yourself be in the moment, observing movement, changing colors, shadows, sounds, etc. No need to label, describe, narrate, or judge.

— Attune inwardly and observe feelings and sensations arising in you as you connect with the natural world.

— If you get caught in any other mental activity, use your inner lasso to bring it back to connecting mindfully with nature in this moment.

---

There are countless ways to direct your attention to the here and now. The exercises and tips included here aren't prescriptive, nor do they mark the "right" way to build your BRITE lasso. Be as creative as you want with this or take a more fundamental approach. Remember: It's not about breathing, eating, moving, listening, or describing. It's about lassoing. All that matters is you practice.

## Using PMA and your BRITE lasso to find your way

This section highlights how PMA and your BRITE lasso help find *your* way through your journey with breast implants. No matter where you are on the BRITE Roadmap, I suggest reading through each roundabout's section because they contain exercises and tips that are helpful across the entire journey. It also shows how PMA can help you prepare for something that feels hard and reorient yourself after taking a reversal route. Guided audios are available for each section's material.

### Rationalizing Roundabout

When you are delighted with your breast implants, your inner fixer might urge you to overlook things. Unfortunately, this sets a dangerous precedent of disconnecting from your experience with devices that become more problem-prone the longer they're in your body. So, early in your journey with breast implants, your work with PMA is akin to the

**Describe Without Judging** exercise outlined previously. Use that approach to notice what you enjoy about your implanted breasts *and* recognize unanticipated ways they impact your body or lifestyle.

Guided Audio 7.8 helps you use PMA to nonjudgmentally explore and describe your full experience with breast implants. It helps you notice what you enjoy about having them *and* the ways they impact your body or lifestyle.

Even when you're long past this part of your journey, you can use the following tips to practice nonjudgmentally describing your full experience with breast implants:

— First, take a few slow belly breaths as you shift yourself into **P**.

— Direct your awareness to your implanted breasts. Describe the observable facts about them by noting your current bra size, each breast's shape (e.g., round, sloped, conical), temperature compared to the rest of your body (e.g., warmer, same, colder), any capsular contracture, visible rippling, or implant edges, etc.

— Describe how you feel about yourself with them and what you enjoy most about having them.

— Describe any impacts on your body, such as tingling in your arm, hypersensitive areas of your breasts, implant distortion with specific arm movements, pain in your neck, shoulder, or back, etc.

— Describe any impacts on your lifestyle, including interfering with working out, jogging, sleeping in your favorite position, etc.

— Acknowledge any other experiences related to your breast implants, such as implant displacement during mammograms or clashes with any of your values.

— When you get caught in feeling defensive, indignant, resistant, or scared, use your BRITE lasso to return your awareness to describing without judgment your full experience of having breast implants in your body.

Know that showing up for your entire experience doesn't mean that you have to *do* anything about your implant-related problems right now. As the BRITE Roadmap shows, at this point, you may be quite far from making any decisions about your breast implants. But using your BRITE lasso to be present to your *entire* experience (not just those with your inner fixer's stamp of approval) is an important part of busting free. Remember, you can work to reclaim your mind, irrespective of where you are in your physical journey with breast implants. You respect yourself by giving yourself permission to like aspects of your breast implants while also acknowledging any way they disappoint you. There's no need to choose between your positive and negative experiences. Both can be true.

## Reasoning Roundabout

As you reason through the pros and cons of living with problematic implants versus doing something about them, your inner fixer disorients you with future-focused images and reminders of painful past moments. When you're a mastectomy patient who reconstructed your breasts using implants, she recycles your original apprehension over losing your breasts. Her moves interfere with fully considering how you feel about living with problematic implants or possibly making a change.

Guided Audio 7. 9 walks you through how to use PMA and your BRITE lasso when you want to consider how your breast implants impact you and your readiness for change.

LISTEN TO GUIDED AUDIO 7.9

The following tips also outline how to use your BRITE lasso to mindfully reason through your experience with breast implants:

— Before starting, consult your BRITE compass to remind yourself why doing this kind of inner exploration matters to you. Validate that it's natural to feel uncomfortable when reflecting on the reality that you have temporary implants in your body that are known to cause more problems the longer you keep them.

— Set a timer for three minutes. Close your eyes and do several cycles of belly breathing as you direct your awareness inwardly to the ways your breast implants give you more than you bargained for. Acknowledge their pros and cons in your life. As you direct your awareness to your breast-implant-related problems, use curiosity to gently consider questions you have and what might be helpful for you to learn.

— When your mind wanders to a feared future or a painful past, or gets caught in ambivalence, doubt, deal-making, or negative self-regard, lasso back to this moment. Consider how you are impacted right here, right now by your implants. Include any nonphysical impacts, such as worry over their black-box status, recalls, ruptures, or association with cancer.

— Remind yourself that this work isn't about convincing, pressuring, or deciding; it's about reasoning through your implant-related problems and solutions; it's about getting ready to be ready.

## Readying Roundabout

As you ready yourself for the significant change of breast implant removal, your BRITE lasso might get a bit worn and frayed. No matter your reasons for explanting, you might end up doom-scrolling every awful possibility as you investigate safe ways to explant. Your inner fixer might detour you with mental rabbit holes. You might get overwhelmed with conflicting information. None of this helps you put together an explant plan. And it certainly doesn't help you care for the part of you that might be grieving how this all turned out.

At this point, using your BRITE lasso is all about catching when you're doing stuff (inside and out) that interferes with preparing yourself. It's about noticing every time your mind wanders back to words you saw on a website predicting that you will be disappointed in your aesthetics after explant, or making it seem like implant replacement is the only reasonable option. It's about catching when you're doom-scrolling and fanning the flames of overwhelm, confusion, and self-doubt. It's about noticing when avoidance has immobilized you. And, it's about returning your focus to your BRITE compass and treating yourself like the person you most want to be.

When you're serious about removing and not replacing your breast implants, PMA is essential to catch when your attention has wandered to one of these inevitable and natural detours, edging you closer to a reversal route. It also helps you notice when you're explant planning while gripping the Breast Rulebook. Whenever you realize that you've drifted into Inner Fixer Lane, use your BRITE lasso to return your focus to your BRITE compass and holistic explant planning as described in Chapter 11.

Though you might need to use your lasso repeatedly, it doesn't mean you're *not ready*, *making a mistake*, *too weak*, or whatever self-appraisal your inner fixer puts upon you. It means you're doing something important that feels risky, like surgically removing bags from your breasts while battling inner beliefs that those bags in your breasts make you better somehow. You struggle because you're defying the Breast Rulebook. Remember to use your inner BRAKE if you ever find yourself circling the Readying Roundabout in a way that feels out of control.

Guided Audio 7.10 helps you nonjudgmentally observe your approach to explant planning and identify mental detours that might be getting in your way. And it ends by presenting you with a process for moving forward and using PMA while explant planning.

**LISTEN TO GUIDED AUDIO 7.10**

## Repairing Roundabout

Remember, the Repairing Roundabout is when change happens. No matter how you feel about removing your breast implants, your inner experience will naturally intensify beforehand. Depending on how threatened you feel by breast implant loss, the surgery, or recovery (or all these things), your nervous system revs up. That's just normal biology. So, in addition to uncomfortable inner body sensations such as anxiety, rapid heart rate, tension, and difficulty sleeping, you might be struggling with grief, loss, sadness, betrayal, anger, fear, and regret.

PMA in the Repairing Roundabout shines a light on your inner experience so you can be there for yourself. You use your BRITE lasso to redirect your awareness to companioning rather than abandoning your inner pain (as explained in Chapter 9). In other words, when you're facing something difficult on either side of explant (which you undoubtedly will), use PMA to plug in and:

— Acknowledge and genuinely validate your struggle. Remember, this isn't about minimizing or putting a positive spin on things. Be *real* with yourself. Acknowledge when something is hard or scary for you, like seeing yourself unwrapped for the first time. Validate that what you are doing is difficult for any woman who grows up in a breast-obsessed culture. This acknowledgment isn't going to get rid of your inner pain, but attuning toward it can soothe you while it's with you.

— Use your BRITE lasso to return your awareness to the here and now; then look at your BRITE compass to bring your whole self forward and move through surgery and recovery as the woman you most want to be.

— Notice when you're super overwhelmed. Then use your inner BRAKE to ground and center yourself.

Guided Audio 7.11 helps you use PMA while you are attending surgical consults, selecting a surgeon, scheduling and having surgery, talking with others about their decision, and in the initial phase of explant recovery.

 LISTEN TO GUIDED AUDIO 7.11

By following this approach, you *will* show up in ways that repair your relationship with yourself and heal from the inside out. Be ready to use this approach in the Repairing Roundabout when:

— facing something that's likely to send you circling, such as surgical consults, going to bed the night before surgery, or waking up after surgery to an entirely different breast shape and size or the complete absence of breast mounds;

— encountering barriers such as being told you must lose weight or quit smoking before surgery, or when doctors have different opinions about the best approach for you or have views different from yours;

— you realize that you're circling Inner Fixer Lane instead of taking care of yourself and problems needing your attention in the here and now.

## Reclaiming Roundabout

Using PMA in the Reclaiming Roundabout empowers you to have your own back, live with self-attunement, and take care of yourself and your needs moment by moment. PMA of your inner experience helps you catch when something around you has threatened your sense of belonging and sends you circling Inner Fixer Lane, such as seeing a woman with breasts you judge as better, bigger, fuller, sexier, or more attractive than yours. (Yes, this can happen to you, even when you have no regrets over explanting. It can be even more painful when something about explant doesn't turn out as you'd hoped.) PMA helps you catch when comparative thinking inevitably shows up and leads you to feel *less than*, insecure, angry, resentful, disappointed over how things turned out for you, etc. It also enables you to catch when your inner fixer is pressuring you for another self-improvement project without regard for its potential risks and long-term impacts.

Using PMA in the Reclaiming Roundabout is about noticing when life inevitably hands you inner pain related to any ongoing, private struggle with your body or new self-judgment and urges to "fix" yourself as you age in a youth-oriented society. Remember, there's nothing wrong with wanting to look your best, so long as the innate drive to belong doesn't lead you to disregard your safety or compromise your values. When these things happen, use your BRITE lasso to redirect your focus and attention back to caring for your inner pain in more helpful ways. Lasso your awareness back to your hard-fought sense of belonging *within* yourself and back to your BRITE compass and other BRITE Inner Healing skills. They help you companion yourself through any difficulty, for the rest of your life. They will never leave you. You simply need to use them.

Guided Audio 7.12 helps you continually reclaim yourself by using PMA to have your own back, live with self-attunement, and take care of yourself and your needs moment by moment.

No matter what unhelpful messaging or predatory marketing you encounter moving forward, follow these tips to return your awareness to reclaiming yourself:

— Acknowledge that the pain of comparative thinking is with you in the moment.

— Genuinely validate your feelings as a woman in an appearance-, youth-, and breast-oriented culture.

— Lasso your awareness back to your chosen values of how you want to treat yourself when feeling *less than*, unworthy, or unsafe.

— Proceed by showing up for yourself in values-guided ways.

## Using PMA and your BRITE lasso before something hard

When you need to do something important, and you know it will kick up disorienting thoughts and feelings, approach it like one of the exercises in this chapter. For example, let's say you doom scroll through distressing images every time you explore explant surgeons. To approach this important work, use the four essential parts of staying connected to the present moment:

— Set your focus. *(e.g., I will explore doctors nearby me who perform en bloc).*

— Set the amount of time to practice and (ideally) set a quiet timer. *(e.g., I will do this research for the next 15 minutes).*

— Direct your attention to whatever you set as your focus. (i.e., explore explant surgeons.)

— Notice when your attention wanders to other people's testimonies, stories, or unhelpful pictures. Keep your BRITE lasso ready to redirect your awareness to searching for a surgeon whenever your attention wanders away.

## Using PMA and your BRITE lasso after a reversal route

Early in this chapter, we explored that success with practicing PMA isn't about preventing your focus from wandering. Instead, success is about catching when it has wandered, and lassoing it back to your stated intention and focus. The same principles and processes apply to reversal routes. There will be times when you're so overwhelmed with moving forward or tackling a challenge that you retreat. Sometimes, PMA will help you catch this, and you will lasso yourself back to the task at hand. And other times, you might overlook your reversal route for a long time. Other times, you know you retreated but have no idea how to recover.

Anytime you realize you've lost your way on your journey to reclaim yourself, gently and without judgment, acknowledge that reality. Take stock of where you are, notice what propelled you to the reversal route, and check your BRITE compass. Use PMA to stay attuned as you move forward. Then follow the steps in the preceding section for using PMA and your BRITE lasso the next time you move through that part of your journey.

## How I used PMA and my BRITE lasso

As you know, I spent decades of my life listening to my inner fixer's judgments and predictions. I also dreaded the surgery—so much so that I tolerated problematic breast implants in my body for years. So, it's no understatement to say that for me to move through my explant journey, I used the hell out of my BRITE lasso.

— During the days leading up to my surgery, I was terrified of not waking up. That was a strong foothold for my inner fixer's last stand against the surgery. So I used PMA to notice when my terror was escalating and overwhelming my nervous system. I used my inner BRAKE to ground and center myself, and I used my BRITE compass to remind me why the surgery mattered to me.

— When my husband wasn't allowed to be with me before surgery, my lasso and compass helped me be kind and caring to myself. Yes, I was angry, and I validated that anger. But I also knew that getting all amped up before the surgery was not a self-care move. If I couldn't benefit from his presence, I needed to show up even more for myself.

— Waking up from my surgery, I was bound so tightly that my chest was completely flat. As my inner fixer wept and wailed, I used PMA to take in what I saw and felt. I observed the striking difference between what I was accustomed to seeing and what I saw at that moment. I lassoed my awareness toward my BRITE compass to genuinely validate my feelings of disorientation and shock by silently saying to myself, *Yes, this is hard. The way I feel right now makes sense, given the significant difference in how my breasts appear. My body looks very different. It's natural to feel disoriented and shocked.*

— When I realized that my inner fixer was convincing me to "fix" The Crease in ways that were hurting me emotionally and physically, I knew I'd lost my way. I used PMA to describe my thoughts, feelings, and behaviors nonjudgmentally. That helped me recognize the physical pain I experienced by cupping and the psychic pain I created each time my hopes would rise and fall. I used my BRITE lasso to direct my awareness back to my compass, ditch the suction cups, and pursue self-acceptance.

— To this day, I use PMA when I see my aesthetically disappointing post-explant reflection. I acknowledge when self-judgment shows up and validate how it makes sense in our breast-obsessed culture. I use my BRITE lasso to return my attention to my BRITE compass and being the woman I most want to be. By giving myself compassion and treating my body respectfully, I don't let my judgment send me circling Inner Fixer Lane. No way are those suction cups finding their way back onto my breast!

## Taking PMA and your BRITE lasso with you

Your BRITE lasso plays a vital role in busting free, so please don't make the mistake of only reading this chapter. Instead, invest a few mindful moments each day to strengthen the mental muscles that keep you present and put your mind to work for you. Just like you can't build larger body muscles by reading about lifting weights, you build the mental muscles needed for PMA and lassoing only by doing exercises.

Remember: This isn't a formal practice requiring you to carve out a block of time, sit on a cushion, and listen to an app on your phone. You can do those things if you want, but this is an on-the-go skill. Choose one or two of the exercises at the beginning of this chapter. Practice them randomly throughout your day. Find ones that are easiest for you to integrate into your life, set your focus, and do the exercises for whatever amount of time, duration, or distance you choose. Most importantly, try to have fun building this helpful inner skill that will serve you the rest of your life. Like daytime running lights on a car, use PMA to constantly illuminate your thoughts, feelings, body sensations, and urges. Monitoring your unfolding inner experience is fundamentally important to companioning yourself and showing up to life on *your* terms.

In addition to staying present and lassoing yourself back to the here and now, busting free and reclaiming *you* means catching when you're automatically following the Breast Rulebook. The next chapter shows you how to create distance between you and it so you can separate what you *do* from what you think.

Chapter **8**

# Let Go of Your Breast Rulebook

Your mind is a problem-solving, storytelling, keep-you-safe machine. As a result, you're quite accustomed to following its ability to ferret out problems. For example, if you wake up one morning to a kitchen filled with ants, your problem-solving mind (i.e., the **Thinking Self**) guides you through figuring out what's drawing them in, how they're getting inside, and how to stop the invasion.

If you're like most people, you strongly identify with your Thinking Self. Why would you not? It solves your problems, helps you get things done, and keeps you safe. Over time, it can be hard to remember that there's a difference between *you* and it. You lose sight that *you* are not your thoughts. When that happens, you automatically follow your thoughts, without seeing them as an experience taking place inside you. They're treated as the truth, the way, and the be-all and end-all. In ACT, you're said to be **fused** with your thoughts when you treat them like commands you *must* obey. When fused, your thoughts dominate your awareness, choices, and actions. You forget there's a difference between what you think and *do*.

To get a feel for what it's like to be fused with your thoughts, take a moment to imagine that all the things you care about, the people you love, and the activities you enjoy doing are across the room from you right now. Visualize what you would see and hear over there. In a moment, I want you to hold *this* book directly in front of your eyes. As you do so, consider what it would be like to engage with the things across the room. Imagine what it would be like to do the things that matter to you with a book in front of your face.

Go ahead now and ponder those things while holding this book immediately in front of your eyes for the next minute.

When I do this exercise with a client, she nearly always says that the book is super distracting and interferes with her ability to interact with everything across the room from her. That's exactly what it's like when you're fused with your thinking. It dominates your awareness and how you interact with the world.

Being fused with your thinking can be helpful or harmful; it all depends on the bigger picture. For example, being fused with *I'm responsible for my home's integrity* leads you to avoid a major infestation when ants appear in your kitchen. But consider what happens when you're fused with the things you learned while growing up in a breast-obsessed society.

## Your breast rulebook

As introduced in Chapter 1, your mind forms rules about breasts, such as how they *should* look (*breasts should be full ,round, perky, youthful, symmetrical*), how women's bodies *ought* to be proportioned (*breasts ought to project out farther than your tummy*), and what breasts mean to intimacy and social acceptance (*breasts make women sexy and desirable*).

In response to these rules, your mind forms judgments about your breasts and how they measure up. These include positive and negative judgments (e.g., *My breasts are my best feature* or *I'd be better with better breasts*). As discussed in Chapter 1, these things form your breast-related self-concept. They're appended to the Breast Rulebook, personalizing it specifically to you.

Over time, your Breast Rulebook becomes quite massive. Imagine how much it would interfere with your life to hold *that* book right in front of your head! When you do, it dominates how you see yourself and the world around you. Every time you look in the mirror, there it sits. You consult your rulebook to determine if you are adequate, balanced, sexy, whole, and womanly. You use it to choose what to wear, which bra you *need*, what photo to post, how sexy to behave, and what surgeries to have.

When fused like this, you might think that you opted for breast implants on your terms or got them entirely for yourself. But that's the same as a person who has only ever viewed the world through pink-tinted glasses thinking that clouds are pink. When you grow up in a breast-obsessed society, it's hard to see how fused you are with your breast-related thinking or how much it controls you. But your Breast Rulebook is there, sitting between you and everything else in your life.

This becomes particularly problematic when you get more than you bargained for from breast implants because your Thinking Self tries to problem-solve problematic breast implants while simultaneously holding your Breast Rulebook. It's accustomed to following your rulebook's solutions for fixing small, "misshapen," "lop-sided," "saggy," or cancer-stolen breasts. There's no chapter titled "Just Kidding, Breasts Don't Really *Matter*."

Not surprisingly, your inner fixer fears that violating your Breast Rulebook means bad things for your future. So, as you navigate the

BRITE Roundabouts, she fills your car with backseat drivers—one for each rule in your book. Like real-life backseat drivers, these metaphorical ones spend their time cautioning you to follow the rules. For example, there's a "Better Breasts Make You Better" passenger. It warns that explant will make you *less than*. To prove its rule is correct, it reminds you of painful memories or shows you distressing images (both real and imagined). As you move through your journey with breast implants, your car can fill with rule-spouting backseat drivers. Their predictions feel threatening; their ruminations are often painful. They quiet down and leave you alone when you circle Inner Fixer Lane rather than act on your behalf. As a result, their words take over your awareness and control your choices and you're no longer in charge of the drive.

## Keeping yourself stuck

One of the ways you might move toward explant is by telling yourself that your rulebook is wrong. For example, if you ever held tightly to the rule, *I need breast implants to feel like a woman,* it will distress you to think about removing them. You know that you will feel better if you can convince yourself that the rule is wrong. So to move forward, you point out the rule's irrationality. Whenever you think, *I need breast implants to feel like a woman,* you try to counter it with, *I can feel like a woman, even without breast implants.* You see others do the same on social media.

Therapists and coaches popularize this approach as a reasonable way to respond to unreasonable information. Most self-help books suggest it as well.

The problem, however, is that when you counter thoughts that show up in response to a long-ago-learned breast-related rule, *you continue thinking about the rule.* That keeps it front of mind and can paradoxically increase the rule's impact on you. This mental trap keeps you stuck thinking about the very thing that brings you distress. It also prevents you from busting free.

Alternatively, you might tell yourself to just forget about your Breast Rulebook and stop thinking about its rules. But trying to deny or push away your thoughts sets the same mental trap. (Remember how well it went when you tried *not* to think about a puppy in Chapter 4?) Ironically, thought suppression brings to the forefront of your mind the very thing you are trying to forget. As a result, each time you try to not think about all the ways you learned that breasts matter, you confront the reality that you live in a society where they do.

You certainly can use these approaches to help you move toward and through explant, but they won't reclaim *you.* Explant only removes problematic breast implants from your body. It doesn't remove you from the problematic messaging around your breasts, nor does it remove your Breast Rulebook. Even when you no longer agree with your rulebook, your mind can't ever fully unlearn its contents. That's why you might be thrilled to be implant-free or committed to bucking unhealthy beauty standards, yet still care a great deal about your breasts' appearance. This leads to confusing moments on even the most beautiful of self-acceptance journeys. Bottom line: To bust free, you need a different way to deal with your breast-related thinking.

This chapter gives you that different way. It introduces you to the ACT process known as **cognitive defusion.** It helps you navigate your journey without your Breast Rulebook, or backseat drivers, calling the shots. This chapter helps you learn this inner skill by providing you with several techniques to watch your thinking and choose whether you follow it. Ultimately, these help you learn to look *at* your Breast Rulebook, rather than be dominated by its content. Though these approaches don't eliminate the social rules you learned about breasts, they help you bust free from the tyranny of following them.

Guided Audio 8.1 takes you through the previous material and experiential of being fused with your Breast Rulebook. It also helps you experience what it's like to lower your breast rulebook as described in the next section. It's an eyes-open exercise that you will want to do when you feel comfortable and safe holding a book in front of your face.

**((•))) LISTEN TO GUIDED AUDIO 8.1**

## Separating *you* from your thoughts

To get a feel for cognitive defusion, imagine again that everything you care about in life is across the room from you. But this time, after spending a few moments literally holding this book in front of your face, pay close attention to what happens as you lower the book and let it rest on your lap.[31] Notice how it impacts you much less. Though you're still in contact with the book, it no longer dominates your awareness. You can more fully engage with the other things that matter to you.

ACT's process of cognitive defusion is the inner equivalent of lowering your Breast Rulebook. Because cognitive defusion is a rather

---

[31] Doing this small act (adapted from Russ Harris) helps you relate differently to the rest of this chapter's material, so it's best to not skip it. If for some reason you cannot do it right now, visualize doing so in your mind for now, and commit to experiencing it with the actual book as soon as you can.

technical term, I refer to it throughout this chapter as creating space between you and your Breast Rulebook, stepping back from your thoughts, or watching your thinking. No matter what you call it, it's about looking *at* your breast-related thinking, rather than *from* it. It's also about noticing when your mind offers up solutions from your Breast Rulebook. It helps you catch when you're automatically following your rulebook and the unworkable solutions its rules inspire, instead of bringing your entire self forward to choose what's best for your breasts, body, and life.

There are literally hundreds of ways to practice watching your thinking. It's such an important part of BRITE Inner Healing, I've planted seeds for doing so throughout this book. For example, referring to "your mind" and the "Thinking Self" creates a sense that *you* are separate from what you think. The metaphors of your inner fixer, backseat drivers, and circling the BRITE roundabouts also help you look *at* your inner experience and see how you react to it. You also experienced watching your thinking while mindfully observing your thoughts and lassoing your awareness throughout Chapter 7.

Now you're ready to put in the behind-the-wheel time to develop the inner ability to step back from even your most dominating breast-related thoughts. Please keep in mind that the goal is to build an inner skill that helps you notice when your breast-related thinking dictates the choices you make for your body and life. It's not about challenging how true, right, or believable your thoughts and feelings may be.

I know all of this is easier said than done. I also know it might feel quite different from other things you've tried. But the following exercises do build an inner skill known to help you be less impacted by dominating thoughts. I can personally attest that although I still have backseat drivers who occasionally remind me that my distorted post-explant breasts are out of compliance with the Breast Rulebook, they do not drive the decisions I make for my body. One of the ways I stay in charge is by using the exact same defusion skills I've taught to countless women. Now it's your turn to learn them as well.

## Watch a passing train

To get started, the following mindfulness-based exercise helps you watch your thinking the same way you might watch a passing train. Just like you wouldn't attempt to do anything to passing train cars, you're not trying to manipulate or control your thoughts in any way. For this exercise, it doesn't matter what thoughts go through your mind. This technique simply gets you a feel for watching your thoughts without being taken for a ride by them. It helps you get a sense that your thoughts come, stay, and go on their own, *including unpleasant ones.* I suggest completely reading through the prompts below beforehand or listening to Guided Audio 8.2.

**LISTEN TO GUIDED AUDIO 8.2**

— Mentally shift yourself into **P** and take some time to watch your thoughts as if they are train cars on an endless freight train. For the next several moments, simply notice if your mind is busy with thoughts that quickly pass by like blurry train cars or slowly lumber along. Notice if your thought train has stopped on its tracks, leaving you with one or two unmoving thoughts to observe.

— Now, spend several moments watching each of your thoughts as they come to your awareness, linger, and fade away. Take 30 seconds and practice tracking your thoughts.

You might notice memories, predictions, or thoughts about things you need to get done, that you care about, what you want to eat, and so on. Your thoughts might appear as images or you might register them as an inner voice in your head. Notice any repetitive thoughts that show up like sequential train cars that look the same. If judgments about the exercise or how you're doing it show up, notice that they pass as well.

— When your awareness gets taken for a ride by one of your thoughts, acknowledge it. Then redirect your awareness to observing your thoughts as if you are waiting for a train to pass.

You may feel like this exercise doesn't "work" for you. Over the years, I've learned that feeling most often indicates you were trying to clear your mind, control your thoughts, or relax. Don't be too hard on yourself when that happens, especially if you're accustomed to the popularized idea that *mindfulness=clearing your mind* or *sitting quietly=relaxing*. Remember, those things might happen. But they aren't what you're going for here. You're simply learning to watch your thoughts without trying to control them or allowing them to take you for a ride.

Please take a few moments to do the exercise again, keeping those things in mind.

The main thing to take from this exercise is that your thoughts continuously come, linger, and go. Being aware of their fleeting nature is helpful because your mind often focuses on what can go wrong, especially when you're doing something that feels risky, hard, or overly vulnerable (such as removing breast implants). When you notice that your awareness has been taken for a ride by one of those attention-grabbing thoughts, it can be helpful to know that even those thoughts will pass eventually.

## Don't follow your thoughts

No matter what your mind says, you don't have to follow your thoughts. You can test this concept for yourself by thinking, *I can't possibly raise my right hand,* while raising it high above your head. Go ahead and do that now. To drive this point home, try mixing up some of your routines. For example, you most likely have a sequence you follow while showering (e.g., wet hair first, then shampoo and condition, finish with body wash). Though you mindlessly follow your shower routine, many thoughts are behind it. When you mix up the routine, your mind will likely disapprove. But *you* can still mix up the order. You can also look for other ways *not* to follow your thoughts as you go about your day. For example, maybe you always sit in the same spot or check on social media or the news at the same time. Although your mind directs those actions, *you* can choose to do things differently.

After mixing up a few routines, experiment with not following more-powerful thoughts. Usually, the more dominating a thought is to you, the more fused you are with it. For example, I'm rather fused with the thought *I'd better do something about my cellulite.* To create space between me and it, I sometimes run little experiments when that backseat driver mouths off at me. I observe what happens when I don't respond in the same old unhelpful ways (e.g., adjusting how I sit, smoothing out my shorts, wearing a cover-up, wrapping in a towel, etc.). It turns out...nothing happens. Of course, people around me might notice and even judge my cellulite, but no one runs away, screaming in horror, as my inner fixer predicts. No one stops loving me. No one treats me any differently.

If you're comfortable, run the experiment of not following one of your backseat drivers. You don't have to make a declaration or even let anyone around you know what you're doing. Instead, simply use present moment awareness to observe what you feel on the inside and what happens in the world around you when you don't follow an old unhelpful thought.

## Separating from your breast-related thinking

For the next several techniques, it's helpful to revisit your answer to Chapter 2's prompts exploring how your inner fixer sends you circling. Then bring to mind or make a written list of the breast-related rules that most often dominate your awareness and actions. Before moving on, please sit for a moment and allow yourself to connect with the thoughts, feelings, and body sensations that you experience when fused with these rules.

Now, please mentally put yourself in **P** while experimenting with the following techniques. I encourage you to work with these until you find at least two that help you create a sense of lowering your Breast Rulebook. As previously stated, these techniques are not about challenging how true, right, or believable your rules may be. (I wouldn't do that to you. I know firsthand how real and hard this stuff can be.) Instead, these techniques help you step back, watch your thinking, and see that you don't have to automatically follow your backseat drivers or the rules they represent.

# I'm having the thought that...[32]

This approach to defusion literally creates a sense of separation between you and your thoughts. Notice any differences as you do the following:

— Choose a breast-related thought that pushes you around and put it in a short sentence. It helps to use the following sentence: "I am _____." For example, *I am too afraid to explant* or *I am afraid I won't feel better after explant* or *I am less than because of how my chest appears.*
— Grab on to this thought, get caught up in it, and let it send you circling for the next several moments. Maybe say it aloud or repeat it mentally a couple of times. Make sure you let it get right on top of you.
— Take a step back from this thought by replaying your painful thought and adding this phrase at the beginning: "<u>I'm having the thought</u> that..." For example, *I'm having the thought that I'm too afraid to explant.*
— Take another step back by replaying the thought with another phrase added upfront: "<u>I notice</u> I'm having the thought that..." For example, *I notice I'm having the thought that I'm too afraid to explant.* You can modify this with phrases like, "I notice my inner fixer telling me to..." or "I notice a backseat driver warning me about...."

What did you experience as you added those phrases? Did you get a sense of what it feels like to create distance between you and a thought? If you didn't get that sense, and even if you did,

---

[32] Adapted from a classic ACT technique introduced in 1999 by Hayes, Strosahl, and Wilson in their book *Acceptance and Commitment Therapy: An Experiential Approach to Behavior Change.*

it's important to do it again, using another thought. As you do this simple exercise, if your mind starts arguing that the thought is true or real, give it reassurance that you're not debating its believability. You can still separate from something that's true, especially when holding tightly to it prevents you from taking meaningful action in your life (like when you had this book in front of your face).

You can take this simple technique on the go to train yourself to look *at your thoughts* rather than be *caught up in your thoughts*. This doesn't require you to carve out time, stop what you are doing, or add something else to your to-do list. Instead, practice this throughout your day. You don't have to wait until a difficult thought shows up. Just practice it silently in your awareness. Although it might be awkward at first, it becomes more natural after practicing it.

## Thank your mind

This approach is another ACT classic, and it's one of my favorite ways to step back from your thinking. It's built on the premise that one of your mind's main jobs is to keep you safe. Your inner fixer represents a part of your mind that tries to keep you safe from judgment, abandonment, rejection, and the pain of feeling *less than* by fixing the way you appear. So, when she fills your car with dominating backseat drivers, why not thank your mind for trying to do its job? Doing so helps you see the purpose of your thinking rather than automatically following its content.

To thank your mind, simply notice when your inner fixer hammers away at you to do something about your appearance. Notice when a backseat driver is warning you to comply with your Breast Rulebook. Then, acknowledge the well-meaning, albeit misplaced, attempt to keep you safe by simply saying, *Thanks, Mind.* You can even give a thumbs-up, half-smile, or nod your head. Doing so often has the benefit of alerting you that something in your mind, heart, or the world around you activated your inner fixer's threat response or violates a deeply held breast-related rule. It helps you attune to yourself and do something more helpful, like give yourself some compassion (discussed further in Chapter 9).

## "Bless her heart"

Having lived in the southern USA for most of my life, I borrowed a Southern expression to help my clients also acknowledge that your mind sometimes gets confused about how to keep you safe. "Bless your heart" can convey "You're dumb and can't help it." It's also used to express sympathy or concern, or to convey, "You poor thing! You're confused and don't know any better."

Using those latter conveyances reminds you that your inner fixer is a part of your mind that means well, gets confused, and may not know any better. Chapter 3 discussed how these things happen when you have problematic breast implants. Your inner fixer truly thinks that having them is in your best interest. But you don't have to share her confusion or follow her backseat drivers. You know where you're headed and why it's important to you. So, when you notice your inner fixer sounding the threat alarm over explant, or a backseat driver warning of a rule violation, you can simply acknowledge, "There she goes again. Bless her heart." (Please, do not use this technique to mock your inner experience or label your thinking as dumb.)

## Naming

The simple act of naming something helps us experience it differently. When something has a name, we can say: "Here is so-and-so." It feels defined and separate. There's also a practicality to giving something a name. Imagine if every time you wanted to acknowledge a beautiful sunset, you had to say, "Look upward toward the sky at how the colors appear, due to the movement of Earth relative to the sun!" The word "sunset" provides a quick and concise way to refer to all that.

Naming also helps us quickly alert each other like, "Watch out for the pothole!" The word "pothole" quickly conveys helpful information to the other person to slow down, watch the road, and proceed with caution. By naming my left breast's disappointing crease "The Crease", I acknowledge my thoughts and feelings around it without getting entangled in their details.

The same applies when it comes to naming your inner experiences. Naming your thinking creates a sense that it is something separate from you. There are a few ways to do this with your breast-related thinking. I suggest experimenting with all of these throughout the next several days and choosing one or two that you find most helpful in helping you to look at your breast-related thinking with less entanglement.

— Use "rulebook" to quickly convey all the disturbing thoughts, rules, judgments, beliefs, memories, and images that come to mind when you regard your breasts. By acknowledging to yourself, *My rulebook is right on top of me,* you avoid the mental trap of trying to pretend that your difficult thoughts aren't there or convincing yourself that they don't bother you. It helps you acknowledge when your mind is flooded with complex breast-related thinking and has the bonus of keeping you from getting entangled in it.

— Refer to your breast-related thoughts and feelings like chapters in your Breast Rulebook. For example, when you explant with hopes of improving your physical well-being but struggle with self-doubt, you can name that thinking the *I'll Never Feel Better* chapter. I titled my unhelpful thinking about dying under general anesthesia the *I Don't Want to Die for Fake Boobs* chapter. Naming your thinking as if it were a chapter helps you choose whether you want to dive into its detailed content.

— Personalize a name for your inner fixer. If you like alliteration, use an adjective that describes this part of your mind using the first letter of your name, like Anxious Alyssa, Critical Chloe, or Vigilant Victoria. You can also choose a name based on a fictional or historical character that you feel embodies your inner fixer. Selecting a name that doesn't vilify her acts as a reminder that your inner fixer is just a part of your mind that worries and tries to protect you from judgment, rejection, and abandonment.

No matter what you choose to name her, when you notice she's sounding the inner alarm, silently note to yourself, *(inner fixer's name) is sounding her alarm.* I know this might seem odd at first, but it's based on solid research around cognitive defusion. The idea is that each time you do this, it helps you see that your inner fixer's distress is an experience within and separate from *you.* It's something you can regard with curiosity rather than automatically follow.

— Name your backseat drivers according to the rule they mouth off about, such as Mr. Bigger Breasts Are Better, Ms. No One

Will Ever Want You Without Implants, Miss Flat Chests Are for Boys, Mr. Breasts Make Women Sexy, etc.

— Create a passenger manifest. First, list your backseat drivers' names in the leftmost column. Then note the feelings that come over you when each one warns you to honor their rule. In the last column, describe how you usually respond. Here's a sample passenger manifest for someone who feels disappointed with her post-explant aesthetics:

| Backseat Driver | How I feel when they remind me of their rule | How their words impact what I do |
|---|---|---|
| Ms. Breasts Make Women Sexy | Sadness, longing, regret | Be less playful with my partner |
| Mr. There's a Right Way for Breasts to Appear | Shame, regret, longing, anger, urge to fix | Avoid intimacy and stop doing things that require a bathing suit |
| Miss Breasts *Matter* | Scared, devalued | Compensate with weight loss, Botox, body sculpting |

Having a passenger manifest like this helps you notice when your Breast Rulebook is blocking your view from the driver's seat. When you observe yourself feeling or doing the things on the manifest, create space between yourself and that rule by using any of the techniques in this chapter. Then you can see your BRITE compass better and show up more like the woman you most want to be.

Your Busting Free digital library includes a fillable worksheet to help you complete your own passenger manifest.

COMPLETE THE PASSENGER MANIFEST WORKSHEET

— You can also use irreverence when naming your backseat drivers. This approach isn't to mock, minimize, or invalidate your thinking; rather, irreverence helps you purposefully disregard their presumed authority. For example, I sometimes irreverently refer to my backseat driver who fixates on my creased left breast as Cartman (the South Park character whose double chin is reminiscent of The Crease). He's super mouthy, opinionated, and manipulative. My Cartman-inspired backseat driver says things like, *Of course, this would happen to you; imagine how much happier you'd be without this crease; better hope your partner doesn't die—just imagine letting someone else see that.*

I feel disempowered, damaged, and fearful when I get hooked by those thoughts. All because of a small crease on one of my breasts! But when I imagine those thoughts coming from a Cartman-esque backseat driver, I don't take them so damn seriously, even though The Crease disappoints me. By irreverently naming that thinking when it shows up (again and again), it helps me disregard the authority of that backseat driver's commands to do something about The Crease. (I am not judging anyone who makes a different choice than me about post-explant surgeries or procedures. Instead, I'm honoring that for me, at this point and given my history and sensitivities, busting free means *not* making that choice.)

Note: If you choose to use irreverence to refer to any of your breast-related cognitions, be sure *not* to mock yourself. For example, consider what would happen if I used "Pity-Party Passenger" to name my crease-related cognitions instead of "Cartman." The latter helps me step back and acknowledge that sometimes my mind is opinionated and manipulative in ways that lead me to feel bad. The former comes across as judgmental, dismissive, and condescending.

## Do I want to follow this backseat driver?

This straightforward question-based approach reminds you that sometimes even the most annoying backseat driver gives useful information. To put it another way: Sometimes even "negative" or painful thoughts are helpful. They alert you to problems needing your attention. For example, when a backseat driver mouths off that your breast implants are unnaturally firm, listening to it helps you acknowledge capsular contracture.

It's a bit trickier when a backseat driver warns, *You're going to be judged post-explant.* It may or may not be helpful to follow it, depending on the bigger picture and what matters to you. For example, when following that warning encourages you to approach intimacy cautiously, you might slow down and talk about your feelings with a safe partner. But when listening to that backseat driver sends you circling Inner Fixer Lane and leads you to avoid doing things that are important to you, it's essential to ask yourself if it's helpful to follow its warning.

Doing so reminds you that you can pursue what matters to *you* and take that unhelpful backseat driver along for the ride. (Of course, it can be uncomfortable to disregard a backseat driver, so the next chapter shows you how to companion yourself every step of the way.)

# Separating from disturbing images

This section includes techniques to help you be less impacted by images that push you around throughout this journey. No matter their content, be it related to your breasts' aesthetics or not, images are powerful tools that your inner fixer uses to keep you circling Inner Fixer Lane before, during, and long after explant. The images that distress you are highly nuanced, depending on your history, sensitivities, and support system. They might depict your chest flat, scarred, concave or distorted, your partner's disappointed expression, people talking judgmentally about (or to) you, or post-explant complications.

Using defusion to work with disturbing images serves a very different purpose than the more popular approach of visualizing desired outcomes. While that might help soothe your nervous system, it's important to loosen your mind's fearful grip of distressing images. Otherwise, your inner fixer continues to view the scenarios they represent as threatening possibilities. Because your mind wants to keep you safe, it recycles disturbing images to ensure that you know what you're doing. Though it's trying to keep you safe, the result is more inner distress.

Just as defusing a bomb doesn't make the bomb disappear, cognitive defusion doesn't erase your disturbing mental pictures. It also doesn't trick your mind into seeing the images in a more "positive" light. Instead, it helps your mind relate to images in ways that lessen their unhelpful influence on your awareness, inner wellbeing, and choices.

## Redesign your inner billboards

To practice this technique, I strongly recommend listening to Guided Audio 8.3 to experience what it feels like to mentally defuse an image.

## 🔊))) LISTEN TO GUIDED AUDIO 8.3

Alternatively, mentally shift yourself into **P** and ground yourself with several cycles of belly breathing. Then bring to your awareness a disturbing image that pushes you around as you move through the BRITE Roadmap. Choose one that your inner fixer puts on billboards to keep you circling. (Note: Remember to use your inner BRAKE if this image leads you to feel overwhelmed.)

Spend several moments viewing one of these mental billboards, re-creating its details in your mind. Once the image is front and center of your mind, there are several mental ways to manipulate it that are akin to defusing a bomb:

— See the image as if it's on a billboard that you're viewing through a heavy rainfall or dense fog. Watch the image ripple, wave, and lose focus, crispness, and clarity.

— Look at the image as if it's on an old billboard in need of maintenance. See different parts of the image ripped, tattered, and faded.

— Add a seasonal flair to the billboard, perhaps by doing something whimsical to the image to reflect an important holiday in your culture.

— Add text to the billboard, representing the thoughts that show up when your inner fixer is using this image to prevent you from exiting your current roundabout, such as *Super distorted breasts, Next Exit* or *Want to feel less than about your breasts and femininity? Exit Right!*

Please keep in mind that viewing these alternate images isn't designed to give a sense of relief. Instead, it helps your mind loosen its grip on them so they impact you differently moving forward (discussed further after the following section on selfies).

## Special considerations for selfies

There are special considerations for selfies, both the ones you take and those posted on social media. They prominently feature images of breasts before and after explant. I believe that you are more likely to see pictures from women who are pleased with their results or track an encouraging amount of improvement over time. Though these photos can be inspiring, they can also trigger comparative thinking. For example, when you are concerned about your aesthetic outcome, your inner fixer blasts other women's outcomes on new billboards with a side-by-side comparison to yours.

However, selfies present you with a unique opportunity to practice defusion using a photo editing app. Using the app's many features, you can modify the image in many ways. For example, you can personify your breasts by adding facial features. You can write words or thought bubbles on the image as if your breasts can talk. Doodle over the image, add an inspirational quote, or pretend you're a tattoo artist adding an element that means something to you.

After practicing these approaches, notice any differences in how you respond to these powerful images moving forward. Ideally, when an unpleasant image comes to mind, its ability to overpower you is weakened. You can use this technique on any billboards your inner fixer erects, whether they're related to your breasts or not.

If you have trouble connecting with this technique, try it again later. When you do, remember that you're not trying to erase or put a positive spin on your images, although those things may happen over time. Nor are you using this to get rid of, invalidate, or minimize the feelings evoked by these disturbing images. You're simply manipulating the image in ways that help it hold less power over you.

I once used a photo markup feature to make my creased left breast appear like Rudolph the Red-Nosed Reindeer. I had the nipple stand in for Rudolph's nose, The Crease gave him a smile, and I drew eyes, antlers, and ears. I wasn't trying to turn a negative into a positive or make light of The Crease. I simply modified the image in a way that helped my mind step back from its usual way of seeing and responding to it.

## Driving with a book on your lap

Driving with your Breast Rulebook on your lap is the only option to find *your* way through this journey. There's no inner equivalent of throwing it out the window. And you absolutely can't take charge of the drive while holding a big book in front of your face. But with it resting on your lap, you freely choose what *you* want to do with problematic breast implants, and you reclaim your mind and heart from its contents.

The more you take these exercises off these pages and into your life, the more you separate yourself from your Breast Rulebook. You'll start to catch when your mind is churning out thoughts driven by your long-ago-learned socially derived beliefs about breasts. You will notice when you're doing things completely driven by the rulebook. The more distance you create between yourself and it, the more you can bring your whole self to bear on the decisions you make for your body moving forward.

By doing things each day to separate yourself from your thinking (no matter the content of your thoughts), you will see that your thinking is just another internal experience. You start to regard your thinking the same way you view your stomach growling. Just because your stomach growls, you don't immediately act. You most likely attune to yourself and discern if you're hungry, unwell, or just making random noises. You choose how to respond, if at all. You can do the same with your thinking. You can attune to it, look for its source, and decide if you want to respond.

Please don't be hard on yourself when you struggle with your Breast Rulebook. It's easy to get pulled into its content. You might have rules that manage to push you around before implants, the entire time you have them in your body, and long after explant. You might have backseat drivers that are very loud at specific parts of your journey and utterly silent at other points. Plus, your inner fixer grips tightly to your Breast Rulebook and continually gives you advice, recommendations, and feedback based on it.

Also, remember that your mind isn't the only one who knows its content. Everyone who grows up in a breast-obsessed society carries this book with them. As a result, entire industries exist around "improving," preserving, and monetizing breast aesthetics. Partners might grieve your implant loss. Doctors might warn that you'll be miserable without replacement. Because most things in society encourage you to follow the Breast Rulebook, including some of your own lived experiences, you must continuously watch your thinking.

Your mind will inevitably revisit the rulebook. Sometimes following the rulebook leads you to do helpful things, such as finding an experienced explant surgeon. But it can also lead you to feel conflicted when you want to be implant-free. After all, the rulebook decries explant is a mistake. Following the Breast Rulebook can lead you to consider additional surgeries, even when you long to leave your body alone after explant. It can lead to harsh self-judgment when you want to be loving toward yourself no matter how your breasts look. It insists that breast aesthetics are all that matter, when the rest of your mind, body, and heart tells you something else does too. When these things happen, I suggest using the mantra *defuse and choose* to remember to separate yourself from the rulebook and choose what matters to *you*.

I notice all kinds of thoughts about my breasts' appearance. Some are fueled entirely by the Breast Rulebook. They give rise to annoying backseat drivers telling me, *I really ought to fix The Crease*, that *I would be so much happier if I would just get a fat transfer*, and *There is no way in hell my partner is okay with my breasts' appearance*. Other thoughts about my breasts have nothing to do with the rulebook. They're more focused on how to care for my post-explant breasts, inside and out. They encourage me to stay on top of cancer screening, especially given the significant scar tissue inside my naturally dense breasts. I follow the thoughts about my breasts that help me show up like the woman I most want to be, and take the rest along for the ride.

Defusion doesn't end the quest for *better* breasts, but it helps you heal the parts of your body and mind scarred by it. *The secret is to acknowledge what you are thinking rather than counter, challenge, or deny it.* Then choose if you want to get involved with it or not. You do this every day of your life with other things, including growling tummies and setting suns. Sometimes you direct your awareness to a sunset. You might even do things differently—sit outside or take pictures—because it's happening. Other days, you do other things even though you know the sun is setting.

You can respond to your breast-related thinking the same way. Sometimes it might be helpful to get involved with it, and other times, it's best to let it happen in the background. You always have a choice. An essential part of making that choice means knowing how to care for the unpleasant feelings that inevitably show up. To that end, Chapter 9 explores how to accept yourself when even the most painful or uncomfortable feelings are with you.

Chapter 9

# How to Give Yourself Acceptance

Unpleasant feelings are among the most noticeable challenges on this journey. Though it's easy to view them as the problem, it's your response to them that keeps you circling—and suffering. Don't get me wrong. You're probably responding in ways that make perfect sense. You're hard-wired to move away from pain. You're also surrounded by social messaging encouraging you to be happy, relaxed, and positive. As a result, you quite naturally try avoiding, getting rid of, or distracting yourself from painful feelings.

Unfortunately, attempting to avoid or rid yourself of unwanted feelings is like playing with a toy finger trap (i.e., a narrow tube made of colorful woven bamboo). When you place a finger in each of its ends, the tube constricts when you try pulling your fingers out. The harder you pull, the more the finger trap tightens. But no matter how long you persist, pulling will never work. It's "unworkable." The only way to loosen this kind of trap is to do something unnatural: make more contact with it. By pressing your fingers deeper inside, the tube expands, and you get room to move.

As you'll see in the following section, trying to avoid or get rid of unpleasant or difficult feelings is also unworkable. Your inner fixer knows this. So, to catch you in the trap of struggling against your feelings, she recruits mouthy backseat drivers, erects scary billboards, plays Bad Boobs Radio, and covers your rearview mirror with painful scenes from your past. Trying to avoid the heartfelt way you feel in response to those things (and the beliefs, social learning, judgments, memories, and concerns they represent) is like driving a car with your fingers in a trap. It doesn't work.

But you can bust free from the trap of struggling against your painful breast-related thoughts and feelings by doing something unnatural: Be with them. Just like an expanded finger trap gives you room to move, when you drop your struggle against your unpleasant feelings, you free yourself. You stop investing your energy in escaping your emotions. Instead, you extend willingness toward them, even when you don't like, want, or approve of them. But that doesn't mean you must suffer. As you'll see, inner pain is often an ally when you approach it with the heart of a companion.

## Acceptance

**Acceptance** is the ACT process that teaches you how to open up to your full experience, even the unwanted parts. Please remember that in ACT, acceptance is not about tolerating, agreeing with, or giving in to your inner pain—it's about allowing it to be there. By not struggling against inner pain, you can be there for yourself when it's with you. In BRITE Inner Healing, acceptance is also about holding your breast-related feelings more gently, with curiosity, kindness, and validation. I refer to this as **companioning**. It changes your relationship with your inner fixer and is key to busting free.

This chapter helps you learn how to companion your inner experience through acceptance. I'm excited for you to read it because if your mind is like mine, and those of the women I sit across from in session, you probably long to accept yourself but don't know how. I've lost count of how many times in my life someone told me that I'd struggle less with my body and sense of belonging by learning to accept myself. I know that advice was well-intended, but it left me feeling like everyone but me knew how to do it. Plus, honestly, I feared that accepting myself might lead me to become careless about my appearance or "let myself go."

I now know that acceptance is a change process. It's not about resignation or caring less. I also learned that few people know how to offer themselves acceptance. As it turns out, acceptance is not a complicated, mysterious, or overly advanced process. But it is something that you must commit to fully. Just like you can't half-jump, you can't partially accept your inner experience. You must be willing to open yourself to all of it, including the parts you don't like or want. I know that's a big ask.

Though you might be totally on board with giving yourself acceptance, you might be asking, *Why should I accept something I don't want, like, or agree with?* That's a valid question with two responses. First, offering acceptance to your inner experience has nothing to do with liking, approving, or tolerating it. Tolerating means putting up with something because you feel powerless, hopeless, or unable to change it. For example, when you want to remove your breast implants but cannot cover the surgery's costs, you tolerate living with breast implants you no longer want. Tolerance is not change-oriented; it's about getting through the worst of something. It can be depressing, demoralizing, and disempowering. (I look forward to the day when women no longer must tolerate living with problematic breast implants inside their body because they can't pay for their removal.) I would never include a process in BRITE Inner Healing that taught anyone to tolerate *more* suffering related to breast implants. Although acceptance doesn't get rid of the hard parts of this journey, it does help you suffer less while they're with you.

The second response to *why should I accept something I don't like, want, or agree with* is that you've probably tried everything else. To be willing to try something new with your most unpleasant thoughts and feelings about your breasts, it's helpful to nonjudgmentally look at what strategies you've tried in the past to free yourself from them. It's also helpful to track how those worked out for you and consider what they cost you in the long run. The following section helps you do that.

The rest of the chapter then teaches you how to give yourself acceptance. It provides you with several ways to open up to your inner experience and respond to it with the stance of a companion. I close the chapter by sharing how I companioned myself through the early days of post-explant intimacy.

## Taking a PASS on inner pain

As previously discussed, when you grow up in a breast-obsessed society and compare yourself to the Breast Rulebook, you might struggle for many years (or your entire life) with internalized breast shame. Alternatively, you might live without breast shame until something ushers it in, such as age, pregnancy, weight changes, or cancer. Either way, it's unpleasant and affects how you see yourself and show up to relationships.

These unpleasant feelings are deeply felt. You understandably try many ways to get them to ease off or leave you alone, including wearing padded bras; using bra inserts; using "breast-enhancing" supplements, creams, or oils; opting for breast implants or other surgical "solutions." Alternatively, you may have told yourself to *Stop feeling like that.* Yet some feelings hang on to your heart the entire journey. Others evolve, ebb, and flow depending on your current roundabout and the quality of support you have in your life.

The previous chapter explored how you unknowingly keep yourself stuck in the Breast Rulebook by challenging its content. You can also create problems for yourself by struggling against your feelings (e.g., internalized breast shame, aesthetic anxiety, surgery-related fear, intimacy avoidance, fear of rejection, abandonment, judgment or BII-related guilt, sadness, regret, anger). Recall what happened when you experimented in Chapter 4 with commanding yourself to love the next person you met—you learned that it wasn't possible to turn *on* a feeling. You also learned that inability to control your emotions goes both ways—you cannot turn them *off.*

Unfortunately, the myth of emotion control runs rather deep in our culture. It's likely been offered up to you, again and again, by well-meaning others. You might experience criticism or be taken less seriously when you don't "control" your emotions. As a woman in a patriarchal society, failure to achieve this fallacy earns you the label "weak." No matter your history, this mindset is pervasive. It fuels the unworkable agenda of controlling, eliminating, or avoiding your unwanted feelings. Unfortunately, your mind will continue buying into it as you move through the BRITE Roadmap.

To help catch when you're buying into this old, familiar, unworkable advice, and to empower you to do something different, let's explore how it's influenced you in the past. Please note that I foster a very compassionate stance when doing this work with clients. So, as you go through the material on your own, remember that you're honoring how hard you've worked to cope with unwanted thoughts and feelings about your breasts, given your natural human desire to belong, be wanted, and be safe. Reviewing your past efforts to ease inner pain isn't about judging them as bad, wrong, unreasonable, or worthless; it's about motivating you to try something different.

The acronym **PASS** (Problem-Solve, Avoid, Sidetrack, Something else) helps you reflect on the different ways you pass on your painful feelings. Your *Busting Free* digital library include a worksheet to look at the ways you try to PASS on breast-related shame and other painful feelings (adapted from Russ Harris' DOTS worksheet). It covers the remaining material in this section.

 ## COMPLETE THE PASS WORKSHEET

If you dislike filling out worksheets, it's okay to mentally shift yourself into **P** and use the following prompts to reflect on how you PASS on unpleasant feelings.

— P: How have you tried **problem-solving** your inner experience? This includes comparing yourself to others to prove you don't have it so bad, thinking positively, or using positive affirmations. These also include efforts to challenge, counter, or dispute the Breast Rulebook, clear your mind, worry, fantasize, revisit or rewrite the past, look for someone or something else to blame, chase that "aha!" moment of figuring out yourself, the situation, or other people, or insist you *can* rationalize away your pain.

— A: What have you done to **avoid** inner pain? This includes times when you quit, decline, renounce, say no thanks, opt-out, convince yourself that you're "not into" something, or tell yourself it's not worth doing because you anticipate feeling bad about your breasts or body.

— **S:** How do you **sidetrack** yourself from uncomfortable feelings? This includes things you do mentally or physically to shift gears, distract yourself, do something else, think about something else, or swap "bad" feelings with "good" ones. For example, if you fear the discovery of a **silent rupture**, you might sidetrack yourself with reassurances of breast implant safety rather than scheduling an MRI. You can also use positive affirmations to sidetrack your mind.

— **S:** How do you seek relief from inner pain by putting **something else** into your body or mind (e.g., breast implants, recreational drugs, prescription drugs, supplements, comforting or pleasurable food, alcohol, coffee, tea, sugar). Also consider when you do something else because you hope it will get rid of your inner suffering, such as therapy, coaching, meditation, yoga, exercise, or detoxing.

By reflecting on all that you've tried, you can see how hard you've worked. You might also see that you've been at this for a really long time. Please know this isn't just a "you" thing. Nearly everyone tries to PASS on pain because those strategies often provide some relief.

It's equally important to look at how taking a PASS on your painful feelings works in the long run. Gently reflect on whether any of these approaches got rid of your unwanted thoughts and feelings once and for all. Explore if any of them were permanent solutions. Consider their long-term impact on your health, well-being, relationships, and sense of safety with yourself. Do you notice any patterns? Does painful stuff keep coming back?

If you're reading this book, and if you're like almost everyone else in the history of the world, painful stuff continues to push you around despite all your hard work to avoid, control, or be relieved from it. Though you get some temporary relief, consider whether:

— **Problem-solving** your pain ever led you to feel stuck in your head, or like you were so busy doing those things, you were missing out on the rest of your life? Has it ever interfered with your ability to focus or experience deep, restorative sleep?

— **Avoidance** led you to miss out on the things that matter to you in life?

— **Sidetracking** yourself led you to invest in things you didn't care about, waste your time and energy, or not take care of problems needing your attention?

— Putting **something else** into your body (like breast implants), or doing something else entirely to get rid of suffering, has ever damaged your health, cost a lot of money, fueled unhelpful hopes, or set you up for emotional letdown?

Please don't beat yourself up if you answered "Yes" to any of these questions. It's normal to problem-solve pain, avoid unpleasant stuff, distract yourself, or use something else (like breast implants) in hopes of feeling better. And when those things give you any relief, you continue doing them.

But over time, these things take a toll, especially when you got more than you bargained for from breast implants. Taking a PASS on the difficult thoughts and feelings that show up before, during, or after breast implant removal is a powerful and insidious trap. It leads you to tolerate problematic breast implants, interferes with steadying yourself before surgery, and stands in the way of truly reclaiming you. Your energy goes into the struggle against your feelings rather than taking care of *you*.

# Dropping the struggle

Acceptance offers a way out of this trap because it's a completely different way to respond to your feelings. Let's modify Chapter 8's book-in-front-of-face exercise to understand what's involved. I still want you to imagine that directly across from you are all the people you love, things you enjoy doing, and everything that truly matters to you. But this time, when you hold this book in front of you, I want you to imagine that it holds your life's collection of difficult thoughts and painful feelings about your breasts. Tucked into its pages are your painful breast-related memories and disappointments. There's a long chapter featuring your breast-related self-concept.

To symbolize your struggle against your painful feelings about your breasts, you'll hold *this* book between both hands while fully extending your arms and locking your elbows.[33] To represent the reality that breasts *matter,* imagine something pushing the book toward you. If your life circumstances permit, ask someone to push against the book while you hold it. If you cannot physically do this or prefer not to, please watch the Dropping the Struggle demo video included in your *Busting Free* digital library.

 **WATCH THE DROPPING THE STRUGGLE DEMO VIDEO**

When you do this exercise in a moment, notice where your energy, awareness, and effort go. Consider how your efforts affect other things. Assess how well you can interact with the things across the room while caught in this struggle. Imagine what it would be like to do anything

---

[33] Adapted from Russ Harris' Pushing Away Paper exercise.

purposeful or fun while struggling with this book. How well could you meet your responsibilities? Also, notice how quickly you fatigue.

Please do these reflections for the next minute while holding this book as far from you as possible. After the minute has passed, lower the book. Then sit for half a minute and notice what changes.

Please do this acceptance-based experiential now.

This exercise helps you directly experience that when you drop your struggle, it no longer affects everything you do. Although the book (i.e., the struggle) is still with you, you interact with it and everything else differently. You can focus, engage, and connect with all those things across the room. You can move, play, work, hug, and do other things that matter to you.

The same things happen when you stop trying to PASS on your painful breast-related feelings. By dropping your struggle against internalized breast shame, you free yourself to handle them (and life) differently. That distinction is notable because when you try to PASS on the painful feelings around breast implant loss, you miss out on the valuable information they convey. For example, when you worry that your partner won't feel attracted to you without your breast implants, fear alerts you that you care about being accepted. By opening up to that feeling, you free yourself to care for it—something you can't do when trying to PASS on it. So, rather than abandoning the part of you that feels fearful, companion it. Listen to your fear with curiosity to receive what it's truly conveying: You simply want to be accepted, loved, and safe. When you make room for your fear, you bust free and can do other, more-helpful things, such as seek assurance from a safe partner or leave one whose "love" depends on implants.

Of course, opening up to your entire experience connects you with the unwanted, uncomfortable, unpleasant parts. So, when you're dealing with profound inner pain, acceptance can be hard work. Whenever you take on any challenge, it helps to know why you're doing it. The same holds true when it comes to practicing acceptance. As you explored earlier, though other ways to manage painful feelings give you temporary relief, inner pain keeps showing up. After all, it comes with being alive. You will experience many painful losses far beyond this journey. So, as you do the following exercises, keep in mind that *you're learning a new way to be with inner pain.* Acceptance frees you to become your own companion through any of life's hardships. It promotes your inner healing and is key to busting free.

## The ABCs of Acceptance

In BRITE Inner Healing, acceptance is a choice you make and an action you take. Through it, you foster a different kind of self-acceptance practice. It doesn't involve "positive thinking" or "turning negative or critical thoughts into positive ones." Those well-meaning tips reinforce the myth that you can turn on positive thoughts and feelings to sidestep unwanted ones. They tighten the trap of struggling against inner pain. Self-acceptance in BRITE Inner Healing is simply a practice where you open up to your *entire* inner experience, even the unwanted parts. It frees you to companion yourself through the hard parts of this journey.

Offering yourself acceptance is a practice rather than a mindset. So to remind you that acceptance is something you *do*, I created the ABCs of acceptance. They offer three tangible categories describing how to *be with* your inner experience: **Acknowledge**, **Breathe and embody**, and **Companion**.

The following material offers you several ways to practice the ABCs of acceptance. I encourage you to read through each approach first, then practice it for yourself. I also recommend listening to each of the guided audios. Because acceptance is about turning toward and allowing your inner experience, you can use whatever you feel in the here and now while practicing. I indicate when a technique is more effective by connecting with a specific struggle. During those, please use your inner BRAKE if you feel unsteady.

You don't have to master all these approaches, but I encourage you to try each one. Your goal is to find a few that resonate with you. If your mind tries convincing you to skim or skip this section, that's just another attempt to PASS on your inner experience. Thank it for looking out for you, bless its heart, and still practice these techniques.

## Acknowledge

To be with your inner experience, you must first acknowledge it. This acknowledgment happens when you inwardly direct your present moment awareness skills (from Chapter 7) toward your feelings, urges, body sensations, thoughts, images, judgments, etc. By doing so, you regard yourself on the inside beyond your usual self-awareness. This heightened awareness helps you be more discerning about how to show up for yourself. By knowing *what* you feel, you can more wisely choose how to meet your needs. The following techniques offer different ways to acknowledge yourself on the inside.

### Name the Now

Naming your inner experience helps you look at what's going on inside you and decide how to support yourself in that moment. It's like pulling over when your car isn't operating normally. You respond differently to a flat tire versus an empty gas tank. It's the same with your inner experience. Naming what's with you (e.g., sadness, fear, anger) helps you respond more helpfully than trying to PASS on your feelings.

To name what's with you in this moment, right now:

— Look inward at your emotions, sensations, and urges. No need to overthink it; just simply notice, without judgment, whatever is with you now.

— Notice contentment, boredom, neutrality, curiosity, anxiety, worry, discomfort, hunger, anger, physical pain, etc.

— Check inwardly again, and name whatever is most noticeable by completing the phrase: "_____ *is with me now.*"

Practice this simple, on-the-go acceptance skill randomly, multiple times each day, by turning inwardly and naming whatever is with you in that moment. Over time, when uncomfortable feelings show up, naming them will come more naturally to you. To this day, when I see the crease on my left breast, I name the feelings that show up by saying to myself, *Longing is with me now.* Putting a name to the longing inspires me to respond with self-kindness rather than self-judgment.

## "What in me needs attention?"

The following technique encourages you to explore your inner experience with a willingness to help, the same way you notice and respond to a "check engine" light while driving. Like these lights, your painful feelings often alert you that something needs your attention. They alert you to "check in" on your inner needs. Perhaps there's a scared, angry, ashamed, or sad part of you that needs you to show up with self-compassion or bravery. Maybe that uncomfortable feeling is alerting you to pay attention, be careful, slow down, show up, reassure, speak up, say no, keep trying, etc.

To get a feel for this technique:

— Turn your attention inwardly.

— Complete a few cycles of belly breathing.

— Spend one to two minutes mindfully observing your thoughts, feelings, urges, and body sensations.

— Then silently ask yourself: *What in me needs attention?*

When first practicing this exercise, you might easily notice your physical needs, such as hunger, thirst, or fatigue. But inner healing requires awareness of less apparent things as well. So spend time intentionally exploring your nonphysical needs, such as longing for connection, assurance, or to be understood. It can be challenging to reconnect with your more-vulnerable inner needs when you've spent years prioritizing your physical appearance, keeping an externally focused vigil, or being invalidated by others. When that's your experience, spend a moment or two gently asking yourself, *What* else *in me needs attention?*

As you move through the BRITE Roadmap, this helps you connect with your deeper unmet emotional needs that are often overlooked when traveling with a panicked inner fixer and surrounded by loud backseat drivers. For example, sadness usually sits farther in the back, overshadowed by more-demanding passengers, such as anger and fear.

## Your Inner Ocean

This visualization technique helps you acknowledge your inner experience by viewing your thoughts, urges, sensations, and feelings as waves in the ocean. Visualizing your inner ocean helps you observe how your inner experience is always changing and that your feelings come, stay, and go on their own. It helps you watch how much they impact you. You see some gently swell and pass you by. While others loom quite large and temporarily lift you off your feet. Others are so powerful, that they knock your feet out from under you. Perhaps most importantly, this visualization reminds you that struggling against your difficult, powerful, or unwanted feelings can be as futile as trying to control the ocean's waves. It highlights the importance of acknowledging your inner experience so you know how to maneuver it and keep yourself afloat.

Because this is about building a skill to help you acknowledge your feelings in the here and now, there's no need to evoke difficult emotions while practicing this visualization. Simply work with whatever you are feeling in this moment. Guided Audio 9.1 helps you fully experience this for yourself.

## 🔊)) LISTEN TO GUIDED AUDIO 9.1

Alternatively, you can read through the prompts below, then mentally shift into **P**, and practice acknowledging your inner ocean.

— Begin by completing a few cycles of belly breathing.
— Then attune inwardly to your mind, body, and heart.
— Observe your self-talk in this moment. Notice any self-judgment. Check on your inner fixer.
— Notice your physical sensations such as tension, discomfort, pain, hunger, thirst, etc.

— Notice any urges in this moment such as a desire to shift position or a longing to move on to another activity.

— Notice any feelings and emotions such as curiosity, annoyance, frustration, confusion, contentment, eagerness, and so forth.

— As you float in your inner ocean, visualize any fleeting or neutral sensations as barely noticeable ripples. Visualize more-noticeable feelings, sensations, or urges as individual waves with sizes that reflect how intensely you feel them. Watch how they rise, reach their peak, and lose their energy. See yourself floating along their surfaces as they come, stay, and go on their own. If a mighty wave lifts you off your feet, remind yourself that it too will pass.

---

Remember, the point of acknowledging your inner experience isn't to change or control it. It's about building the inner skill to watch what's going on inside you. By practicing the preceding approaches throughout your day–including neutral moments–you become more adept at knowing yourself from the inside out. By acknowledging what you're experiencing on the inside, you can show up for yourself in more helpful ways throughout this journey.

## Breathe and Embody

Just as an expanded finger trap gives you room to move, your breath and body can soften tension and assist you in making room for your feelings. This helps you expand around your inner pain rather than entrapping yourself by struggling against it.

## BRAKE instead of PASS

You can't pull over and see what needs your attention without pressing the brakes. BRAKE was introduced as a grounding technique in Chapter 5. It also works well as a body-based acceptance technique. As an acceptance technique, BRAKE is modified in the following ways:

**BR**: Breathe slowly in and out; make room for your feelings.

**A**: Attune inwardly to your feelings and urges; notice and name them.

**K**: Keep connecting to the body sensations showing up with your feelings.

**E**: Expand your awareness beyond your most noticeable feelings and sensations; look for more subtle ones that are easy to overlook.

## Belly Breathing

Belly breathing (introduced in Chapter 5) is also a stand-alone tool to help you make room for your inner experience. Place a hand on your belly, making sure it rises each time you inhale. As you bring oxygen into your distressed body, visualize yourself expanding around your feelings, sensations, and urges. As your belly expands like a balloon, notice how you literally create space within yourself. As you slowly exhale, drop your shoulders down your back and soften any tension within you. As you experiment with dropping your struggle against your inner experience, silently remind yourself: *Make room, open up, allow,* or *soften.*

## Embody

One meaning of the word "embody" is to represent something in a physical, concrete, or visible form. As an acceptance technique, embodying helps you connect with your harder-to-see abstract inner experience in a more tangible way. Embodying inner pain doesn't change it, rather it assists you in turning toward it. For example, typically, when you feel afraid or fearful, you might do things to PASS on those feelings. To embody them, you would describe how they feel inside your body: *hot and cold, a fluttering sensation, most intense in my chest, spreading throughout the rest of my body.* Over time, embodying your feelings might help you understand that an odd fluttering sensation in your chest is your body's way of alerting you to proceed with caution. Guided Audio 9.2 helps you fully experience this for yourself.

 LISTEN TO GUIDED AUDIO 9.2

Alternatively, you can read through the prompts below, then mentally shift into **P**, and practice expressing your abstract inner experience in concrete ways.

— Begin by taking a few centering belly breaths.
— Now turn your awareness inward.
— Notice your feelings and body sensations.
— Choose a feeling or sensation that is particularly noticeable right now.
— To embody it, simply notice where you feel it most in your body.

— Notice if you feel it just under the surface of your skin or deep within you.
— Does this feeling have a shape or is it more like a blob?
— How big is it?
— Does it have a shape or remind you of something, like a spiky ball, heavy anvil, whirlpool, or swarm of bees?
— Does it move or stay still?
— Does it feel heavy or light?
— Does it feel hot, cold, or the same temperature as you?
— What color fits it? Would it be clear or opaque?
— Does it feel like a solid, liquid, or gas? If it feels solid, notice if it feels smooth or rough? Slippery or full of friction?

As you move through your journey with breast implants, embodying your inner experience helps you gain more awareness of how your body silently communicates with you. With practice, it helps you get to know your body's signals and discern between helpful alerts and false alarms from your inner fixer.

## Companion

This part of acceptance is where you approach your inner pain with the heart of a companion, rather than the hammer of a fixer. You walk alongside your feelings, making room for whatever shows up, allowing it to be there, and receiving what it offers. The following approaches are the foundation of my self-acceptance practice. I also consistently observe helpful shifts in clients who use these techniques to companion themselves.

## Genuinely Validate *You*

You're probably familiar with validating others. For example, when someone is crying, you validate them by saying, "I see you're hurting." If someone is trembling, you validate them by saying, "I can tell you're afraid." When done in a genuine and sincere way, it usually helps them feel seen and less alone in the experience. Validating someone has nothing to do with whether you agree with them, see things the same way, or would react the same. It's like acknowledging when a child is afraid of thunder, even though you know it cannot hurt them. You acknowledge *their* experience. You validate it by telling them you see what they're going through.

Though you might do this for someone you care about, you might rarely do it for yourself. Perhaps you never considered validating your own emotions. Either way, self-validation facilitates acceptance of your feelings. It offers a tangible alternative to taking a PASS on them. This validation must be genuine and sincere, however, otherwise, it's just another attempt to sidetrack yourself. Guided Audio 9.3 helps you fully experience this for yourself.

 LISTEN TO GUIDED AUDIO 9.3

Alternatively, you can read through the prompts below, then mentally shift into **P**, and practice validating your own feelings.

Begin by taking a few moments to connect to a part of this journey that's hard for you. Choose something where your struggle is ongoing and difficult feelings quickly show up when you think about it. (Remember to use your inner BRAKE if needed.) Alternatively, you can work with a difficult memory.

Give yourself some time to direct your awareness to this struggle. You're not trying to change or fix anything. You don't have to figure anything out or convince yourself to feel differently. You're simply sitting quietly and attuning to your inner experience until you can complete the phrase, *This is _____ for me right now.* Fill in the blank with whatever you genuinely notice at this moment. Perhaps it feels hard, scary, overwhelming, uncomfortable, embarrassing, sad, disappointing, etc.

Then acknowledge that it's normal to feel distressed when your reality is vastly different from how you want it to be. Validate yourself with statements like *Anyone experiencing this would feel the same* or *No one goes into breast implants hoping they won't work out well.* Validate yourself further by acknowledging, *My inner experience goes deeper than my breasts' appearance.* Acknowledge: *It's normal to feel heartfelt concern over my sense of belonging.* Genuinely validate: *Humans want to feel accepted, valued, and secure; I feel this way because I am a caring human,* and *I hurt where I care.*

Though genuine self-validation like this puts you in more contact with your difficult feelings, it also gives you room to companion yourself while they are with you. It's very different from abandoning yourself while trying to make them ease off or go away.

## See Your Inner Fixer

This acceptance-based approach helps you open up to your inner experience by offering compassion to your inner fixer.

Compassion is what you feel when you see another person's suffering and want to help. It's natural *not* to feel compassion toward your inner fixer as she hammers away at you about fixing your body. It's more likely that you feel exhausted, maybe even demoralized, from keeping up with her projects. Believe it or not, she probably feels the same.

However, this technique isn't about feeling sorry for your inner fixer. Nor is it about learning to love, like, or approve of this part of your mind. It's about seeing this part of you more fully and responding to it in more helpful ways. When I do this type of inner work with clients, I ask them to close their eyes when willing. Guided Audio 9.4 helps you fully experience this for yourself.

 LISTEN TO GUIDED AUDIO 9.4

Alternatively, you can completely read through the following written description of this technique before shifting yourself into **P** and closing your eyes to practice it. It's okay to work with one paragraph at a time, opening your eyes in between to read what you should do next.

Take a moment and turn your awareness inward, completing a few cycles of belly breathing. As you slow your breathing, bring to mind this part of you that has worked so hard throughout your life to avoid harsh judgment from others, fit in, be *good enough*, belong, and improve, fix, or hide your imperfections.

Try visualizing your inner fixer. What image comes to mind? Perhaps she looks a lot like you (given she's the product of your mind's desire to keep you safe). Or maybe another image comes to mind entirely. There is no right or wrong image; work with whatever shows up for you.

Spend some time personifying her image. See her gripping tightly to her metaphorical hammer, sweat beaded on her brow, exhausted from her nonstop efforts to help you avoid the pain of judgment, ridicule, or abandonment. See her facial expression—without menace. See how seriously she takes her job of fixing you in hopes of keeping you safe. Spend some unrushed moments seeing this part of you.

See yourself alongside her, like a companion who cares and is curious about her experience. Listen to her thoughts and feelings about how this particular "remodel project" turned out for you. Remember, she was all for the idea of getting breast implants. Does she feel anger, regret, longing, sadness, guilt, shame, or any other feelings? Do post-explant chests distress her? Does she fear you'll believe that your post-explant chest makes you *less than*? Does she fear judgment from others, your own self-judgment, or both? Spend some moments now, listening with your heart to this part of your inner experience.

Try responding compassionately to this part of your inner experience. Offer this part of your mind the same tenderness or gentleness you would give a scared baby, kitten, or puppy. Try companioning this part of you in whatever way feels comfortable and authentic. Perhaps reassure her by letting her know, *I've got you/this/me.* If this feels uncomfortable or unnatural for you, experiment with acknowledging this part of your inner pain simply by saying, *Yes.*

Try responding this way anytime she starts hammering away at you. Mine shows up pretty much every time I see The Crease. But I don't try to PASS on her concern. I compassionately acknowledge her (and my) disappointment by saying, *I know. This is hard.* Sometimes I thank her for trying to keep me safe, and I assure her by silently saying, *I've got this; I'm here for this sadness.* I like to imagine she puts down her hammer and rests. That image gives me a sense of peace because I know that part of me has been working very hard for a very long time.

## Lend a Hand

The following technique works well after the **See your inner fixer** exercise and as a stand-alone approach to companioning your inner pain. It's an adaptation of a well-known self-compassion technique where you rest a supportive hand wherever you most intensely feel your inner pain. It's often an area where your body holds tension, such as your shoulders, jaw, forehead, chest, or stomach, but it can be anywhere in your body.

When you receive a supportive and gentle touch, the tend-and-befriend part of your nervous system triggers the release of oxytocin. It's a hormone that promotes human bonding. Oxytocin increases your sense of compassion, trust, connection, safety, and calm. (I often tell clients that we would have world peace if we could bottle oxytocin.) You release it when you give or receive a tender touch, including when connecting with yourself.[34]

Sadly, we don't often do this for ourselves. Knowing this, I walk nearly all my clients through this exercise. They typically report getting a lot out of it. I've modified it here specifically for women anywhere on the BRITE Roadmap. I hope it's useful to you too. Lending a hand to my inner fixer was pivotal to changing the course of my journey. I described that moment in Chapter 6. Now I'll walk you through doing the same for yourself. It's most impactful to close your eyes and allow yourself to be guided through this experiential, so I strongly encourage you to listen to Guided Audio 9.5.

**LISTEN TO GUIDED AUDIO 9.5**

Alternatively, you can completely read through the following written description of this technique before shifting yourself into **P** and closing your eyes to practice it. It's okay to work with one paragraph at a time, opening your eyes in between to read what you should do next.

For this exercise, bring to mind any of your inner fixer's ongoing projects. Perhaps she is actively resisting the threatening remodel that comes with explant or working on fixing the appearance of your post-explant chest. She also might be hammering away on some other aspect of your body and self-worth. Choose something that quickly brings up difficult feelings

---

[34] To learn more about self-compassion research, visit self-compassion.org featuring the work by Kristen Neff, Ph.D.

when you think about it, something that you actively struggle against.

Whatever the project, turn your awareness inward toward the struggle it represents. Complete a few cycles of slow belly breathing. Make room for your feelings around this part of your body or appearance by gently doing the following:

— Notice and name your disappointment, sadness, longing, fear, regret, self-doubt, the unhelpful comparisons you make, or whatever else is there.

— Notice how intensely your inner fixer wants to "fix" this part of you. Without judgment, bring to mind how many times you look at this part of you with disappointment or longing for it to be different. See how you manipulate it in hopes of improving its appearance. Notice when you touch it in hopes of finding it "better." See your attempts to ignore it. Recall how often you dress to hide or improve its appearance, delete a picture of yourself or do other things because of your feelings about this part of your body.

— While slowly breathing in and out, gently rest your hand on this part of your body. Connect with it like you would a distressed family member or friend. Notice how your hand feels as it supports this body part. Notice how the body part feels to be supported. Know that this tender touch activates your tend-and-befriend wiring.

— Notice how you feel while connecting with and supporting this part of your body (perhaps for the first time ever). Notice how this physical gesture metaphorically lends a hand to your inner fixer, as if you're helping her with this part of your body in a completely different way. Open up to any self-compassion, self-trust, self-connection, safety, or calm that may naturally arise from the oxytocin released by giving *and* receiving this tender touch.

— Bring to mind what this part of your body does *for you*, despite what you may have done *to it*. Consider how it never consented to be targeted. Notice how it continues functioning, despite its lack of acceptance. If your hand is resting atop an implanted breast, contemplate your body's efforts to create a barrier between you and this unnatural guest. If your hand is resting atop an explanted chest, consider how it has been surgically altered, at least twice, without its permission. Contemplate its scars as proof of your body's commitment to healing and moving on. Your body's willingness to heal and keep you well is nothing less than magical; your scars are sacred wounds, reminding you of your journey. They are proof that you can heal. Know that *this* work, right now, is part of deeper healing.

To bring this acceptance exercise to a close, mindfully observe what you notice as you remove your hand. Notice how the temperature cools as air once again touches this part of your body. Notice any differences in how you regard your body and what it does for you. Gently consider how you might use this approach to always lend yourself a hand whenever your inner fixer shows up with her hammer.

---

The following table shows the ABCs of opening up to your inner experience. It's important to put in behind-the-wheel time with them by working with your everyday inner experiences. Then during distressing times, you use these approaches rather than taking a PASS on inner pain and entrapping yourself in that struggle.

I recommend using your phone to take a picture of this table so that you have it with you on the go. If your life circumstances permit, it's also helpful to make a copy of it and put it in useful places around your life to remind you to practice new ways of responding to your inner experience.

## The ABCs of Acceptance

| Acknowledge | Breathe and embody | Companion |
|---|---|---|
| Name the now | BRAKE instead of PASS | Genuinely validate *you* |
| Ask: "What in me needs attention?" | Do belly breathing | See your inner fixer* |
| Float in your inner ocean | Embody your inner experience | Lend a hand to your inner fixer* |

*You don't need to always shift into **P** to benefit from these more formal experiences. You can re-experience them by simply bringing the image of your hardworking inner fixer to mind or taking a compassionate stance toward her.

## Companioning the vulnerability of post-explant intimacy

Initial experiences with intimacy after explant are notable points in these journeys. These moments can be painful, powerful, or both, depending on your circumstances. Without the artificial barrier between your chests, you might feel more connected to your partner. You might be intensely aware of your implants' absence. Your mind might fill with distracting thoughts, while your heart floods with uncomfortable and unwanted feelings.

My explant surgery took place just three weeks before my 20th wedding anniversary. Months earlier, my husband and I planned an overseas trip to celebrate that milestone. Thankfully I was well enough to maintain our plans. In fact, I was rapidly recovering from unrecognized BII and feeling more energized than I had felt in years.

While we were away, we shared our first intimate moments without my cold, barely moving, never-liked-to-be-touched breasts. I was thrilled to be free of those things. But there was also a sense of loss, sadness, and apprehension. My breasts looked profoundly different than ever before. They were early in their recovery and still very distorted. Because of the Breast Rulebook, my mind quite naturally determined that my distorted breasts made *me* not sexy, at all, period, end of the story.

My inner fixer insisted that I wear something to keep them covered. I dutifully slipped into something sheer and distractingly pretty. As I stood before the mirror, appraising this never-seen-before reflection, I could hear the volume turning up on my inner fixer. My mind filled with mouthy backseat drivers pointing out the aftermath of willingly defying the Breast Rulebook. And although my breast implants were problematic for me and I didn't want to keep them, my heart was heavy with grief.

If ever there was a time to companion myself, this was it. I didn't want to get caught up in self-conscious assessment. I was busting my ass to repair my relationship with myself. I didn't want to engage in self-abandonment and disconnect from the moment. I wanted to be right there, on our trip, enjoying my renewed health and vitality. I wanted to use my body, which was now in so much less pain, to connect meaningfully with this man who I knew loved and accepted me completely. I also knew that to be the kind of partner I wanted to be, live with the vivaciousness I enjoyed, and bust free of the Breast Rulebook, I had to bring all my inner skills forward.

But I want you to know that I didn't have some perfect formula to follow. Using your BRITE inner healing skills to companion yourself through difficult moments isn't some rigid, off-the-shelf distress-tolerance protocol. It's just about entering the moment, as you are, knowing that you are willing to help yourself, no matter what thoughts or feelings show up.

Here's how I companioned myself through this tender part of my post-explant journey. Though this might seem like it required some deep meditative state, it didn't. It was a matter of showing up to my inner experience with the heart of a companion.

To do that, I first acknowledged my inner fixer's distress as she appraised my reflection. I validated how it made sense for her to be concerned. I asked myself, *What if she is not my enemy but my ally?* That curiosity helped me understand that my inner fixer was genuinely worried about what my distorted breasts *meant* to my sex appeal, desire, and worth. She feared that being intimate with distorted breasts might threaten my belonging. Her distress helped me discover that, despite my husband's unwavering acceptance of me, my mind deeply feared he might be disappointed or turned off by my breasts' appearance.

By opening up to myself like this, I saw that I was scared to walk out that bathroom door—what if I appeared foolish? It didn't matter if that feeling was justified; it mattered that it was there alerting me to something important. I didn't need to talk myself out of it, give myself positive affirmations, or spin it in ways that unintentionally invalidated the rule it represented.

Instead, I connected with my fear even more. Like pressing farther into a finger trap, this freed me to show up differently for myself. It's my nature to comfort someone who's scared; I won't abandon them. So I stayed *with all of me*. I comforted my fear-filled thoughts, feelings, judgments, and beliefs with genuine validation. I recognized the painful gap between the breasts I wanted and the ones now on my body. I acknowledged that gaps this wide often fill with pain.

I didn't try taking a PASS on this painful inner experience. I knew all too well the path of self-abandonment. It led away from inner awareness and knowing what care to give myself. Instead, I practiced mindful awareness of my unwanted thoughts and feelings. I opened up to the feelings of vulnerability. I saw my inner fixer gripping tightly to the Breast Rulebook. So I thanked her for her concern and assured her I had my own back. She gently lowered the book.

That distance helped me make different choices for myself. A quick check on my internalized BRITE compass helped me choose to act bravely. So I opened the door, walked out, and named my shame, out loud, to my husband and myself. I honestly described my inner experience without any judgment. I told him, "I feel sad about my breasts. I don't feel sexy right now. I regret having done all this to my body."

As a result of being open and authentic, I received helpful and loving reassurance. I practiced mindful awareness of his attunement to me. I took in his assuring response and his continued engagement. I pursued trust and decided to believe that he meant the words he spoke. By choosing to be there for my pain, fear, regret, vulnerability, and distorted breasts, I showed up for all of me.

By companioning myself, I experienced true self-acceptance.

## Be your own companion

Moments like this are peppered throughout your journey to bust free. Though explant changes your outward appearance, your inner experience is much more private. Unlike other losses, where others might rally around you with support, you can feel alone and vulnerable as you go through the more personal aspects of this journey. You might have support leading up to and after the surgery, but as you know, there is much more to it.

The only way through the inner journey is *through* it. There are just simply no shortcuts, expressways, or detours around it. It's not "fixable" through approaches such as avoidance, control, distraction, denial, etc. When you use strategies to PASS on your inner pain, you *can* push yourself through the physical side of breast implant removal. But it makes for quite a rough ride. It also sets you up to continue struggling with your inner fixer for the remainder of your life. That part of your mind will never stop anticipating appearance-based threats to your belonging. Though she means well, her solutions never truly resolve your inner pain. They entrap you within it.

By becoming your own companion, on the other hand, you show up to your entire inner journey with curiosity and heartfelt listening. You are willing to be there for yourself and make room for whatever you think and feel along the way. You change your relationship with yourself by learning to be there for all of *you*, even the parts you don't like (e.g., unwanted thoughts, feelings, and body parts). When you have your own back, you truly bust free.

Imagine if you learned to companion yourself while growing up surrounded by toxic messaging about breasts. Rather than turning to your inner fixer for advice on how to problem-solve your breasts, you would know to validate yourself when feeling *less than* compared to the Breast Rulebook. Rather than opting into expensive, problem-prone, repetitive surgeries, you would bear witness to your painful self-judgment and longing to belong. Curiosity would help you discover your perfectly natural human aversion to feeling *not good enough*. And though you might not know how to get rid of that pain, you would at least walk beside yourself while in it. Rather than self-abandonment, you would give yourself exactly what humans need when sad or distressed: connection, caring, and companionship.

Though you can't go back in time and give yourself those things, you can offer them to yourself now and as you move forward. The next chapter reconnects you with a powerful inner resource that extends your ability to offer yourself acceptance. It helps you move through your journey with the ability to tap into pure awareness and see far beyond your breast-related self-concept.

# Chapter 10

# See Yourself from a Different Point of View

Your breast-related self-concept (discussed in Chapter 1) stems from all the self-judgment, opinions, narratives, stories, and beliefs you accumulate across your life and append to your Breast Rulebook. It's woven into your identity and body image. It influences how you feel about yourself (i.e., self-esteem) and how you show up as a partner, parent, co-worker, friend, etc. It can be negative and harsh: *My breasts make me defective, deformed, damaged, unlovable, not a real woman; incapable of being sexy, flirty, confident, or playful*; and so on. On the other hand, it can involve positive self-assessments: *My breasts make me sexy, worthy, desirable, better, good enough, who I am, complete, whole, a woman,* etc.

When fused with your breast-related self-concept, it's nearly impossible to see past it. As a result, it dictates the kind of bras you buy, the types of clothes you wear, how sexy or confident you're "allowed" to be, and how accepting you are (or are not) of yourself. You don't live life on *your* terms. It plays a considerable role in choosing to get, keep, replace, or remove breast implants.

Understandably, when breast implants are central to your breast-related self-concept, removing them might feel like losing an integral part of yourself. You might worry that you will no longer be *you*. When you have breast implants for augmentation, removing them might return (or intensify) your former negative breast-related self-concept. When you have them for breast reconstruction, removing them ushers in a foreign sense of self. Without learning to see beyond your breast-related self-concept, it continues pushing you around on the other side of explant.

Fortunately, you have a powerful inner resource that sees beyond your breast-related self-concept. In ACT and many other disciplines and traditions, it's called your **Observing Self**.[35] It's there for you, irrespective of whether your breast-related self-concept is negative, positive, dependent upon implants, or new and disorienting. And it works the same no matter what breasts *mean* to you or how tightly you hold your breast-related self-concept. From its perspective, you experience pure awareness and an enduring sense of self. Both are *incredibly* helpful to finding your way through this journey to reclaim *you*.

In BRITE Inner Healing, I call this inner resource your **Aware and Enduring Self**. This chapter features ACT's process for reconnecting with this important and overlooked part of yourself. This chapter helps you conceptualize and directly experience this part of yourself through metaphors and mindfulness-based exercises. Then you'll see how to use

---

[35] The concept of Observing Self is sometimes referred to by other names, such as Observer Self, continuous you, perspective-taking self, enduring you, and pure awareness. You're free to call it what you like. Though I refer to it as your Aware and Enduring Self, please think of it however helps you conceptualize it best. A word of caution: you will find the concept of the Observing Self used in many different ways. Some of these promote the idea of using it to control your thoughts or feelings. Those applications put you back in the trap of struggling against and trying to PASS on your inner experience. They should not be confused with the ACT-based approaches in this book.

its aware and enduring aspects to navigate the BRITE Roadmap, prepare for something difficult, and reorient yourself after a reversal route. Finally, I share how I use this part of me to stay in the Reclaiming Roundabout, despite my rule-breaking breasts.

## Your Aware and Enduring Self

Your Aware and Enduring Self isn't something that you can point to or touch. There are no X-rays, MRIs, or medical tools for measuring it. Rather than a physical part of you, it's more like a viewpoint. It's the *you* behind your eyes; it's your awareness of your awareness. It watches your life play out without adding or subtracting anything. It's there, even when you're not thinking about it. As its name suggests, your Aware and Enduring Self remains steady your entire life, silently noticing everything taking place inside you and your life.

It's also separate from your Thinking Self. That means it's incapable of judging, predicting, or ruminating. Like your ears hear sounds they don't make, your Aware and Enduring Self observes thoughts, feelings, and experiences that it doesn't create. It's also not impacted by them. Given that it doesn't generate ideas, stories, or narratives, it's fully aware of the various roles in your life but not invested in changing or maintaining them.

To help you grasp this, ACT practitioners use many different metaphors. One likens this part of you to the sky, and your thoughts, feelings, and body sensations to the weather: Though in full contact with the weather, the sky does nothing to manipulate it. Another metaphor compares this part of you to bookshelves: They hold the books sitting on them but don't change depending on the books' contents. Another likens this part of yourself to a chessboard: It's entirely in contact with the games played on its surface, but the board remains constant irrespective of the players, their moves, the style of chess pieces, or winning color.

The main thing for you to keep in mind is that the *you* behind your eyes helps you see things very differently. Its viewpoint is outside the Breast Rulebook's content, so it offers you **pure awareness** outside the labels you put on yourself. Its viewpoint remains steady, whether you have breast implants or not. From its continuous perspective on your life, you see yourself living in a patriarchal society where breasts *matter*. You observe the messaging about breast implants preying upon your innate human drive to belong. You witness yourself getting more than you bargained for from breast implants and coming to terms with their loss. This broader perspective awakens in you a willingness, even eagerness, to offer yourself the abiding acceptance and self-compassion necessary for true inner healing.

To visualize how pure awareness helps you see beyond your breast-related self-concept, consider how differently the sky and clouds appear during a plane's ascent to a cruising altitude. As the plane rises through the cloud line, all you see is white. However, you see much more once you pass through, such as the vastness of the sky, the clouds' shapes, and the sunlight's colors. Though the clouds completely blocked your view moments earlier, you now see they are only a part of the sky. In the same way, your breast-related self-concept clouds everything your Thinking Self sees (including yourself). Reconnecting with your Aware and Enduring Self's perspective is like breaking through the cloud line and seeing that there is much more to *you* than your breasts. From its perspective, you see that your breast-related self-concept does not define *you*. Instead, it's a part of you—a relatively small and surprisingly noisy part.

There's another aspect to your Aware and Enduring Self that's invaluable when facing or recovering from explant. This part of *you* endures no matter how your breasts change. To grasp this, consider the body you had in your earliest memories. It literally doesn't exist anymore.

Nearly all those cells have been replaced countless times as you've grown. As a result, your body's skin, hair, size, and shape are entirely different. And yet, your Aware and Enduring Self remains the same as it watches your life unfold from behind your eyes. Your awareness of your awareness never changes, no matter how much your body does. You can lose a body part, even a highly sexualized one like breasts, and this part of you endures.

Not only does this part of you endure over time, but it also cannot be harmed by any of your feelings, sensations, thoughts, judgments, beliefs, self-concepts, or roles you take on. Like blizzards, hurricanes, and thunderstorms cannot hurt the sky, this enduring part of you cannot be harmed by even your most distressing thoughts, uncomfortable feelings, or painful body sensations on this journey. This aware part of you knows the inner turmoil you feel over changes to this part of your body, and the enduring part of you remains steady through it all.

Because the BRITE Inner Healing processes are interconnected, you have been indirectly using this inner resource throughout this book. It plays a role in promoting your present moment awareness. It notices your wandering attention and alerts you to wield your BRITE lasso. It helps you catch when you're automatically following your Breast Rulebook or trapped by your efforts to PASS on internalized breast shame.

Now it's time to work directly with your Aware and Enduring Self.

## Reconnecting with your Aware and Enduring Self

As with the other BRITE Inner Healing skills, it's not enough to simply read about your Aware and Enduring Self. So this section offers several ways to reconnect with it. Some help you conceptualize this part of yourself, and others enable you to experience it directly. You don't have to master these exercises and do them repeatedly. Instead, simply use them to reconnect with this inner resource's pure awareness and enduring sense of *you*.

If your mind tries to convince you to read (rather than *do*) the exercises or urges you to do them "later," use your defusion skills to notice and not follow those thoughts. You deserve to rediscover this part of yourself. It's a game-changer for busting free from your breast-related self-concept.

## Thinking Self vs. Aware and Enduring Self

If you're like most people, you're nearly always in your Thinking Self. You were educated by a system focused primarily on analytical thinking, reasoning, logic, memory, problem-solving, organizing, planning, etc. As a result, your mind naturally thinks rather highly of itself and the content it holds. You might rarely consider that there's more to *you* than what you think. When living primarily from your Thinking Self, you seldom experience nonjudgmental self-awareness, which is critical to busting free and reclaiming *you*.

To help you notice the difference between your Thinking Self and your Aware and Enduring Self, spend half a minute with your eyes closed while listening to everything your mind says. It's literally constantly chattering, so this is as easy as closing your eyes and purposefully paying attention to it. So please do that for half a minute now. Guided Audio 10.1 helps you fully experience this (and the following exercise) for yourself.

 LISTEN TO GUIDED AUDIO 10.1

In that half-minute, did you notice the chattiness of your Thinking Self? What about the silent listening of your Aware and Enduring Self? Go ahead and invest another half-minute in yourself by repeating this brief exercise. This time, purposefully pay attention to the part of you that's silently observing your thoughts. It's the *you* behind your eyes; it's your Aware and Enduring Self.

If this distinction isn't immediately apparent to you, don't panic. Your Aware and Enduring self is there. The exercises and experientials in this section will help you reconnect with it.

## Am I

An extension of the previous exercise is to ask yourself the following two questions:

1. Am I the thoughts going through my head?
2. Or am I the one who is aware of the thoughts going through my head?

Please take a moment now, and quietly ask yourself these questions while noticing your inner experience. Randomly ask yourself these two questions over the next week. Be sure to ask them during times when your mind is really absorbed in its content. It can be helpful to write "Am I?" on sticky notes, phone alarms, or your hand to remind yourself to do this simple exercise. Though there isn't much to this exercise, doing it reminds you that there *is* more to you than you think.

## I am...

This is a popular exercise in ACT that helps you experience this part of yourself by making a list of "I am" statements. To do this, write the words "I am" at the top of a sheet of paper or on a digital note. Then, write 20 statements about yourself, each starting with "I am." Each statement should be written on a separate numbered line. For brevity, here's a sample of how half of my list appears:

*I am*

1. I am Amanda.
2. I am compassionate.
3. I am an ACT practitioner.
4. I am a BII survivor.
5. I am an American.
6. I am a cat mom.
7. I am a wife.
8. I am a mother.
9. I am middle-aged.
10. I am a *Star Wars* fan.

Go ahead and complete yours now. **Note: Your list needs to be physically written out.**

Once you complete your list, go back and strikethrough (or delete) whatever is written on the last line. Mindfully notice your Thinking Self's reaction to crossing off that statement. Then repeat this process of striking through and noticing your Thinking Self's reaction, one line at a time.

Notice if some lines feel harder to remove. (Usually, your Thinking Self dislikes crossing off the ones tied more tightly to how you see yourself. There's nothing wrong with that; it's simply worth noticing.) Continue until you have lined through each entry.

Finally, notice what remains on your page. It's the simple statement at the top, "I am." *That* is like your Aware and Enduring Self. It's always there, simply aware of *you*, no matter how long your list of self-labels might be, how those labels might change over time, what role you're serving, or what quality you believe you have or lack.

## Experiencing your Aware and Enduring Self

Guided Audio 10.2 is an adaptation of ACT's classic exercise to experience this part of yourself. ACT co-founder Steve Hayes and colleagues developed the original version in 1999. I adapted it to include your breast-implant-related experiences. It enables you to reconnect with the *you* behind your eyes who watches your thinking and notices your feelings. Because this experiential helps you directly experience your Aware and Enduring Self, **please don't skip it**. If you don't have time or the ability to do it right now, please set a reminder to do this exercise during a part of your day where you can invest about 20 minutes into an important and helpful eyes-closed activity.

## Enduring Beyond any Change to Your Breasts

This exercise helps you experience the part of you that endures no matter how your breasts appear, even if they're surgically removed. To fully experience this for yourself, I strongly recommend listening to Guided Audio 10.3.

Alternatively, you can read through the following prompts, being sure to pause between each one and closing your eyes to fully reconnect with that moment. (Note: If you have trouble recalling any of these moments, it's okay to imagine how you experienced them from behind your eyes.)

— Settle in by mentally shifting yourself into **P**, completing a few cycles of centering belly breathing, and intentionally reconnecting with the silently aware and enduring part of yourself that's been with you throughout your quest for *better* breasts.

— Begin by revisiting the moments in your life before and early into puberty, as you wondered about your developing breasts. Explore these moments from the inside out, as you looked down upon your chest or stared into the mirror. From this perspective, see if you can recall the thoughts and feelings that moved through your mind and heart during those moments.

— Now move forward in time to when you tried on your first bra, stuffed your bra to see how you would look with larger breast mounds, or wore your first push-up bra. Recall any of these moments as your Aware and Enduring Self watched them unfold from behind your eyes. Reconnect with that part of you that is always there, silently observing your life from behind your eyes. See how it was there watching your life unfold as you kept vigil for breast development, dressed in ways to reveal their development, or relied on bras to create their illusion. Recall the thoughts and feelings that moved through you during those moments. Notice that although your breast mounds, thoughts, and feelings changed from early in puberty, your Aware and Enduring Self remained the same.

— Now move forward in time to the moment just before being put to sleep for your breast implant surgery. Recall that moment from the silent point of view from behind your eyes. Just notice that a part of *you* was there then, just as it always was and as it's always been.

— Allow yourself to move forward in time to when you saw yourself for the first time with breast implants. Reconnect with that silent part of yourself that was there in that moment, aware of the changes to your body, registering your thoughts and feelings about those changes. See how that part of yourself remained unchanged despite the change in your breast mounds and how you regarded them. It was the same before breast implants and remains the same long after their removal.

— Now bring to mind any moment that was enhanced or negatively affected by having breast implants (e.g., hugging, sleeping, exercising, dressing, intimacy). It doesn't matter what memory you choose, and you can explore more than one. Simply notice that in each of these moments, the *you* behind your eyes is the same as it always was and always will be. No matter how sexy or uncomfortable you feel on the inside, what thoughts move through your mind about your breasts, or the labels you put on yourself because of your breasts, notice that your Aware and Enduring Self is there–unchanged.

— Finally, connect with the *you* behind your eyes, right now, as you read these words. Notice how this part of you is the same as she has always been, no matter how your breasts or post-explant chest appear.

Notice that there's a familiar and stable sense of yourself across each of those moments. Though fully aware of the changes to your body–and the thoughts and feelings that came with them–your Aware and

Enduring Self didn't change. No matter how your breasts appear in those moments, the *you* behind your eyes is the one you've always been and will always be.

You will always have this continuous you, no matter what thoughts go through your mind or feelings fill your heart—even if you dramatically change or completely lose a highly sexualized part of your body. Connecting with this sense of yourself provides a sense of familiarity while your body weathers the physical changes throughout this journey and beyond. Though you will inevitably be caught in your Thinking Self, you can direct your awareness to this silent, reliable, and stable sense of *you* that helps you see yourself, your body, and life with a perspective that's free of all the psychological content contained in your breast rulebook.

## See Beyond Your Breast-Related Self-Concept by Taking a Bigger View

Sometimes, when passing through the cloud line on an airplane, the blinding white outside the plane's window feels suffocating to me. So I contemplate how the clouds look from the broader perspective of the vast sky. I know that from the sky's perspective, the smothering clouds are only part of the bigger picture.

Like a plane in the cloud line, it can be hard to see beyond your breast-related self-concept. There are many times before, during, and long after breast implant removal when your mind clouds with self-judgments, predictions, worries, memories, beliefs, and self-labels. When that happens, it can help to tap into the broader perspective of your Aware and Enduring Self. From there, you see that your breast-related self-concept is something you contain rather than something that holds you.

This exercise helps you take a bigger view. To fully experience this for yourself, I recommend listening to Guided Audio 10.4.

Alternatively, you can use the following prompts:

— Begin by mentally shifting yourself into **P** and completing a few cycles of centering belly breathing.

— Allow your breath to return to normal and spend the next several moments intentionally clouding your mind with your breast-related self-concept. Without any judgment or resistance, mentally pass through your breast rulebook and consider all the beliefs your mind holds about women, breasts, and belonging.

  – Did your mind learn long ago that *women have breasts*?
  – Did it derive that *better* breasts make women *better*?
  – Observe what image comes to mind when you think of an idealized breast or ideal proportions for your body.
  – Does it hold any rules about how confident, sexy, or worthy you are allowed to be or feel because of your breasts or post-explant chest?
  – Are there any rules about how you ought to dress?
  – According to your breast rulebook, is your chest something to display or something to hide?

— As you peruse your breast rulebook, notice how its content shapes your breast-related self-concept. Notice how you feel about yourself when your mind is clouded by these rules, judgments, and beliefs.

— Notice that in this very moment there is a part of you regarding all this. There is a silent, observing part of you that is here now, aware of your breast-related self-concept. *Don't try to grab this sense of yourself and look at it—just touch this awareness lightly.*

— Notice that you are here, aware in this moment of your life, and separate from your breast-related self-concept.

— Notice that you contain your breast rulebook and that you are not bound by it.

— Just as the sky doesn't try to change or control the clouds, use your Aware and Enduring self's perspective to watch your breast-related thoughts, feelings, and judgments as they move through your awareness. Notice that even the darkest clouds on this journey (e.g., internalized breast shame) are an experience that *you* contain.

As you move forward, you can quickly remind yourself to take the bigger view by asking yourself: *Am I stuck in my inner cloud line?* Then use your Aware and Enduring Self's perspective to view your breast-related thoughts, feelings, and beliefs as experiences moving through you and to remind yourself that there's more to you than you think.

## See the Screen

Another way to remind yourself to use your Aware and Enduring Self's viewpoint is to take advantage of your daily exposure to phone, tablet, computer, and TV screens. The screen is like your Aware and Enduring Self. The content on the screen is like your Thinking Self's continuous output of thoughts, judgments, beliefs, comparisons, etc. Though the screen shows you different content as you stream a movie, scroll through social media, or shop online, it remains unchanged. To remind yourself that *you* are unchanged by your Thinking Self's content (and your breast-related self-concept), see the screens in your life. Each time you do, check on the observing, enduring, and aware *you* behind your eyes.

The idea here is to form a habit that helps you remember that there is a difference between *you* and the content of your mind. This habit might benefit you over time by reminding you of a place within yourself that's not affected by the comparative thinking, unwanted feelings, and self-judgments that show up when you see breasts objectified on posters, ads, social media, and billboards (the kind you pass on the road and those erected by your inner fixer). It doesn't get rid of those inner experiences, but it reminds you that not all of you is affected by them.

## See Yourself from a Different Perspective

Just as your Aware and Enduring Self offers you moment-by-moment awareness of yourself, it also enables you to see your struggles, heartache, and fears from different perspectives. It helps you flexibly see things from inside and outside yourself, from *here* and *there*, and from *now* and *then*. When you use it to see yourself from the outside, it awakens the same desire to help that shows up when you see someone else in pain. It facilitates a self-compassionate response and helps you show up for yourself as you do for so many others. I do this experiential with nearly all my clients; they consistently find it helpful. To help you experience this for yourself, I created Guided Audio 10.5. Because this experiential helps you directly experience self-compassion, **please don't skip it.**

 **LISTEN TO GUIDED AUDIO 10.5**

If you don't have time or the ability to do it right now, set a reminder to do this perspective-taking exercise during a part of your day where you can spend about 10 minutes with your eyes closed. Once you've done the guided audio, you are welcome to repeat it as often as you find helpful, but there's no need to repeat it. You can simply close your eyes (or not) and visualize yourself and your struggles from across the room and genuinely show up for yourself.

---

The preceding exercises aim to reconnect you with your aware and enduring viewpoint. It gives you moments of clarity outside your Thinking Self's judgments, the Breast Rulebook, and your breast-related self-concept. But just as quickly as you experience this clarity, it nearly instantly clouds again by your mind's continuous self-appraisal, judgments, comparisons, and storytelling. Because of the ongoing behind-the-scenes process, described in Chapter 1, your mind naturally does those things throughout life. But that doesn't mean you shouldn't strive for moments of clarity, especially when finding your way through this journey while holding an unhelpful breast-related self-concept. That would be like refusing to use windshield wipers in a storm because they don't stop the rain. In fact, it might help you to regard your Aware and Enduring Self as inner windshield wipers. You can use them whenever you realize you're caught in your Thinking Self's storm and unable to see beyond your breast-related self-concept. They won't get rid of those things, but they will help you find *your* way.

## Using your Aware and Enduring Self across the BRITE Roadmap

This section provides you with tips for using your Aware and Enduring Self to see beyond your breast-related self-concept in each roundabout. For the most complete picture, you might want to read through them all. But it's also okay to focus on your current roundabout. The prompts for each roundabout are designed to be used in the here and now. So when you are early in your journey, come back to this section each time you move into a new roundabout and keep its prompts in mind to help you tap into this inner resource. When reading this book later in your journey or after explant, you might focus on the Repairing and Reclaiming Roundabouts. However, if you notice yourself being pushed around by your breast-related self-concept, please also work through the earlier roundabouts.

## Rationalizing Roundabout

Your Aware and Enduring Self nonjudgmentally watches as you circle the Rationalizing Roundabout. Use its awareness to notice when you're doing something that is driven entirely by your breast-related self-concept (e.g., downplaying or denying disappointments or problems with your implants, changing the way you dress to accentuate or downplay your breasts, avoiding MRIs because you "don't want to know"). In those moments:

— Watch your thoughts, judgments, beliefs, and feelings about yourself, your breasts, and your body. Observe your inner fixer's justifications for tolerating problems or disappointments with them. Remember, you are not trying to change them; you're using this perspective to simply be aware of them. Ask yourself if *you* are those thoughts and beliefs or the person having them?

— Watch a mini-documentary featuring the ways your breast-related self-concept clouds your existence. Then get out of the mental cloud line and into the viewpoint of your Aware and Enduring Self. From there, look beyond your breast-related self-concept. Notice when it's driving you. Curiously consider what *you* might do differently by bringing your whole self forward.

## Reasoning Roundabout

You need a clear mind when coming to terms with getting more than you bargained for from breast implants. But often, your breast-related self-concept clouds your perspective. To see beyond it, use your Aware and Enduring Self to:

— Notice the part of you holding tightly to the belief that this highly sexualized body part defines your worth.

— Observe your mind's brewing inner storm. Notice thoughts that grab your attention like lighting in a night sky. Notice feelings that rumble through you like thunder. Acknowledge that although your thoughts and feelings might be powerful, they cannot impact this part of *you*.

— Look for aspects of *you* and your life that didn't change because of breast implants.

— Look for how *you* and your life *have* changed, independently of having breast implants.

— Look for parts of your Thinking Self that are *not* caught in the storm. Listen for what they say about your breasts, body, and belonging.

## Readying Roundabout

In this roundabout, your Thinking Self helps you prepare for explant while holding on to the Breast Rulebook. When you find yourself caught in your conflicted Thinking Self's storm, use your Aware and Enduring Self again and again like windshield wipers to:

— See your inner fixer's moves from this part of yourself that doesn't engage with them. Nonjudgmentally observe when you're reacting in unhelpful ways.

— Notice when you take a PASS on your feelings rather than caring for your underlying needs. Notice when you entrap yourself by struggling against the uncomfortable aspects of breast implant removal rather than companioning yourself through them.

— Use these moments of clarity to also see the part of you committed to removing your breast implants and that there are things that matter to you beyond your breast-related self-concept.

## Repairing Roundabout

All of *you* goes through explant. Your body holds the surgical discomfort and has the job of physically healing. Your Thinking Self grapples with what your new silhouette *means*. And your Aware and Enduring Self offers you a safe place to watch all the physical changes unfold. It's unchanged by the thoughts and feelings that come with this change.

In the Repairing Roundabout, using your Aware and Enduring Self goes well beyond that of an inner windshield wiper. This familiar *you* behind your eyes is there when you look at your breasts for the first time after explant, while you wait for the Fluff Fairy to show up, or when you feel vulnerable during physical intimacy. This enduring inner resource provides you a sense of stability and sanctuary as you adjust to your new silhouette. It provides a safe place to weather your inner fixer's panic when you wake up, tightly bound, with those icons of femininity completely changed or gone.

During this point in your journey, use your Aware and Enduring Self's viewpoint to:

— Notice the physical sensations of your body working to repair.
— Observe your nonphysical feelings. For example, in addition to feeling surgical discomfort, you might feel proud or relieved.

— See your body, once again healing and serving you, despite the scars it never consented to carry. Observe what shows up in your heart and mind when you see your body, not as an object to fix, hate, or improve, but as something impacted by compelling beliefs in a breast-obsessed society.

— Notice what's playing out in your Thinking Self. Observe when you compare your recovery to others' recoveries. Observe when your mind urges you to put something off, such as looking at your post-explant chest or being seen by others. Watch your thoughts, feelings, and urges change like the weather from this skylike vantage. Notice the familiar part of you watching your thoughts and urges unfold.

— Know there is a part of you that's not impacted by these physical changes or your thoughts and feelings about it. From there, watch for efforts from your inner fixer to *fix* your aesthetic outcome, speed up recovery, or bribe the Fluff Fairy. Look for and companion your inner fixer's distress.

— Take a more distanced perspective. See that there's more to *you* than your breast-related self-concept. Observe that *you* acted independently of the Breast Rulebook.

## Reclaiming Roundabout

Your Aware and Enduring Self's viewpoint helps you continually pursue a reclaimed relationship with yourself. It helps you watch how you go about life as a post-explant woman in a breast-obsessed culture. It enables you to see your journey, the Breast Rulebook, and yourself in a much bigger context.

From its vantage, you see that there are times when society's toxic messaging leads you to feel concerned about your appearance. You notice when your Thinking Self's old wiring lights up in response to images on social media, store posters, billboards, old photos of you with implants, or other women. You observe when you consider or engage in an inner fixer project without regard to long-term impacts on your well-being. From the broader perspective of your Aware and Enduring Self, you see that none of this means you're failing at reclaiming yourself; it means you're human.

Busting free isn't like flipping a switch and walking away. It's an ongoing practice. Your Aware and Enduring Self helps you notice comparative thinking, watch as feelings of *less than* show up, and catch when you're being pushed around by any rulebook. From its perspective, you see those inner experiences and observe how you react. By tapping into moments of pure awareness, you pivot toward your BRITE compass and continually reclaim *you*.

## Using your Aware and Enduring Self before something hard

You can proactively take the perspective of your Aware and Enduring self when tackling a challenge (e.g., telling a breast-obsessed partner that your implants must go). When you see yourself navigating a mental and emotional storm, evoke or repeat the **See Yourself From a Different Perspective** exercise from earlier in this chapter to bring forth an accepting and compassionate stance. Notice how you want to show up for yourself. Then choose one or two of your BRITE compass points to guide yourself through the actual experience while being the woman you most want to be. Chapter 11 helps you explore actions you take on your behalf during times like these, such as talking about your discomfort and asking for the reassurance you want.

## Use your Aware and Enduring Self after a reversal route

You can also use your Aware and Enduring Self's viewpoint to step back and observe what overwhelmed you after a reversal route. Just as the vast sky lets you see that even smothering clouds have beginnings and ends, your Aware and Enduring Self offers a different perspective on whatever seemed impassable. For example, when you take a reversal route after being told you can't proceed with explant unless you lose weight, quit smoking, or receive clearance from a cardiologist, your Aware and Enduring Self's perspective allows you to see that even those barriers are discrete experiences that you can work through.

## How I use my Aware and Enduring Self to stay in the Reclaiming Roundabout

I use my Aware and Enduring Self to help me continually reclaim myself in two helpful ways. First, it's aware of my awareness, even when I'm not. It helps me notice when I'm heading down the mental superhighways of comparative thinking and self-judgment. Both behaviors are easy for my mind to do each time I'm confronted with The Crease. That awareness helps me know something (e.g., my reflection, another woman, an airbrushed image) tripped up my old wiring. My Aware and Enduring Self sees how my mind quickly, and without my permission, determines that I am *less than*. It watches that interpretation play across my mind. It helps me acknowledge when my sense of worth and belonging feels threatened.

Do I like that my mind can still push me in that direction? No. Do I agree with those thoughts? No, absolutely not. Does the fact that these thoughts and feelings show up mean that I'm failing at self-acceptance, that explant was a mistake, or that I shouldn't write this book? A thousand times, no! I don't buy into those unhelpful thoughts because my Aware and Enduring Self helps me see that the Breast Rulebook is simply part of my mind. It also helps me see the bigger picture: I live in a breast-obsessed society. Seeing these things helps me contextualize why my mind struggles with the rule-defying crease. I don't have to assign any great meaning to that struggle. Instead, this broader perspective reminds me that busting free is a continual process.

The second way my Aware and Enduring Self helps me continually reclaim myself is akin to the comfort I experience on a plane by *knowing* even the most suffocating clouds are only a fraction of the vast sky. I do the same perspective-taking when thoughts around The Crease cloud my mind: I consider them from the much broader perspective of my Aware and Enduring Self. From that vantage point, I see that The Crease is a very small part of *me*. I see that despite my body's extra crease, *I* am not damaged. I observe that my mind is having unpleasant (and socially conditioned) thoughts about my body. I also see that The Crease is actually a very small part of my life with essentially no impact on any of my relationships or interactions.

Does this alternate perspective deliver me to great inner peace? Not necessarily. But these moments of pure awareness remind me that in addition to having these thoughts and feelings, *I also have a choice over how I react*. So I acknowledge that a part of me is inwardly storming and see that there is much more to me. The rest of me can companion myself and compassionately validate that my breast's crease disappoints me. *I* can show up as the partner, mother, sister, daughter, friend, therapist, and woman that *I* care about being, even when my mind clouds with concern over The Crease.

When I see The Crease from outside my breast-related self-concept, I know that it's there because I busted free. When everything is said and done, I sometimes even feel proud of The Crease. My hope is that you can also take perspective on yourself and show up like the woman you most want to be, no matter how your breasts or post-explant chest appear. With practice, you can do this for the rest of your life as you and your body age, change, and defy all sorts of other rulebooks.

## Be the Sky

From behind your eyes, you see that *you* are separate from this journey and its outcomes. When you tap into this viewpoint, you notice when you're gripping tightly to your Breast Rulebook, circling Inner Fixer Lane, and struggling against feelings that make sense in the bigger picture. Your awareness of your awareness alerts you to lasso back to the here and now, where you can companion yourself through any difficulty.

No matter where you are on the BRITE Roadmap or why you move through it, tap into this part of yourself to see far beyond your breast-related self-concept. Its pure awareness gives you a perspective that helps you come to terms with getting more than you bargained for from breast implants. It helps *you* choose what's best for your body, even when it means defying your Breast Rulebook. When you explant, this enduring viewpoint gives you a sense of inner continuity. Turn to it while your mind remaps your body's changing contours. You can also use it to see that you are still *you*, even when your post-explant breasts break the rules (e.g., they're smaller, deflated, scarred, flat, floppy, saggy, creased, dented, wrinkled, misshapen, or completely missing). Finally, use your Aware and Enduring self to see when old wiring lights up and you feel *less than* as a woman. Then bring forward everything you've got, show up for yourself on *your* terms, and keep busting free.

Over the years, I created a three-word mantra to remind clients to take the bigger view when caught in a Thinking Self storm: *Be the Sky*. I know that might sound all woo-woo, but it's intended to remind you to elevate above society's programming around your body, see beyond your threatened breast-related self-concept, and take a much bigger perspective on *you*.

Even the briefest moment of pure awareness allows you to step back and use your BRITE Inner Healing skills to bust free. Chapter 11 shows you how to pull them all together to reclaim your body, mind, and heart—long before and long after explant.

# ACTing on Your Behalf Before, During, and Long After Explant

You made it to the final chapter! You arrive with the full set of BRITE Inner Healing skills and tools to steady and guide yourself, stay in the here and now, watch your thinking, companion your inner pain, and see far beyond your breast-related self-concept. You have the BRITE flexibility to find *your* way through the mental and emotional barriers that inevitably arise when temporary and problem-prone breast implants impact your life. With that flexibility, you bring your whole self forward as you choose to replace or remove them, develop a holistic explant plan, and find *your* way as a post-explant woman living in a breast-obsessed society. Your BRITE Inner Healing skills let your tired inner fixer rest while you live a vital and meaningful life. But they don't build that life for you. For that, you must take **driven action**.

Driven action in BRITE Inner Healing is based on the remaining ACT process known as committed action. In ACT, *commitment* is the fuel for change. It means doing things, no matter how small, to move toward the life outcomes you desire. But taking driven action is different from pushing yourself forward begrudgingly or *in spite of it all*. Instead, it reflects your inner drive to act on your own behalf while using BRITE Inner Healing skills, no matter what your inner fixer says about it.

Several things help you take driven action. First, you need to know the life you're driving toward, especially on this harder-to-see inner journey. You might long for inner healing, and a life liberated from the Breast Rulebook, but it's challenging to drive toward something when you don't really know what it *means* to you or see the differences it would make in *your* life. This chapter helps you visualize both. Second, you're more likely to do what matters to you when you know how to pull all this together and apply it in real life. This chapter provides you with a straightforward three-step process to do just that. You're also more likely to take driven actions when you know what they look like. I've sat across from countless women who know what they're driving toward and are willing to act on their behalf, but they simply don't know what to do. I don't want that to happen to you. So this chapter provides you with many driven actions to consider in each roundabout.

Finally, these journeys are challenging, rewarding, and ongoing. There will be times when taking driven action comes more easily, and there will be periods when you struggle. To help with the latter, I close the chapter with a shame-free mini guide to use whenever you know what you want to do, but you just aren't doing it.

## How would your life change by busting free?

It might seem odd to ask you this question in the final chapter, but now you can be realistic about your answer. For example, you now know that your mind learned and derived countless beliefs about women, breasts, and belonging without your awareness or permission. You understand that it holds those beliefs in a vast breast rulebook filled with content you can never fully unlearn. You also know that humans are wired for connection. In response to our innate drive for group belonging, we naturally engage in comparative thinking and self-judgment. You understand the ongoing behind-the-scenes process fueling these inner behaviors—and your inner fixer—are here to stay. You know that she represents a part of your mind that convinces you to PASS (problem-solve, avoid, sidetrack, something else) on feeling *less than* or *not good enough*. And now you know that although those approaches provide temporary relief, they can amplify your suffering in the long run.

By knowing these things, you move forward without setting "dead people" goals, such as, *Stop comparing myself to others* or *Stop caring about what other people think of me* or *Stop feeling regret, doubt, anxiety, etc.* You know to guard against placing unrealistic expectations on yourself just to *be happy, grateful,* or *positive.* You understand that liberating your mind and heart comes by opening up to your thoughts and feelings, even the unwanted ones. And you recognize that although you might reclaim yourself from the Breast Rulebook, you will always care about belonging.

Knowing all this helps you envision how your life would change by busting free. Because that vision plays an integral part in your willingness to take driven action, the following section helps you visualize it for yourself.

## Your BRITE Inner Healing sequel

In Chapter 2, you used Movie Mind to look across your life and watch how you responded to your inner fixer. Now you're going to use it to watch a long-anticipated sequel of your life with inner healing. It helps you see how you will companion yourself through life instead of being steered by your inner fixer. As you watch this sequel, assume you can tell what you're doing on the inside, just as you can infer a character's inner experience when watching a movie based on a book you know well. Keep in mind that your inner healing sequel isn't a fantasy film showing you living a pain-free life. You will still occasionally circle Inner Fixer Lane. But in this sequel, you see yourself using BRITE flexibility to find your way out.

Because BRITE flexibility helps you stop rigidly following *any* rulebook, you don't have to limit this sequel to breast-related issues. For example, I enjoy trail biking, but I'm constantly distracted by how my cellulite and saddlebags violate the Leg Rulebook. Inner healing for me means no longer allowing my life's moments to be hijacked by fear of being *less than* according to any rulebook. So, in my sequel, I see myself acknowledging my cellulite-related thoughts and still doing what matters to me while biking. For example, I'm in the moment noticing leaves fluttering in the breeze, birds floating in the sky, and the wind passing like waves over a field of prairie grass. Instead of getting caught up in my self-judgment, I validate that wanting group approval is just part of being human. That frees me to appreciate my body's ability to bike long distances when only a few years earlier, I was in disabling pain.

Spoiler alert: This is exactly how biking goes for me now. I still have thoughts about my cellulite, but they do *not* control me. I wear shorts on summer days without spending the entire time pulling them down or strategically positioning myself in hopes of avoiding judgment from others. When my inner fixer warns me against taking these risks, I thank my mind for looking out for me, validate the urge to avoid being judged, and still do what matters *to me*. I even ask myself, *If this were my last time to go biking, how would I want to spend it?* As morbid as that might be, it helps me spend my time wisely. Each time I head out for a bike ride, I rewatch this part of my sequel and remind myself about the driven actions I want to take.

Before doing this version of Movie Mind, check your BRITE compass and remind yourself about the kind of woman you most want to be deep down in your heart, underneath your social conditioning about you *ought* to behave and appear. Even when you already have this vital tool internalized, it's helpful to revisit Chapter 6's values list and ensure that your BRITE compass is dialed in. Afterward, hold those values close to your heart and listen to Guided Audio 11.1.

## 🔊 LISTEN TO GUIDED AUDIO 11.1

Alternatively, you can shift yourself mentally into **P** and use the following prompts to help you visualize what busting free from the Breast Rulebook looks like in your life. Please don't overthink this or worry about coming up with the *right* answers. Allow this to be more of a heartfelt reflection.

— To begin, take some time to come into this moment of reflection and visualization. Center yourself by slowing your next inhale, allowing your belly to fill like a balloon, and then softening your body while you slowly and completely exhale. Take a few more centering breaths, softening your body on each exhale and bringing your awareness fully to this moment.

— Now turn your awareness inward and begin visualizing what you would do differently on the outside when using BRITE Inner Healing skills and tools rather than automatically following the Breast Rulebook or appeasing your inner fixer.

   – Is there anything you would start, stop, or do more or less often?

- Are there people, places, or activities you'd approach differently?

- If you still have breast implants, what would BRITE Inner Healing skills help you do differently than you do now?

- If you are moving through explant, how would your BRITE Inner Healing skills help you show up to breast implant loss as the woman you most want to be?

- If you already explanted, watch scenes that show you using BRITE Inner Healing skills to show up to post-explant intimacy, hugs, health-related appointments where you're undressed above the waist, and so on. Those scenes show what busting free means to you.

— How would your life be different if your inner fixer, backseat drivers, and the Breast Rulebook came along for the ride instead of dictating your course? What would change about your relationship with yourself if you used inner skills when your inner fixer was distressed or pressuring you? Can you think of anything you'd like to see yourself do differently?

— What would you do differently on the inside when flooded with self-judgment, internalized breast shame, or fear of judgment from others? Remember, BRITE Inner Healing has given you skills to help with things you can control, such as your focus, engagement, attentiveness, self-compassion, and validation. Take some time to see yourself using those things when inner pain is with you.

— Now think about any challenges that lie ahead for you or an area where you keep getting stuck. See yourself approaching them with your BRITE Inner Healing skills at the ready. Watch how you companion yourself through the complex parts of this journey and the rest of your life. What scenes would get you cheering for yourself because you know they show you living life on *your* terms?

The scenes in your sequel reveal *your* **Life Worth Driving Toward.** It's important to put words to this vision and transform it into a succinct goal for yourself. Take some time now and gently listen to your inner wisdom on how to summarize your Life Worth Driving Toward. It might help to simply ask yourself: *What does Busting Free mean to me?* Trust yourself to answer this question realistically now that you understand the ongoing behind-the-scenes process driving the quest for better breasts, your innate drive to belong, and the futility of trying to PASS on inner pain.

Here are some examples shared with me by other women on these journeys:

*Speak and live my truth, even when fearing I'm not enough.*
*Live a full and purposeful life based on what I care about most.*
*Make decisions for my body on my terms, not solely based on what society deems important.*
*Have my own back, inside and out, especially as I age.*
*Do what I want to do, even when worried about how I look.*
*Get my life back and be the person I was meant to be in this world.*
*Reconnect with and be loving toward myself no matter how my chest appears.*
*Know how to take care of myself when I feel worried about my breasts or any part of my body so I can live my best life.*

Your Life Worth Driving Toward might change over time as you continue to reconnect with yourself. For that reason, I suggest revisiting this section's prompts whenever you move into a different phase of your journey. You might also want to write out your responses because writing often helps inner goals seem more concrete and tangible.

## Using your Life Worth Driving Toward

To put your overarching goal to use, think back to Chapter 7's PMA (present moment awareness) exercises. In each of those exercises, you chose something to focus on, specified an amount of time to watch your awareness, and then used your BRITE lasso to bring your mind back whenever you noticed it wandering. Remember, the point of those exercises was to build your ability to direct your focus rather than have it hijacked by your inner fixer.

Reclaiming your body, mind and heart is basically a giant version of those exercises. You focus on your Life Worth Driving Toward rather than appeasing your inner fixer and automatically following the Breast Rulebook. However, there is one important caveat for using your Life Worth Driving Toward. You don't get to set a timer on this work. You never declare yourself done.

As previously discussed, you must stay at it for three reasons. First, you live in a society that preys upon your innate human drive to belong. Second, you can never fully unlearn the Breast Rulebook. Third, your inner fixer is here to stay. Even when she leaves you alone about your breasts, she's got plenty of other threats to manage, including aging in a youth-obsessed society. That's why you pursue your Life Worth Driving Toward *for the rest of your life.* When you wander off course or behave unlike the woman you most want to be, use your internalized compass and mental lasso to return to reclaiming *you.*

Remember that success isn't the absence of losing your way; it's catching when you've wandered off course and returning to your Life Worth Driving Toward. Often, a visceral feeling comes over you when you've lost your way, like a part of you is contracting or crying on the inside. It's also described as mounting pressure, a sense of frustration, and a return to old, familiar struggles.

You can improve your chances of staying on track by creating a PMA-based habit of regularly asking yourself, *In this very moment, what do I think? What do I feel? What matters most to me? Are my current actions taking me toward or away from my Life Worth Driving Toward?*

## *ACT* on your inner healing

You're more likely to do what matters to *you* when you know how to pull all this together. This alternative take on ACT gives you a straightforward three-step process to *ACT* on your inner healing:

— **Accept** your present reality and your reactions to it
— **Choose** one or two values that you want to be guided by or take a stand for
— **Take driven action**

Whenever you know there's a gap between how you're living right now and the life you're driving toward, *ACT* (accept, choose, and take action) on it. Let's explore how to *ACT* on the following scenario: The beach is your happy place, but you avoid it after explant. First, accept your reality; gently acknowledge to yourself, *I really enjoy the beach, and I avoid going because of my post-explant chest.* You don't have to analyze this, convince yourself to get over it, or anything like that. Those things often just help you PASS on your reality. Instead, open up to the thoughts and feelings keeping you off the sand. Then choose one or two values to help you respond differently to them, be the woman you most want to be, and live life on *your* terms. Finally, take action. Follow through on doing things that get you back on the sand, such as shopping for a top with camouflaging layers or ruffles. Even though your inner healing sequel might show beach scenes with you wearing whatever you want, it's okay to work up to that—one step at a time.

In ACT, we often point out that you don't have an odometer or speedometer. So please don't judge how much progress you make or how quickly you progress. Instead, continually *ACT* on your inner healing no matter how small or insignificant your steps might seem. Even small steps can be bold steps that inspire you to take the next one. Often, it's the first tender step that's most difficult. But when you do it from the stance of a companion, it often becomes more manageable.

By taking driven action, you realize the benefits of living life on *your* terms. Of course, that doesn't mean you're chasing happiness. For example, in the beach scenario, you might grieve your former silhouette before, during, and after a beach trip. But, you will *also* be in your happy place. It's only by doing both that you benefit from the joy you feel when there.

As you move forward, use your Aware and Enduring Self to watch the choices you make and how they play out for you. From its perspective, notice when you're doing things that appease your inner fixer versus doing things that support your Life Worth Driving Toward. Understandably, you will see yourself doing both. But when you *ACT* on your own behalf until you reach the end of your days, your life turns out differently. Rather than regretting all the moments you sat out because something was *wrong* with you, you look back on your life and reflect: *That was a life worth living.*

# Driven actions across the BRITE Roadmap

After a lifetime of following the Breast Rulebook and appeasing your inner fixer, you might want to *ACT* on your behalf and be willing to do so, but simply not know what that looks like for you. Within our driving metaphor, this kind of stuckness is like idling your engine. It doesn't get you anywhere. To help you stop idling, this section provides examples of driven actions across the BRITE Roadmap. They show how to bust free from the Breast Rulebook, no matter where you are in your journey with breast implants.

The following lists aren't prescriptive or inclusive. Some actions might not be an option (or even necessary) on your journey. Some might feel like doable next steps. Others might require preliminary work. You might need to break others down into a series of smaller steps. Either way, these lists are intended to inspire you to harness your BRITE flexibility and take driven action to reclaim your body, mind, and heart from society's Breast Rulebook. Because your journey is highly nuanced depending on your history, circumstances, and support, always consider potential driven actions in the context of your values and what busting free means to you.

This section is long. Reading through it gives you a complete picture of busting free throughout this journey, but you can act only in the here and now. So, it's okay to focus on your current roundabout. When reading this book early in your journey with breast implants, you might want to skim the other sections to understand what lies ahead, and then revisit each roundabout's section as you move along. When reading this book after explant, it's okay to focus on the Repairing and Reclaiming Roundabouts and skim the others for ideas on how to promote your inner healing.

## Rationalizing Roundabout

Driven action in the Rationalizing Roundabout is primarily about ensuring that you are informed and aware while breast implants are in your body, rather than following your inner fixer's smoke and mirrors. By recognizing that they are temporary and problem-prone devices, you can:

— Follow through on screening breast MRIs or ultrasounds, even though they might reveal that one (or both) of your implants is ruptured and force you to face the decision to replace or remove them sooner than you might like.

— Follow groups that provide reliable, evidence-based, unbiased, and timely updates about breast implant safety.[36]

— Reach out to the surgeon who placed your implants to possibly secure a copy of your surgical notes and to learn what kind of implants were placed inside your body.

— If you have an implant card, keep it in a safe spot, make a digital copy, store it in the cloud.

— Set reminders every six months to check for recalls from your breast implant manufacturer.

— Ensure that you are informed and aware of potential impacts to your health from breast implants, irrespective of whatever you may have signed as part of your pre-op informed consent.

— Inform your health providers that you have breast implants. Know and ask for appropriate breast cancer and implant integrity screening.

---

[36] Resource list available at amandasavagebrown.com.

— Use integrative or functional practitioners who recognize and consider systemic impacts on your body related to having an implanted device.

— Regularly check in with yourself by doing the exercises specific to this roundabout in Chapters 7 and 10. Consider linking them to another event that you do with regularity, such as monthly breast self-exams or paying bills.

## Reasoning Roundabout

Taking driven action through the Reasoning Roundabout must be done on a mindful and intentional middle path that allows for the reality that breasts *matter* and that you got more than you bargained for from breast implants. Driven action in this roundabout honors your total experience rather than following your inner fixer's urging to take a PASS on disappointments or worsening problems. Some ways you can do that include:

— Acknowledge any conflict you might feel between wanting to have *better*, restored, or reconstructed breasts and not wanting to live with problematic breast implants. Use Chapter 9's exercise to allow both experiences.

— Use the **Describe Without Judging** approach in Chapter 7 to nonjudgmentally describe the different ways your breasts are impacted by having implants inside them (e.g., pain, discomfort, capsular contracture, distortion, rippling, cold to the touch, loss of sensitivity, hypersensitivity, etc.). Write out a list of these things and date it. Then, set a reminder to revisit your list every few months to see if it improves, persists, or worsens.

— Nonjudgmentally describe and list any lifestyle effects that you experience related to your breast implants (e.g., compromised hugs, miss sleeping on your stomach, weightlifting restrictions, unable to feel your child's or partner's heartbeat against your chest, etc.). Write out a list of these things and date it. Then set a reminder to review your list every few months to see if it improves, persists, or worsens.

— Reflect on other ways breast implants impact your health and well-being. For example, consider if your implants interfere with mammograms, remind you of something painful in your past, or keep part of your mind in constant fear of having another surgery. Write out a list of these things and date it. Then set a reminder to review your list every few months to see if it improves, persists, or worsens.

— Track unexplained health declines associated with BII. Monitor the financial, practical, and health costs of continuing to seek diagnosis and treatment.

— Acknowledge any values violations you experience by having breast implants.

— While taking the stance of a companion, explore what it will be like to continue tolerating your current or worsening circumstances.

— Companion yourself while curiously exploring what concerns you most about taking driven action to address your problematic breast implants. Acknowledge that you're not ready to act, but that you must inevitably choose to remove or replace them. Consider how each option might resolve, maintain, or add to your current struggles.

— Thank your mind whenever you notice your inner fixer sounding the alarm, riling up backseat drivers, erecting scary billboards, and playing Bad Boobs Radio so that you PASS on the threatening reality that breast implants might not work out for you.

— Acknowledge that your Thinking Self knows that problem-solving *this* problem might mean defying the Breast Rulebook. Explore what rules push you around the most. Rather than challenging them, validate how you feel when they're right on top of you. And expand your awareness to other things that also matter to you in your life.

## Readying Roundabout

Driven action in the Readying Roundabout is about developing a *values-guided* holistic explant plan. To put together an explant plan on *your* terms that's not dictated by your Breast Rulebook, you must use your BRITE Inner Healing skills to plan on *your* terms rather than your inner fixer's. As discussed in Chapter 4, because these surgeries impact an objectified and sexualized part of your body, holistic explant planning also must address the social and relationship effects. Your *Busting Free* digital library include a holistic explant plan checklist to help you track your efforts to act on your behalf in the Readying, Repairing, and Reclaiming Roundabouts (as discussed in this and the next two sections). Because it covers a significant portion of your explant journey, it's intended to serve as a guide rather than something you sit down with to work through all at once.

 USE THE HOLISTIC EXPLANT PLAN CHECKLIST

## Understanding explant surgery

Remember, breast implant removal is an evolving area of women's health. You will encounter differing opinions, some of which heavily reinforce the Breast Rulebook. There are additional considerations when you remove breast implants under suspicion of BII or after breast cancer reconstruction with implants. For all these reasons, you must access different sources of information to discern what is best for your circumstances.[37] This section does not tell you what to do. Instead, it lists ways to act on your own behalf by understanding:

— **The scar capsule around all breast implants:** Read peer-reviewed research from pathologists and scientists who study them or follow groups that summarize those findings for you. Understand what capsules do, what they contain, and that the body does not reabsorb them over time. Also, explore the risks for BIA-ALCL when capsules are left behind.

— **Surgical approaches to breast implant removal:** Understand the differences between *en bloc* removal, total capsulectomy, and other techniques. Know which procedure is appropriate for your circumstances (e.g., BII, rupture, implant-fill type).

— **Surgical approaches when explanting after breast reconstruction with implants:** Understand the pros and cons of aesthetic flat closure or autologous reconstruction using tissue from another part of your body. Both have many surgical considerations, such as scar shape or donor site. Join groups, participate in discussion boards, and connect with breast cancer survivor advocacy groups.

— **Different approaches to post-operative care** including drains, medications, nerve blocks, scar treatment, compression bras, etc.

---

[37] Resource list available at amandasavagebrown.com.

— **The pros and cons of additional surgeries** such as lifts and fat transfers. Know their costs, recovery, risks, and benefits. Consider these things in the context of your circumstances (e.g., Are you prone to keloid scars? Do you have enough body fat? Do you have lifestyle habits that interfere with surgical healing? Can you afford additional surgeries and reoperations related to them? Do you long to do as little as possible to your body?) Also, research the pros and cons of doing additional surgeries simultaneously versus waiting.

— **Other women's experience with breast implant removal:** Learn about possible outcomes from other women who explant, but guard against setting expectations for yourself. Recognize that everyone comes into these journeys with different histories, sensitivities, and support. Search for personal blogs, Facebook groups, and social media accounts of women who explant and explant surgeons. Even if you do not identify with BII, its groups offer valuable information about explant surgery, surgeons, and recovery. Many have pictures that help you understand what's aesthetically possible after surgery.

— **How to prepare for explant consultation:** BII organizations also provide lists of questions to ask at surgical consults. They raise your awareness of important things to explore during consults, irrespective of whether you identify with BII.

— **Financial and medical insurance considerations.**

— **Ways to support your body leading up to and after explant.**

Remember, change theory shows that thorough planning minimizes regret, remorse, and relapse (i.e., reversal routes). I know countless women who, for varied and valid reasons, rushed through this part of their journey and then struggle with the aftermath. You deserve to be conscientious and thoughtful about these decisions. Even when there is an urgent need to remove breast implants to protect or reclaim your health, you must prepare yourself. Remember to divide explant planning into smaller, doable tasks. It's also helpful to set goals for moving through this learning. For example, you might decide, *By the end of the week, I will finalize my list of consult questions.*

## Using inner skills to explant-plan on *your* terms

Your inner fixer often complicates values-guided explant planning. As explored throughout this book, she views explant as a threat to your well-being. So she ramps up her efforts to encourage a reversal route once you seriously start planning. When you persist, she and her backseat drivers switch tactics. They work to ensure that the Breast Rulebook's content heavily influences your explant plan. To bust free:

— **Use your inner BRAKE** to steady yourself whenever you feel overwhelmed, panicked, or overly distressed so that you can thoughtfully ready yourself physically, emotionally, mentally, and socially.

— **Keep your BRITE compass at the front and center of your awareness.** Choose one or two values to guide you through the surgical side of breast implant removal. For example, I prioritized self-care above everything else. That meant letting my body recover from explant before deciding on any additional surgeries. However, it might mean something different to you. That's why it's so important to know *your* context, what *you* want to take a stand for, and *your* Life Worth Driving Toward.

— **Use your BRITE lasso to continually redirect your awareness back to busting free from the Breast Rulebook.** Remember, you must be intentional about using new pathways in your mind; the old familiar ones are much easier to access and faster to use. With your inner fixer continually pushing your attention toward the Breast Rulebook, you must use your PMA skills to catch when you're prioritizing its content over other things that matter to you as well. Remember, run these inner skills continuously, like a car's daytime running lights.

— **Remind yourself that even though you can never fully unlearn the Breast Rulebook's content, you don't have to follow your thoughts related to it.** Use exercises from Chapter 8 to notice, name, and disentangle from rulebook thinking while planning for breast implant removal. Otherwise, it might lead you to do things that don't align with your Life Worth Driving Toward. For example, you might agree to additional surgeries that you cannot afford or might overly tax your body at this time. Creating distance between you and the Breast Rulebook is essential when you explant after breast reconstruction and prefer aesthetic flat closure. You will encounter many resources encouraging flap reconstruction to comply with the Breast Rulebook and "preserve your body image."

— **Acknowledge that many aspects of this surgery are beyond your control.** Then commit to using exercises from Chapter 9 to companion the distress you might feel because this surgery impacts a highly sexualized landmark on your body. Bring all your acceptance skills forward. Unwanted thoughts, feelings, and beliefs naturally show up when doing something important that feels risky. Companioning yourself is key: Your nervous system will be less agitated when you go into surgery fully attuned to yourself rather than battling against or neglecting your inner experience.

— **Tap into the perspective of Aware and Enduring Self when your mind floods with concern over your body's coming changes.** From its vantage, notice your Thinking Self's storm as it explant-plans while holding the Breast Rulebook. Then, use exercises from Chapter 10 to reconnect with the part of you that sees beyond your breast-related self-concept and endures no matter how your thoughts, feelings, or body change.

— **Stay in constant *Companion Mode*.** Planning and problem-solving soothe your nervous system, but your mind can go looking for trouble once it's completed. It often starts second-guessing, self-doubting, and ensuring that you know that what you are doing is risky. So use PMA to watch your thinking. When caught in unhelpful thinking patterns leading up to explant, lasso yourself back to the life you're driving toward. Then choose one or two exercises from Chapters 8-10 to step back from the Breast Rulebook, companion yourself, and see far beyond your breast-related self-concept. There's no formula to follow; just use whatever approaches help you bust free.

# Readying yourself for social and relationship impacts

As you plan for explant, your mind naturally considers the social impact of breast implant loss. There might be important people or groups in your life that don't know you have breast implants. With some, you might feel disinclined to discuss your surgery but apprehensive about seeing them afterward. You might be very close to other people who don't know you have breast implants but will be affected by your surgery (e.g., children, close relatives, friends, or co-workers). You might want to discuss your surgery with this group of people but feel uncomfortable. Finally, when you are partnered with someone who is "really into boobs" or has never seen you without implants, you might feel apprehensive about their adjustment to your post-explant chest.

When you are a breast cancer survivor, you might relate to some of these concerns. But when you were encouraged, lauded, or pressured to reconstruct with implants, you might dodge the awkwardness of removing implants that people important to you don't know about. Even so, explant after breast cancer reconstruction often means that you are explanting to flat. People in your life might say insensitive things. When you feel misunderstood, judged, or isolated, it's important to be your own companion or join communities where others know your journey.[38]

Whether you're a reconstruction or augmentation patient, the social and relationship impacts of breast implant loss cannot be denied. Remember, your mind perceives that group belonging is just as important to your safety as physical well-being. That's why holistic explant planning must address social and

---

[38] Resource list at amandasavagebrown.com.

relationship concerns. How you go about that varies depending on your circumstances and quality of support in your life. Several suggestions follow.

— Check inwardly with yourself and honor your feelings about the social aspect of breast implant loss. Though explant is a personal decision you make about your body, it's far from private. Spend time discerning how open or closed you want to be about your changing silhouette. Explore middle paths. Plan what you will share, with whom, and when. Keep it on *your* terms.

— Acknowledge that your inner fixer fears strong or judgmental reactions when others see you after explant. Based on the stories of countless women, I can assure you that most people in your outer circles either do not notice or do not comment. Those who do notice something is different most often ask if you've lost weight.

— Acknowledge people in your life with whom you simply do not want to discuss your breasts (e.g., your partner's boss, co-workers, gossipy neighbors, extended family, etc.). Know who they are and develop a plan to care for yourself and any self-awareness you might feel when seeing them after surgery.

— Consider who you want to include on your journey at this point, and if there are others with whom a wait-and-see approach feels more helpful. It's been several years since I explanted, and it hasn't organically come up with most people outside my immediate circle. I don't bring it up because I focus on more than my breasts. However, I openly and easily discuss it when it feels germane.

— Identify people who will be affected by your recovery or intimately involved in your post-explant life. Consider if they already know you have breast implants. Be honest with yourself about whether they are supportive to you. Then, *ACT* on your behalf by planning values-guided conversations with these people.

- Decide when it's most helpful to you to inform supportive people about your plans. Explore their questions, concerns, and how they can best support you moving forward.

- When dealing with unsupportive people, consider what boundaries are necessary to define; know what you want and don't want from them. Write out what you want to say when your boundaries are not respected.

- Identify anyone in your life who doesn't know you have breast implants that you need or want to tell. For example, children who were young when you opted for breast implants or people you became close with after getting breast implants. Determine when you want to discuss your surgery with them. Choose a value to guide your plans for the conversation.

- Also, identify anyone you misled about having breast implants. Determine if you want or need to acknowledge that. Develop a values-guided plan to talk with that person about your earlier decision.

- Consider the effects on your intimate relationships. When you are safely partnered, it's important to talk about your concerns, understand your partner's perspective, and seek reassurance by listening to and trusting your partner. When you are not safely partnered, consider having these conversations with a therapist's support, guidance, and containment. When that is not possible, meet with a therapist or coach on your own.

## Repairing Roundabout

Driven action in the Repairing Roundabout is all about following through on the major milestones on the physical journey (e.g., attending consults, selecting a surgeon, scheduling explant, and caring for yourself before, during, and after surgery) and connecting with others in meaningful ways. But you're not just pushing yourself through those things; you're doing them in ways that repair your relationship with *you*.

### Assemble a BRITE Inner Healing First-Aid Kit

Traditional first-aid kits contain equipment and supplies to provide medical treatment to someone who is injured or suddenly feeling unwell. Your BRITE Inner Healing First-Aid Kit contains various items to care for yourself when inwardly overwhelmed or hurt by painful or unsupportive interactions with others (i.e., gaslighting).

This kit should be a small bag that fits inside a purse or backpack. It should include something that soothes each of your five senses. For example, a printed copy of a favorite picture, a scented oil, a favorite mint, an object with a texture you enjoy touching, and lyrics to a song you cherish. It should also have a printed or handwritten version of your BRITE compass and inner BRAKE. I also suggest writing out a list of your preferred ways to step back and watch your thoughts (Chapter 8) and practice acceptance of your inner experience (Chapter 9).

Once you have this kit assembled, take it with you wherever you go, and use it just like a first-aid kit. Take it with you on consults and use it to ground yourself before meeting with the surgeon. Use it to stay grounded when someone is judging your decision to explant, during the days of heightened anxiety leading up to surgery, and after explant when you want to steady yourself through recovery and beyond.

## Driven action during surgical consults

Most plastic surgery suites surround you with messaging that activates your inner fixer in an unhelpful way. When you know that will pull you away from your Life Worth Driving Toward, bring a book, do something engaging on your phone, or review your list of consult questions. Although distraction is often an unhelpful long-term solution to inner pain, it can be a helpful short-term strategy when it allows you to follow through on something important to you.

To companion myself through the discomfort of sitting in a plastic surgery suite with my agitated inner fixer, I noticed and named that I was in a setting that felt difficult to me. I reminded myself why being there mattered to me. Because it was important to me to reclaim myself from the "fix it" agenda, I used my BRITE lasso when I noticed my focus settling on brochures or getting entangled in lobby videos offering anti-cellulite or anti-aging procedures. I also recommend sitting with your eyes closed and grounding yourself using your inner BRAKE.

## Attune inwardly as you choose a surgeon

Choosing an experienced explant surgeon is a significant decision to your long-term outcome and well-being. I recommend interviewing at least three. Irrespective of whether you identify with BII, consult with surgeons who recognize it and discuss how their approach safeguards your long-term health. When you are explanting after breast reconstruction, interview surgeons who respect your decision to go flat or microsurgeons skilled at flap reconstruction. Bring your list of questions that you prepared in the Readying Roundabout. Use PMA to pay careful attention to how the staff treats you and your feelings while there. Visualize yourself attending pre-ops and several post-ops in that setting. Do not overlook red flags (or even pink ones).

## Reach out to others

Remember, women use tend-and-befriend responses when confronting something difficult. So connecting with others who share this journey is an important driven action in this roundabout. You can do this through social media groups. Many explant and breast reconstruction surgeons offer their own social-media-based groups or pages that you can follow. Each has a different culture and feel, so it's helpful to join a few to ensure you can find the best fit for yourself. I encourage you to look for groups that allow members to share experiences of explant-related relief *and* remorse. These experiences are not all-or-nothing, and you deserve to be fully supported no matter how your journey unfolds.

I also encourage you to put limits on the amount of time you spend in these groups. It's easy to cross the line between helpful information and overload. When engaging with any group, use PMA to stay attuned inwardly to yourself. Consider rating your inner experience using a 1-10 scale, where 1 is "totally calm" and

10 is "overwhelmed." Know what level is helpful for you and take a break when you feel yourself surpassing it.

When social media is not something you want to use, ask your surgeon if they have a list of patients who are willing to connect with you. Read books (like this one) and find online blogs from other women openly sharing about their explant journeys.[39]

Now is when you follow through on plans you made to talk with others who are affected by your surgery. Ask for their support or establish boundaries around your decision. Remember to choose a value from your BRITE compass to guide yourself through these conversations. For example, I spoke honestly while telling our youngest daughter. She was the only one of our three girls who didn't know I had breast implants. I told her that when she was 2 years old, I had elective surgery on my breasts. I disclosed my struggle with the Breast Rulebook after pregnancy and breastfeeding. I described my long-standing struggles with my breast implants, the recent shape change, and increasing pain. I acknowledged that I would look very different to her and assured her that she would get used to it over time. I stopped talking and braced myself for her reaction.

She started cracking up! She wasn't mocking me or being mean. She just immediately saw my awkward position and found humor in it all. Her reaction helped me see that while this was a big deal to me, it might not be to everyone else. It also helped me connect with the reality that there was so much more to me than my changing body. Having my implants removed didn't change *all* of me—it certainly wasn't making me less of a mom.

---

[39] My blog is available at amandasavagebrown.com.

## Steady yourself leading up to surgery

Even when you are eager to remove your breast implants and get the surgery behind you, the weeks and days leading up to the surgery often usher in a sense of unease. You might stay busy preparing your home, meals, arranging backup providers for children, buying recovery supplies, etc. While preparing your environment is helpful, guard against using those tasks to take a PASS on your inner experience. Repairing your relationship with yourself means intentionally caring for your inner fixer's distress, acknowledging when you're feeling apprehensive, and responding in ways that support yourself.

— Use PMA to notice any conflicting but simultaneous feelings you experience, such as dread *and* eagerness or relief *and* sadness. Then offer support to all of it.

— Revisit the acceptance-based exercises in Chapter 9. Choose several to practice each day leading up to your surgery.

— Choose several BRITE compass points to guide you through the pre-surgery jitters (e.g., bravery, self-care, or self-respect).

— Proactively use your inner BRAKE as a grounding technique. Do several cycles of belly breathing each hour.

— Always keep your BRITE Inner Healing First-Aid Kit with you. Use it proactively to soothe your nervous system.

— Create a playlist that inspires you.

— Spend time with people or do things that calm and center you (e.g., yoga, guided relaxation, prayer, reading a favorite novel, watching a beloved movie).

— See the bigger picture and embrace your Life Worth Driving Toward.

## Using your Aware and Enduring Self immediately after surgery

Though some women who explant describe a sense of coming home to their original body, it can be a shock to your mind to go into the surgery with one silhouette and come out with a completely different one–especially when you explant to flat or experience a significant change in your breast volume. You can help yourself (and your inner fixer) adjust to your new silhouette by mindfully scanning your body from the inside out while allowing emotions, judgments, and sensations to come, stay, and go on their own. Because this gentle practice requires no movement of your body, you can offer yourself this type of support even during times of restricted arm movements. Regular practice helps your body spend less time in fight-or-flight mode and more time in rest and digest mode–which is helpful during recovery.

For your convenience, I created two BRITE Inner Healing body scans. They are included in your *Busting Free* digital library. Guided Audio 11.2 is for when you explant to smaller breasts and Guided Audio 11.3 is for when you explant to flat.[40]

 LISTEN TO GUIDED AUDIO 11.2

---

[40] Adapted from the body scan practice originated by Jon Kabat-Zinn, founder of Mindfulness-Based Stress Reduction.

🔊))) LISTEN TO GUIDED AUDIO 11.3

You can use them to soothe your nervous system and help yourself mentally adjust to your new silhouette. Regular use helps you observe that your post-explant discomfort ebbs and flows, including the kind that shows up in your mind and heart. As you deepen this practice, you connect to yourself in ways that go far deeper than your body's appearance.

## Have your back during The Reveal

Seeing yourself unwrapped for the first time is a significant opportunity for repairing your relationship with yourself and your inner fixer. Beforehand, remember your Life Worth Driving Toward and why breast implant removal mattered to you. Use Movie Mind to visualize showing up to this moment as the woman you most want to be. Review your BRITE compass and choose values to guide you through this vulnerable moment. Then, depending on what you choose, list out how you want to treat yourself during this moment. In Chapter 6, I shared how I proactively planned to speak respectfully to myself during this tender moment.

I also chose to have my first look on my own. When I went to the post-op appointment where my doctor removed the wrap, I chose not to look at my breasts in his presence. I wanted to be alone when I saw my traumatized breasts. Making that choice was another way I acted on my behalf while treating myself respectfully. It was part of the life I was driving toward.

Remember that you move through this journey on *your* terms by taking driven actions before, during, and after difficult moments like The Reveal. You do not need to justify, defend, or explain yourself when you *ACT* on your behalf while recovering from breast implant loss.

## Be loving to yourself during recovery

Offering yourself acceptance during post-explant recovery is key to reclaiming yourself. Chances are high that you're quite accustomed to viewing your body as something that lets you down and needs fixing. As your body works hard to repair itself, you can *ACT* intentionally to repair any unhelpful ways you view your body.

— Consider how hard your body is working to heal you from a surgery it never signed up for and had no idea it was facing. Imagine what it's gone through. See the surgeries from its perspective—practice gratitude for its continued perseverance.

— When your journey includes breast cancer or BII, take time to honor the persevering spirit within your body.

— Make a list of actions to treat your body tenderly, gently, kindly, protectively, and respectfully.

— Revisit the **Describe Without Judging** exercise in Chapter 7 to guide how you speak to yourself and about your breasts.

— Use PMA to notice how you regard and treat yourself moment by moment, and use your BRITE lasso to continually support being the person you saw in your BRITE Inner Healing sequel.

## Responding to comparative thinking after explant

No matter how you feel about your post-explant chest, comparative thinking will happen. You compare your aesthetic outcomes to others who made the same surgical decisions. You compare how you once looked in a bathing suit or favorite top to how you look after explant. You compare your post-explant chest to your pre-implant chest. When you have BII, you compare how you're healing and recovering from it. Even when you have no regrets over explant and no longer agree with the Breast Rulebook, you will naturally continue assessing how well you measure up. It's just part of being human.

Taking driven action to repair yourself from the inside out must include:

— Using PMA to notice when comparative thinking shows up and lasso back to your BRITE compass for guidance on how you want to treat yourself (Chapter 7).
— Using defusion to step back from the Breast Rulebook (Chapter 8).
— Companioning your inner fixer any time she fears you might be *less than* (Chapter 9).
— Intentionally seeing beyond your breast-related self-concept (Chapter 10).

Here's what I do when I notice I'm engaging in comparative thinking or feeling *less than*. First, I silently acknowledge, *Comparative thinking is with me* or *Feeling less than is with me*. Then, I genuinely validate that it can be hard to have distorted post-explant breasts in a breast-obsessed society. Next, I thank my mind for trying to keep me safe by reminding me about society's breast rulebook. Finally, I assure my inner fixer that I am safe, and I have my own back. Then, I stand a little straighter, hold my head a little higher, and honor all of me, including my post-explant chest.

## Showing up to post-explant intimacy

Because breasts are highly sexualized landmarks on your body, post-explant intimacy offers another opportunity to repair your relationship with yourself and your inner fixer. It might be quite intense initially. In Chapter 9, I described how I companioned myself and used my BRITE compass through the initial forays with intimacy post-explant. When intimacy is a part of your post-explant life, I encourage you to reread that section. To show up to intimacy like the woman you saw in your inner healing sequel, use your BRITE Inner Healing skills and tools to care for yourself in those moments. Ideally, you are with someone you trust, so it's also another opportunity to *ACT* on your behalf and ask for reassurance.

I want to share a word of caution here: Avoidance begets avoidance. If you avoid post-explant intimacy or only ever show up to it clothed or under cover of darkness, it can lead you to feel dependent on those coping techniques. If your Life Worth Driving Toward looks different from T-shirt sex in the dark, use the *ACT* approach outlined earlier in this chapter to attain the intimacy you want and deserve. For example, you can start as I did by wearing something sheer. Or use candlelight and gradually bring in light over time and as your comfort increases. Buy a beautiful new bra (even if you explant to flat).[41] Use PMA to notice things such as chest-to-chest warmth, the feel of a

---

[41] Visit amandasavagebrown.com for post-explant bra resources.

beating heart, and the absence of breast discomfort or pain. Continue to take small steps toward the level and kind of intimacy you want.

## Reclaiming Roundabout

Taking driven action in the Reclaiming Roundabout is all about maintaining a sense of safety and belonging within yourself. Like values, reclaiming you isn't a goal you ever finish; it's an ongoing way of being. That's why the BRITE Roadmap ends with a roundabout rather than a parking space. Like the other roundabouts, this one has an Inner Fixer Lane. You circle it anytime you automatically follow other rulebooks (e.g., how you *should* age, what you *should* weigh, how you *ought* to dress) and PASS on how you feel through invasive, costly, and problem-prone procedures.

As previously covered, it's perfectly normal to want to look your best. By continually reclaiming your body, mind, and heart from social rulebooks, you avoid things that violate your values, put your body or financial well-being at risk, or feel like you *must* do it to be accepted, worthy, or safe. You live the life you saw in your inner healing sequel.

In many ways, busting free and reclaiming you is simply about your willingness to allow your unwanted thoughts and feelings about parts that don't measure up well to society's rulebook. You bust free each time you companion yourself while doing things on *your* terms, such as going to the beach with your post-explant chest, even when your inner fixer says to stay home. You reclaim yourself by keeping PMA on and lassoing back to your BRITE compass whenever you realize you're caught in your inner fixer's futile agenda. Busting free means you continually ensure that the Breast Rulebook (and any other rulebooks your mind holds) rests on your lap so that you make decisions that honor other things that matter to you as well. It means tapping into the *you* behind your eyes each time you see the sky, and intentionally seeing far beyond toxic social messaging.

## When you know what you want to do, but you just aren't doing it

There will be times when taking driven action comes more easily and times when you struggle. This section provides you with a shame-free mini guide to use when you know what you want to do, but you just aren't doing it. Stalling out like this usually happens because of four barriers represented by the acronym FEAR.[42]

**F=Fusion with the Breast Rulebook's content.** You're listening to your backseat drivers to the exclusion of other important things in your life.

**E=Excessive goals have led you to shut down.** Either your goal overwhelms you, or you have not yet developed the skills or resources to accomplish it.

**A = Avoidance of discomfort.** You're caught in the trap of struggling against your unwanted thoughts and feelings rather than making room for them.

**R=Remoteness from values.** You've forgotten why you want to reclaim your body, mind, and heart from the Breast Rulebook. You've lost touch with your Life Worth Driving Toward.

When you want to change but aren't acting on your own behalf, come back to this section and use the following guide to identify and move past your barriers. Start by putting yourself in **P** and reflecting inwardly. Use the **See Yourself From a Different Perspective** exercise

---

[42] Adapted from Russ Harris, *The Happiness Trap*, 2008.

from Chapter 10 to see yourself struggling and stalling. Use the **Describe Without Judging** exercise from Chapter 7 while you:

## Notice your thoughts

Are you being pushed around by thoughts such as *I can't handle this, I don't have enough support, It won't work out for me,* or *It won't be worth it?* Is your mind telling you what you *ought* to do, how your breasts *must* look, or predicting doom and gloom by defying the rulebook? If so, revisit Chapter 8 and take driven action to create space between you and the Breast Rulebook. Remember, you're not trying to get your pushy thoughts to go away. Instead, you're reminding yourself that you, and what you do, are separate from them. Experiment with:

— Watching your thoughts like passing train cars. See that even your rulebook-related thoughts come, stay, and go on their own.

— Creating distance between *you* and your thoughts by noticing and naming your thinking.

— Thanking your mind for its concern.

— Naming the backseat drivers who are mouthing off.

— Asking yourself if you want to follow your backseat drivers.

— Noticing and naming when Bad Boobs Radio is playing.

— Redesigning any inner billboard images that overwhelm you.

## Be realistic about your next steps

Are you shutting yourself down with unrealistic expectations? Or do you need more health, finances, support, information, or skills to move forward? If so, get real with yourself.

— Set specific goals to learn BRITE Inner Healing skills, perhaps reread and practice one chapter per week to improve your BRITE flexibility.
— Break down intimidating goals into smaller steps.
— Take driven action to improve any resources that you lack. For example, if you want to explant and your health is a barrier, take driven action to improve it.
— If you truly cannot move forward at this time because of finances or something else beyond your ability to change, set a different goal. Avoid all-or-nothing thinking. Look for middle paths that reclaim your body, mind, and heart in other ways.

## Check your avoidance

Are you doing everything *but* dealing with your problems? Are you being pushed around by your difficult thoughts and uncomfortable or painful feelings? Are you unwilling to companion yourself through the anxiety of defying the Breast Rulebook or the fear of being *less than*? If so, revisit Chapter 9 and take driven action to free yourself from the trap of taking a PASS on inner pain. Remember, you're not trying to convince yourself to feel other than you do. Instead, practice the ABCs of acceptance:

— **Acknowledge** that you're on a journey you never wanted to take.

— Use your **breath, body,** and **mind** to make room for *all of you,* even your unwanted thoughts and feelings.

— Walk alongside yourself with the heart of a **companion** rather than the hammer of a fixer.

### Check to see if you can clearly describe your Life Worth Driving Toward

Have you given up on, lost sight of, or failed to really create a clear vision of your Life Worth Driving Toward? When you let go of the Breast Rulebook and take back the wheel, do you feel unsure of what matters to you? If so:

— Settle in and watch your BRITE Inner Healing sequel again.

— Reconnect with what matters to you as a woman impacted by temporary, problem-prone, and inappropriately studied breast implants.

— Revisit the earlier sections in this chapter and choose an area where you most want to *ACT* on your behalf. Then set a goal for yourself that feels purposeful and doable.

— Embrace your values. Hold them close to your heart. Use them to guide you as you take the next step toward reclaiming *you.*

---

## Staying in the driver's seat

No matter where you are on the BRITE Roadmap, how loudly your backseat drivers remind you to follow the Breast Rulebook, what programming you hear on Bad Boobs Radio, or how many distressing billboards or warning signs your inner fixer erects, you have everything you need to bust free and stay in charge of the drive. Your collection of BRITE Inner Healing skills and tools includes:

— an inner BRAKE to steady yourself anytime you feel overwhelmed;

— a BRITE compass to guide you based on what matters deep down in *your* heart;

— present moment awareness to nonjudgmentally acknowledge your full experience and problems needing your attention;

— a BRITE lasso to help redirect yourself when behaving unlike the woman you most want to be;

— the inner abilities to create space between you and society's rulebooks, drive with a car full of backseat drivers, and take your inner fixer along for the ride;

— many ways to companion your inner pain, rather than abandon it;

— a reconnection with an aware and enduring part of you that sees far beyond your self-concept and endures no matter how your body changes;

— a process to *ACT* on your own behalf.

This collection helps you travel a more mindful path through this journey. By using these inner skills and tools, you bring your whole self forward while making decisions before, during, and long after breast implant removal. You liberate yourself from automatically following *any* rulebook so you can finally follow *your* heartfelt values instead. You companion yourself while showing up to life as the woman *you* most want to be.

These ACT-based skills work the same, irrespective of the challenge. They help you prevail whether you're struggling inwardly with how you think and feel about your breasts or something else entirely. So as you move forward, use this powerful collection of inner skills to respond much more helpfully to your inner fixer and innate drive to belong.

BRITE Inner Healing offers you a new way to *be*. Though you've finished this book, please don't declare yourself done with present moment awareness, companioning yourself, watching your thinking, or watching life outside your Thinking Self. Please cherish your compass, create one that's specific to any challenge life throws your way, and never stop *ACT*ing on your own behalf. Your continual use of these skills and tools fosters your ongoing self-acceptance practice.

For my self-acceptance practice, I rely on a subset of BRITE Inner Healing skills, tools, and exercises that help me most. They include belly breathing, describing without judging, thanking my mind and blessing its heart, noticing and naming my thoughts, offering a hand to my inner fixer, genuinely validating myself, and taking perspective on me. Though I use others, these are my go-to tools. I use them and my BRITE compass to live a meaningful life, even though my breasts violate the Breast Rulebook. My self-acceptance practice helps me continue busting free and be the partner, mom, daughter, sister, friend, therapist, coach, and author I most want to be.

Your self-acceptance practice might look different. What matters is that you identify *your* preferred ways to ground, support, and open up to yourself for the remainder of your life. It's okay if you can't list your preferred BRITE Inner Healing skills at this time. There's a lot to cover in this book. It's okay to go back through the material until you find your preferred collection. You can also join one of my groups or workshops.[43] I would be honored to meet and support your efforts.

---

[43] Check for groups and workshops at amandasavagebrown.com.

Either way, keep at it until you have your go-to collection of tools for offering yourself acceptance. Then use them each day as you bravely continue busting free.

# Final Words

I wrote this book for you as one of the millions of women living in a time and place where temporary, problem-prone, and inappropriately studied devices are offered to augment, restore, or reconstruct breasts. I speak with countless women like you, whose lives are irrevocably changed because their quest for *better* breasts led them to the implant table. Because breast implants aren't lifetime devices, you inevitably must choose to replace or remove them. And because they aren't problem-free, the decision is sometimes made for you. Either way, as discussed throughout this book, the impacts of your breast implant journey go far beyond the surgeries to put them in or take them out. My most earnest hope is that this book empowers you to heal inwardly from the very real, but often trivialized, psychosocial impacts that you endure as a woman whose life journey includes breast implants.

I wrote this book for you because coming to terms with getting more than you bargained for from breast implants and healing from their removal is about much more than safely explanting. You learned long ago that breasts *matter*, and you will spend the rest of your days surrounded by images and messaging that continually reinforce their importance.

Understandably, when breast implants don't work out for you, the mental, emotional, and social impacts are significant. This isn't because you are vain, shallow, or suffering from a body-image disorder. It's because you're human. Although you can never fully unlearn or separate from the Breast Rulebook, I hope to empower you to bust free from automatically judging yourself against it. My most sincere hope is that you reclaim your body, mind, and heart from following it at the expense of your health, well-being, or finances.

Throughout the writing of this book, I held an image of you in my mind and close to my heart. In that image, I see three versions of you.

I see you as a very young girl, living with blissful *self-unawareness* before your mind began compiling the Breast Rulebook and comparing you to it. That young version of you is still there, fueling your longing to feel safe within yourself again, urging you to bust free.

I also see you as the woman you are today. A woman who bought this book, knowing deep down that your experience with breast implants is emblematic of so much more. Because you want to truly accept yourself, inside and out, I envision you giving your very best to bring this book's material off these pages and into your life, even when your mind says *it's too much, not worth it,* or *won't work.*

And finally, I also see you emerging from this journey as the woman you most want to be. This version of you appears like a living piece of kintsugi pottery. Only instead of bright golden lacquer mending broken pieces, your BRITE Inner Healing comes shining through. Having healed inwardly from a journey that leaves you scarred but not broken, you are stronger and more radiant than ever before. You feel at home in your body. You show up to life on *your* terms. You love fiercely, do the things that you want to do, and laugh deep to your core. As you (and your body) continue to change and age in a youth-, breast-, and beauty-obsessed culture, you have your own back. And you companion yourself *for the rest of your life.*

# Did you take value from this book?

My fervent hope is that *Busting Free* makes a difference in how you see and treat yourself. If it did, your review will help other women find this book. In fact, it holds tremendous influence over whether other women will find *Busting Free* when searching for help. Much as I'd like to, I don't have the reach of a New York publisher, nor can I run huge ad campaigns. But I do have YOU. And your honest review is what will bring this book to the attention of other women on these journeys.

If this book holds value to you, I would so appreciate it if you spent just a few minutes of your life leaving a review on the book's Amazon page. It can be as short as you like.

You can go directly to the page here:

https://amzn.to/3PGx9O9

From the bottom of my heart, thank you.

# Glossary

**ABCs of acceptance:** three tangible categories describing how to *be with* your inner experience; Acknowledge, Breathe and embody, and Companion

**Acceptance:** the ACT strategy that teaches you how to open up to your full experience, including the unwanted parts; allowing inner pain rather than struggling against it

**Acceptance and Commitment Therapy:** An evidence-based behavioral intervention to help people engage with and overcome painful thoughts and feelings through acceptance and mindfulness techniques, to develop self-compassion and flexibility, and to build life-enhancing patterns of behavior

*ACT:* Accept, Choose, Take Action

**ACT hexaflex:** six-sided figure showing the interconnections among and between the six ACT strategies

**Aesthetic anxiety:** apprehension and concern focused on the aesthetic outcome of explant surgery

**Arbitrary:** assigning meaning to something based on human-made and socially-derived ways of relating things to one another

**Autonomic Nervous System:** the part of the nervous system that controls bodily functions that are not consciously directed, such as breathing, digestion, and heartbeat; has two branches known as the sympathetic and parasympathetic nervous systems

**Aware and Enduring Self:** the *you* behind your eyes; your awareness of your awareness

**Backseat drivers:** metaphor for your mind's concern about following the Breast Rulebook

**Bad Boobs Radio:** metaphor for when your mind replays and turns up the volume on painful memories involving your breasts or feared predictions about your post-explant chest

**BIA-ALCL:** breast-implant-associated anaplastic large cell lymphoma, a type of cancer of the immune system that occurs in women with breast implants

**BRAKE:** an acronym to help you remember to steady yourself by Breathing slowly in and out, Rubbing your lips lightly, Attuning inwardly, Keep connecting with your body, and Expanding your awareness

**Breast implant illness:** systemic health effects in women with breast implants not explained by other known medical reasons

**Breast-related self-concept:** the way you view yourself based on your thoughts, feelings, memories, and comparisons of your breasts and self-worth relative to the Breast Rulebook.

**Breast Rulebook:** a massive network of beliefs about women and breasts that are generated by human minds while growing up in a breast-obsessed society

**BRITE:** an acronym for Breast Implant Through Explant; BRITE™ refers specifically to the strategies, tools, and inner healing program presented throughout *Busting Free*

**BRITE compass:** an inner tool representing the top eight values you want to pursue, be guided by, and take a stand for as you navigate your breast implant through explant journey

**BRITE diamond:** BRITE Inner Healing's adaptation of the ACT hexaflex; translates ACT six strategies for psychological flexibility specifically to the breast implant through explant journey

**BRITE flexibility:** using BRITE Inner Healing's strategies to stay present and do what's important to you as you move through your breast implant through explant journey; helps you respond differently to the challenging thoughts, unpleasant feelings, and uncomfortable body sensations that arise when defying the Breast Rulebook

**BRITE Inner Healing:** an ACT-based program for women whose life journey includes breast implants; it helps you mindfully navigate the inevitable choice to remove or replace breast implants on *your* terms, to fully reclaim your body, mind, and heart from society's Breast Rulebook, and to forge a self-acceptance practice that will serve you for the rest of your life

**BRITE Lasso:** a mental muscle that redirects your awareness and focus back to the present moment whenever you realize your attention has been hijacked by your inner fixer, backseat drivers, or Breast-Rulebook thinking

**BRITE Roadmap:** an adaptation of the Transtheoretical Model of change that models what you typically think, feel, and do when you get more than you bargained for from breast implants, move toward explant, and reclaim yourself from the Breast Rulebook

**BRITE Roundabouts:** used to show that moving through your journey with breast implants is not one-way nor a roundtrip adventure; each roundabout has unique challenges, opportunities, and inside lanes that you circle until something in your life, health, or mindset changes

**Rationalizing Roundabout:** the first BRITE roundabout; you circle it when you are pleased with your breast implants and not experiencing, attributing, or bothered by problems related to them; you are not contemplating replacing or removing them

**Reasoning Roundabout:** the second BRITE roundabout; you circle it while you reason through the pros and cons of life with and without breast implants; you are not ready to make a change, though you acknowledge that your breast implants are creating problems for you

**Readying Roundabout:** the third BRITE roundabout; you circle it once you decide you want to explant and as you ready yourself for the change

**Repairing Roundabout:** the fourth BRITE roundabout; you circle it while you move through explant, help your breasts and body recover, and companion yourself through these events in ways that repair your relationship with yourself

**Reclaiming Roundabout:** the fifth BRITE roundabout; you circle it while continually working to reclaim yourself and practicing ongoing self-acceptance

**Capsular contracture:** when the fibrous scar tissue the forms around all breast implants tightens and squeezes the implant; leads to chronic pain, distortion, and possible displacement on the chest

**Capsules:** a fibrous scar tissue that the body forms around any foreign object placed inside it to create a protective barrier; capsules form around all breast implants

**Capsulectomy:** surgical removal of the fibrous scar tissue surrounding a breast implant; surgeons perform partial, complete, or en bloc capsulectomy

**Cognitive defusion:** an ACT strategy that helps you separate what you do from what you think; it helps you step back from dominating thoughts, beliefs, judgments, and unhelpful interpretations so that they have less hold over you

**Companioning:** opening up to your full experience and showing up for yourself as you would for someone else; staying with yourself through difficult experiences and in the presence of unwanted thoughts and feelings; having your own back

**Dead-person goals:** goals you set for yourself that are done better by a dead person, such as stop worrying, caring, or thinking about something

**Defusion:** see cognitive defusion

**Deeply held beliefs:** things your mind learned and derived long ago, often without your permission or awareness; you may hold tightly to these beliefs and struggle internally when confronting them

**Driven action:** acting on your behalf in values-guided ways; doing what matters to you

**Explant:** removing and not replacing breast implants

**En bloc:** a surgical technique to simultaneously remove a breast implant and its surrounding scar capsule

**Fluff Fairy:** metaphor for when breasts recover from the surgical trauma of explant, increase in volume and regain a more natural shape

**Fused:** a term used in Acceptance and Commitment Therapy to describe when your thoughts dominate your awareness, choices, and actions and you forget there's a difference between what you think and *do*; when fused, you treat your thoughts like commands you *must* obey

**Holistic explant plan:** recognizing that your body, mind, and heart is moving through explant; planning for more than the surgical aspects, such as ways to support yourself mentally, emotionally, and socially

**Inner fixer:** the part of your mind that tries fixing how you feel on the inside by "fixing" how you feel on the outside

**Inner Fixer Lane:** when you circle this metaphorical part of a BRITE roundabout, you are struggling with your inner fixer's moves to honor the Breast Rulebook rather than taking driven action to reclaim your body, mind, and heart from it

**Internalized breast shame:** feeling *less than* as a woman relative to the social standards for breasts

**Life worth driving toward:** the life you want to live by busting free from the Breast Rulebook and using BRITE Inner Healing strategies

**Movie Mind:** a technique to nonjudgmentally observe yourself from the outside; helps you understand how you typically go about life and respond to your inner fixer; helps you visualize what you would like to see yourself doing differently

**Observing Self:** a powerful inner resource that helps you see beyond your self-concept

**Oxytocin:** a hormone that is important to childbirth, lactation, and various human behaviors including mother-infant bonding, romantic attachment, sexual arousal, recognition, trust, and empathy; it's anti-stress effect can be induced by low intensity stimulation of the skin, such as placing your own hand on your body

**Parasympathetic Nervous System (PNS):** the part of your nervous system responsible for the body's rest and digest response when you are relaxed, resting, or feeding; it acts like a brake to slow down your body's response to the fight or flight response after a stressful situation; it decreases respiration and heart rate

**PASS:** an acronym describing ways you seek relief from unwanted thoughts and feelings by Problem-solving, Avoiding, Sidestepping, or Something else

**Patriarchal society:** a society where a male-dominated power structure leads to systemic biases against women and entrenched views of how women "should" behave and appear; in a breast-obsessed society, this underlying power differential plays a role in driving the quest for *better* breasts

**Present moment awareness:** the ACT strategy for learning how to stay in the here and now, no matter what memory or feared prediction your inner fixer conjures; it helps you stay present to yourself and your surroundings

**Psychosocial:** involving mental, emotional, and social aspects

**Psychological flexibility:** staying present and doing what's important to you in any given situation, even with challenging thoughts, unpleasant feelings, and uncomfortable body sensations

**Pure awareness:** the viewpoint offered by your Aware and Enduring Self that allows you to momentarily see yourself and life beyond the labels you put on yourself and your socially-conditioned beliefs

**Putting yourself in Park (P):** a reminder that the current exercise or experiential you are reading in *Busting Free* requires inner reflection that's best experienced with your eyes closed

**Quest for *better* breasts:** experienced by people who grow up in a breast-obsessed society; it's fueled by your life experiences, innate drive to belong, natural tendency to compare yourself to the Breast Rulebook, and a nervous system that's wired to move you away from feeling *not good enough*

**Recall:** when a manufacturer takes action to fix a device that violates FDA safety laws by being defective, a risk to health, or both

**Reversal route:** moving left on the BRITE Roadmap and returning to an earlier roundabout

**Rupture:** where a saline or silicone breast implant sustains a tear or hole

**Silent rupture:** also known as an intracapsular rupture; occurs when a silicone gel-filled implant is ruptured but its contents are maintained within the fibrous scar capsule around the breast implant; can be detected by MRI

**Sympathetic Nervous System (SNS):** the part of the nervous system that directs the body's rapid involuntary response to dangerous or stressful situations; it floods hormones that boosts the body's alertness and heart rate, sending extra blood to the muscles; commonly referred to as your fight-or-flight response

**Tend and befriend:** a stress response where humans affiliate with others when threatened, includes tending to offspring to ensure their survival and affiliating with others for mutual protection and comfort

**Thinking Self:** the part of you that thinks, problem solves, judges, derives, holds the Breast Rulebook, etc.; humans strongly identify with this part and are accustomed to following its solutions

**Transtheoretical Model:** one of the most utilized theories of change; developed in the late 1970s, by Prochaska and DiClemente, to conceptualize how we typically think and feel while moving through five stages of change as we ready ourselves to act on a new, healthier behavior (precontemplation, contemplation, preparation, action, and maintenance)

**Vagus nerve:** the main nerve of your parasympathetic nervous system; it is extremely long and wande

rs through your body, connecting your brain to vital organs, such as your heart, lungs, stomach, and intestines; contributes to many functions including the slowing of your heart rate

**Values:** the ACT strategy for knowing what matters to you and using those things to guide how you show up to life; values are qualities that describe ongoing ways you want to behave

*You*: used throughout *Busting Free* to distinguish between your usual sense of yourself (i.e., your self concept) and bringing your whole self forward to honor what matters to you deep down, instead of automatically following society's rulebooks

# Acknowledgments

When I set out to write *Busting Free*, I had no idea how much I didn't know about writing a book in the digital age. The path from heartfelt inspiration to finished product was anything other than straightforward and many people helped me find my way.

I want to acknowledge the team of professionals who helped *Busting Free* become realized, written, and published. Initially, I worked with author and book coach, Kathie Giorgio, whose constant encouragement helped me "finish the book." My content editor, Chris Nelson, helped me translate my vision for *Busting Free* onto these pages. He tracked my model and concepts with an attention to detail for which I am eternally grateful. I had the distinct pleasure of benefiting from the professional copyedit and proofreading services of Cindy Elavsky; everyone should be so lucky to have a high school friend turned copy chief. Her edits elevated *Busting Free* to a new level. I also want to thank my coach Marla Tabaka for helping me internalize a much more supportive inner voice. I'm extending a special shout-out to my illustrator, Kayli Fradin. I am a rather exacting person and her patience with my requests is laudable! I especially appreciate her manifesting my vision for the cover art. Finally, a huge thank you to Jenn Hanson-dePaula at Mixtusmedia for her mentorship during the most unfamiliar and challenging parts of this journey. Once Jenn joined my team, everything changed. Her energy, enthusiasm, and expertise inspired me to reach farther than I ever hoped.

Though I reference Dr. Russ Harris' work throughout Busting Free, I want to acknowledge his tremendous influence on me as an ACT practitioner. His gift for transforming difficult concepts into practical applications inspired me to translate ACT in relatable ways for women on these journeys. To my greatest joy, he encouraged me throughout the writing of this book. Russ, on behalf of my clients' lives and all the readers of *Busting Free*, thank you.

I'd like to thank my sister for allowing me to share parts of her personal story and for *always* believing in me–especially when I struggle to do that for myself.

I want to thank my husband and three daughters for supporting my passionate commitment to this project. Throughout it, the house wasn't super clean, I'm not sure how we managed to eat meals, and I often remained deep in thought after a day of intense writing. Thank you for listening to me as I found my way through each surprise, disappointment, and challenge. Thank you for cheering me on and celebrating my little successes along the way. To my husband, in particular, thank you for your unequivocal encouragement, faith, and support–in taking on this project and so many other ways. None of this would be possible without your commitment to me.

Finally, to the readers of *Busting Free*, thank you for trusting me with your inner healing journey. Writing a book to companion you is truly among my greatest honors in life.

# Connect with the Author

Amanda Savage Brown lives and works outside Chicago, IL, USA. Her most pursued value is meaningfully connecting with others. Though she's currently on social media @dr.amandasavagebrown, she may not always be. The best way to connect with her is by visiting her digital home at amandasavagebrown.com. From there, you can join her newsletter, comment on her blog, and keep "abreast" of her workshops and other endeavors. And, if the mood strikes you, email her at amanda@amandasavagebrown.com.

Printed in Great Britain
by Amazon

19807941R00183